On April 29, 1992, the "worst riots of the century" (*Los Angeles Times*) erupted. Television newsworkers tried frantically to keep up with what was happening on the streets while, around the city, nation and globe, viewers watched intently as leaders, participants, and fires flashed across their television screens. *Screening the Los Angeles "riots"* zeroes in on the first night of these events, exploring in detail the meanings one news organization found in them, as well as those made by fifteen groups of viewers in the events' aftermath. Combining ethnographic and quasi-experimental methods, Darnell M. Hunt's account reveals how race shapes both television's construction of news and viewers' understandings of it. He engages with the longstanding debates about the power of television to shape our thoughts versus our ability to resist, and concludes with implications for progressive change.

Screening the Los Angeles "riots"

Cambridge Cultural Social Studies

General editors: JEFFREY C. ALEXANDER, *Department of Sociology, University of California, Los Angeles, and* STEVEN SEIDMAN, *Department of Sociology, University at Albany, State University of New York.*

Editorial Board
JEAN COMAROFF, *Department of Anthropology, University of Chicago*
DONNA HARAWAY, *Department of the History of Consciousness, University of California, Santa Cruz*
MICHELE LAMONT, *Department of Sociology, Princeton University*
THOMAS LAQUEUR, *Department of History, University of California, Berkeley*

Cambridge Cultural Social Studies is a forum for the most original and thoughtful work in cultural social studies. This includes theoretical works focusing on conceptual strategies, empirical studies covering specific topics such as gender, sexuality, politics, economics, social movements, and crime, and studies that address broad themes such as the culture of modernity. While the perspectives of the individual studies will vary, they will all share the same innovative reach and scholarly quality.

Titles in the series

ILANA FRIEDRICH SILBER, *Virtuosity, charisma, and social order*
LINDA NICHOLSON AND STEVEN SEIDMAN (eds.), *Social postmodernism*
WILLIAM BOGARD, *The simulation of surveillance*
SUZANNE R. KIRSCHNER, *The religious and Romantic origins of psychoanalysis*
PAUL LITCHTERMAN, *The search for political community*
KENNETH H. TUCKER, *French revolutionary syndicalism and the public sphere*
ERIK RINGMAR, *Identity, interest and action*
ALBERTO MELUCCI, *The playing self*
ALBERTO MELUCCI, *Challenging codes*
SARAH M. CORSE, *Nationalism and literature*

Screening the Los Angeles "riots"

Race, seeing, and resistance

Darnell M. Hunt
University of Southern California

CAMBRIDGE
UNIVERSITY PRESS

Published by the Press Syndicate of the University of Cambridge
The Pitt Building, Trumpington Street, Cambridge CB2 1RP
40 West 20th Street, New York, NY 10011–4211, USA
10 Stamford Road, Melbourne 3166, Australia

First published 1997

Printed in Great Britain at the University Press, Cambridge

A catalogue record for this book is available from the British Library

Library of Congress cataloguing in publication data

Hunt, Darnell M.
    Screening the Los Angeles "riots" : race, seeing, and resistance /
Darnell M. Hunt.
        p.   cm. – (Cambridge cultural social studies)
    Includes bibliographical references and index.
    ISBN 0 521 57087 5 (hc). – ISBN 0 521 57814 0 (pbk.)
    1. Television broadcasting of news – California – Los Angeles.
    2. Race relations and the press – United States.   3. n-us-ca.
    I. Title.   II. Series.
    PN4888.T4H86   1996
    070.1′95 – dc20   96–10443   CIP

ISBN 0 521 57087 5 hardback
ISBN 0 521 57814 0 paperback

To my family, friends, and all those who have lived the struggle.

Contents

Figures

Tables

Preface

Two days after the fires, I spent many hours with my fiancée, brother and a friend riding through South Central Los Angeles. I wanted to see with my own eyes what I had up to that point been witnessing via my television screen. I remember being stunned by both the extent and patterning of the devastation. Liquor stores, banks, and Korean businesses were looted and/or burned to the ground. Many businesses were left untouched, "Black-owned" markers guarding them against harm. Building walls were pregnant with fresh graffiti: "Crips and Bloods Together Forever"; "LA Revolucion"; "Fuck Police"; "Blacks and Mexicans United."

On the way home, we stopped at a South Central shopping center that had been looted, to help other volunteers clean up the debris. Out of the corner of my eye I caught an aging black man looking over the remains of a looted record store. As my fellow travelers and I approached with our brooms, the old man identified himself as the store owner. He pointed out how badly his business had been damaged, noting particular items that had been stolen. But then he turned to us with a nervous smile, "This is all material," he said. "I'd sacrifice it all to help the black man rise."

In just fourteen words the old man had rewritten news depictions of the events. How many others see it this way? I remember wondering. From what position or positions were viewers finding meaning in the flames that danced across their television screens? I would like to thank that old man for awakening me to the idea for this book.

This is a book about mass media, race and resistance; it is a book about the interplay between television news, racial identity, and social change. The case study: the 1992 Los Angeles "riots." To what degree did news media work to depict a privileged view of the "riots?" How did race affect media depictions of the "riots" and audience members' understandings of them? Under what conditions might audience understandings of these depictions constitute acts of resistance, contributions to efforts aimed at social change?

From idea to proposal, from writing to revision, this book has been enriched by timely feedback and advice from a number of fine scholars: Jeffrey C. Alexander, Walter R. Allen, Phillip Bonacich, Steven Clayman, Teshome Gabriel, Barry Glassner, Herman Gray, Angela James, George Lipsitz, Melvin Oliver, Jeffrey Prager, M. Belinda Tucker, Darrell Williams, and my anonymous reviewers. I would especially like to acknowledge Walter R. Allen and Jeffrey Prager for their support in the project's early phases, for the direction they have provided me over the years.

Managing the logistics behind this project was an exercise in stamina and patience. I would like to thank my family – Angela James and Bruce Hunt, in particular – for accommodating me and my mood swings throughout this rather challenging, three-year period. In retrospect, data collection was the most demanding phase of the project. Chapter 4 could not have been written had it not been for the revealing interviews conducted by Margaret Zamudio. Funding provided by the Ford Foundation's Pre-Doctoral Fellowship for Minorities supported the data collection phase of the project, while a rather generous faculty start-up fund provided by the University of Southern California supported the analysis and writing phases.

I would also like to thank Deborah Callahan at Youth Opportunities Unlimited, Toni O'Leary at Community Youth Gang Services, Jackie Harper from First African Methodist Episcopal Church (FAME), and the faculty and staff from Freemont High School for assisting me in identifying potential study groups from South Central Los Angeles.

I am also grateful to the people at Cambridge University Press – especially Catherine Max and Jayne Matthews – for their support in bringing this work to press.

And last, but certainly not least, I would like to thank the sixty-five young women and men who made this study possible by opening up their ways of seeing to me and my camcorder.

1

Introduction

On Wednesday, April 29, 1992, a hazy spring afternoon in Los Angeles, two words leaped forward again and again from the city's electronic media: not guilty, not guilty, not guilty. Within minutes, order was disrupted as some residents of the city took to the streets. Others, trying to make sense of what was happening, monitored television images of rage, hope and despair from the safety of their living rooms.

When the smoke finally cleared a few days later, fifty-one people had died, more than $1 billion worth of property had been reduced to ashes, and thousands had been arrested in what the *Los Angeles Times* described as "the worst riots of the century" (Coffey 1992, p. 49).

News media first informed the world of verdicts in the Rodney King beating case at about 1 pm on April 29. At this time, most people in Los Angeles and across the nation were occupied by the routine demands of day-to-day living. An infinitesimally small segment of these people, of the potential media audience, was present in the Simi Valley courtroom as the verdicts were being read. An even smaller segment had been present over the course of the entire trial. A somewhat larger, but still quite small segment of the potential audience lived in areas the media were to later identify as "riot" areas. In short, only a small segment of the media audience had firsthand knowledge concerning the outbreak of the events or the causes to which they had been attributed by the media. Instead, a large measure of what people "knew" about the events and the conditions leading up to them was undoubtedly based on media depictions.

The events that erupted in Los Angeles undoubtedly meant many things to many people. To the nation's president, the events represented "the brutality of a mob, pure and simple."[1] To the news media, they were "riots," events resembling those that occurred in Watts twenty-seven years earlier.[2] To many observers, they were a direct response to the ten not-guilty verdicts which exonerated four white police officers in the infamous beating of black motorist Rodney King – fifty-six baton blows captured on videotape. To others, however, these events constituted a "rebellion," the explosion of a powder keg of economic, social and political injustices that had oppressed their communities for years.[3] The verdicts just lit the fuse.

The language of race, of course, permeated most discussions of the events. From accounts of black and Latino economic deprivation in South Central Los Angeles, to the Rodney King incident, to the probation of Soon Ja Du, racial understandings loomed large in the discourses surrounding these events. For example, black–white antagonisms served as a key explanation in the *Los Angeles Times'* analysis: "The attack on Reginald Denny would become the flip side of the attack on King – the unofficial, black-on-white answer to the official, white-on-black beating. Within hours Los Angeles would plummet into chaos" (Coffey 1992, p. 45). Scholarly analyses of the events also tended to identify race as a key factor. As Omi and Winant (1993) explained it:

What does the Los Angeles riot tell us about racial politics in the US? Above all else, it serves as an immanent critique of the mainstream political process, of the political convergence which dominates national politics today. It demonstrates the continuing significance, and the continuing complexity, of race in American life.

(pp. 99–100)

In short, many observers understood the events as a sad commentary on race relations in the United States. But is this how all viewers understood television depictions of the Rodney King beating, an incident that news media have associated with the outbreak of the events?

Goodwin (1992), for example, suggests otherwise. While many viewers might interpret the videotaped beating of King as involving "brutality and racism" (p. 122), he argues, the jury in the case did not see it that way. He suggests that the jury "contextualized the images differently" relative to other viewers (p. 123), that the environment in which the images were viewed (i.e., the trial) and the forms in which they were offered (i.e., edited and "enhanced") facilitated the jury's not-guilty verdict. In conclusion, he noted that "In the wider arena of politics, radicals are onto a no-winner if they choose this moment suddenly to start believing in the simple veracity of mediated images" (p. 123). But while mediation surely makes a difference, is it not possible that the "veracity" of *all* images – "simple" or otherwise – is to some degree determined by what people want or are socialized to see? For example, is it merely coincidental that the jury who arrived at this decision was essentially composed of *white* members?[4] Would a jury containing *black* members have reached the same verdict – interpreted these "mediated" images in the same way? In short, what exactly is *race*, and how might this factor have influenced television viewers as they sat in their living rooms, attributing meaning to news coverage of the events?

At the same time, consider the following proposition: television news-workers intended for their reports to provide viewers with a *particular* understanding of the events.[5] That is, just as attorneys in the King beating case relied heavily on images to convince the jury of the validity of their competing claims, television newsworkers undoubtedly covered the events with the goal of reconstructing for their viewers *what-actually-happened*. But the definitions, meanings and understandings various event observers embraced regarding what-actually-happened, as I suggested above, were far from uniform. How does this realization square with newsworker efforts to represent the events in terms of a particular understanding? In other words, how much *power*[6] do news media have to advance a certain view of reality in the face of viewer alternatives? Furthermore, in what ways might race figure in viewer tendencies to resist media influence?

These burning questions motivate the present study; they also expose fundamental gaps in the mass media and race literatures. These gaps, I propose, are the unfortunate legacy of discord between two longstanding research traditions.

Old story, new ending?

Once upon a time, in the land of knowledge, there stood two well-built houses. Residents of the first house sought desperately to document the ways in which mass media bolster ruling class power in society; from time to time, however, these residents bickered amongst themselves over the nature of audience resistance, whether "real" resistance to this power was, in fact, possible. Meanwhile, residents of the second house tried to explain how race exerts its influence in society; toward this end, these owners spent most of their time identifying and analyzing what they understood as out-comes of racial group interaction.

Now the first-time listener might suppose that these neighbors fre-quently hobnobbed with one another – that those who studied media, power and resistance were also likely to have been interested in how race enters into the mix, or that those who studied how race exerts its influence in society were also likely to have been concerned with understanding how mass media help construct and reproduce racial subjectivities. But rarely, we find, did these neighbors venture beyond the confines of their own yards.

In the real world of academia, of course, these houses are commonly known as "Critical Media Studies" and the "Sociology of Race." Assuming for the moment that the point of our little tale is a valid one,[7] we are left with a nagging problem: Just how should one study the *interplay* of mass media and race? How can we avoid treating either concept unproblematically in our analyses, taking its nature for granted? How can we establish – measure, interpret, characterize, demonstrate – not only the social significance of media *or* race, but of their *interaction*? The keys to these questions, I submit, have for too long remained locked inside two houses of knowledge, literatures built for different reasons, with different methods, and in different styles.

Different reasons

It is hardly accidental that researchers working within the Critical Media Studies tradition rarely center race in their analyses.[8] After all, Critical Media Studies grows out of a Marxist theoretical tradition[9] whose main current has tended to treat race as epiphenomenal. Many of the more orthodox proponents of this tradition even understand racial consciousness as "false consciousness," identifying class, instead, as the fundamental analytical category for understanding societal relations.[10]

For example, in her attempt to illustrate how Critical Media Studies differs from more "traditional" media studies, Press (1992) inadvertently reveals the marginality of race in the former paradigm. She begins this comparison by noting that critical approaches are committed to understanding "what might be," while more traditional approaches are primarily concerned with "what is." In other words, Press (1992) rightly argues that Critical Media Studies – unlike traditional studies of the media – embraces a progressive political agenda and couples this agenda to its theoretical one. Underscoring class's dominant position on this consolidated agenda, Press identifies "the relative absence of politically effective working-class movements in the United States" as something she has had to "grapple with" in her work. Note that she makes no mention of the *relative abundance* of racial movements in the United States; it is as if these movements had, and continue to have, little bearing on the Critical Media Studies agenda.

Press (1992), of course, is not alone when she slights race in her discussion. As Gray (1993) illustrates, critical studies of television typically assume that the television apparatus works to normalize, incorporate and commodify differences such as race or gender. But while the work of women scholars such as Press and Radway (1984) has kept the issue of gender up close in the literature, race has been kept at "arm's length" (Gray

1993, p. 192). This situation, it seems, is extremely problematic in a context such as the United States, where race has been, and continues to be, a central axis of social relations (Omi and Winant 1986, 1994).

Equally problematic in a society permeated through and through by electronic communications, the Sociology of Race rarely centers mass media in its analyses.[11] This literature might be crudely divided into two camps: works whose focus is to explain race *per se* and those whose focus is to explain race *relations*. Scholars who start with an analysis of race relations – who expend little effort theorizing the *content* of the category itself – seem to treat race as a mere artifact of more elementary processes. For example, many influential racial scholars share Critical Media Studies' concern with class, conceptualizing the significance of race primarily in economic terms (cf. Cox 1970; Bonacich 1972; Wilson 1978). This observation may seem rather ironic when the failure of these studies to examine mass media is considered in conjunction with our central problem. But then these studies take the meaning of race for granted, defining it once and for all as a rather static category. The shifting complex of meanings that constitutes "race" (Prager 1982; Omi and Winant 1986, 1994), as well as the role that mass media might play in its formation, are defined as marginal concerns by the assumptions of this framework.

In contrast, scholars who attempt to theorize race as an irreducible category – a category in its own right – are more likely to recognize it as a dynamic phenomenon, one composed of ever-evolving meanings and significances.[12] Omi and Winant (1994), perhaps, is the exemplar of this approach. This study's notion of racial formation – "the sociohistorical process by which racial categories are created, inhabited, transformed and destroyed" (p. 55) – clearly implicates mass media as an important player in the construction and reproduction of racial meanings. Unfortunately, mainstream sociology has been slow to develop the connection. This observation, I contend, is due in no small measure to two factors. Firstly, the mainstream sociological discourse on race has been dominated by positivist approaches which conceptualize race in static terms, rather than interpretive ones which center the construction, reproduction and transformation of racial meanings in their analyses. Secondly, the "dominant paradigm" in American communications studies (Gitlin 1978) – a signature positivist enterprise – proclaimed in the 1940s and 1950s that mass media have very little effect on social actors.[13] Mainstream sociology, it seems, accepted this proclamation, discounting media as a topic worthy of serious study.[14] Accordingly, "Mass Media" is conspicuously absent today from the list of thirty-five standing sections of the American Sociological Association, and it is given only cursory attention in most introductory textbooks.[15] Given these observations, it should come as no surprise that mass media are also marginalized in the projects of mainstream sociologists who study race.

Different methods

Over the years, Critical Media Studies concerns with "what is" and "what might be" have generated research questions that seem to demand qualitative analyses of one sort or another. A key concern of Critical Media Studies, as I noted earlier, is the relationship between mass media and societal rule. In order to explore this concern, scholars in the Critical Media Studies tradition devote their energies to one or both of two major projects: exposing the ideological functions of media texts[16] and/or identifying whether and under what conditions real audiences might resist these texts. Neither of these projects has to date found much use for quantitative methodology, a methodology that tends to flatten meaning when it represents complex concepts with numbers.

Text-centered analyses, which continue to dominate the tradition, assume that media are more powerful than audiences in the reception experience. Influenced by a key tenet of Marxist thought – that "[t]he ideas of the ruling class are in every epoch the ruling ideas" (Marx 1972, p. 136) – these studies seek to expose the infestation of ruling ideas in media texts.[17] Toward this end, textual analysis necessarily involves the use of interpretive methods, methods well-suited for teasing out the symbols and other narrative devices in a text that work to activate and support ruling ideas. The formal sampling procedures, statistical tools, and reliability and validity measures so central to quantitative methods do not seem very useful to researchers wrestling with the subtleties of meaning. Indeed, it is this fact that prompts many positivists to view critical works as "idiosyncratic" and speculative at best (Press 1992, p. 93).

Works within Critical Media Studies that endeavor to study audiences are on the rise and yet continue to be controversial within the tradition.[18] Typically, these studies embrace Gramsci's (1971) notion of hegemony, understanding the term to describe an unstable order or equilibrium in society predicated on 'both coercion and consent. The mass media, it follows, facilitate the consent on which hegemony depends. But the process is an unstable one in which ideological cleavages open from time to time, providing space for counter-hegemonic readings and practices. How audiences understand or *decode* a given media message, then, suddenly becomes a meaningful empirical question.[19] Thus qualitative techniques such as ethnography, participant observation, and in-depth and focus-group interviewing are employed to explore how audiences actually make sense of media (cf. Jankowski and Wester 1991), whether and under what conditions they might resist media influence. Again, due to the focus on meaning and interpretation, the research questions in these projects do not lend themselves to easy quantification.

The Sociology of Race, in contrast, has spawned countless quantitative studies. This development has no doubt been motivated by the continued dominance of *positivism* in the social sciences.[20] But this development is also the result, as I point out above, of the tradition's tendency to conceptualize race in static terms. Indeed, these two factors are intertwined. That is, because the meaning of race-as-category is predetermined by the researcher, a relevant population can be easily identified and representative (read "objectively valid") sampling undertaken. Accordingly, many of the more traditional research questions involving race – for example, questions of stratification, segregation or attitude – have focused on clearly defined groups that exhibit quantifiable characteristics. While these projects generally share the concerns of Critical Media Studies with social structure and power, many do so from the vantage point of a competing theoretical framework: pluralism. In recent years, the ethnicity paradigm (and concordant images of cultural and political pluralism) has left an unmistakable imprint on social scientific conceptualizations of race.[21] This paradigm tends to equate race with ethnicity, suggesting that race relations should be understood as a competition between a multitude of different ethnic groups who seek to influence societal outcomes in their favor. Accordingly, an important interest that drives these studies is specifying the balance of power or degree of integration present in society at any particular point in time. This enterprise, of course, generally results in the generation and comparison of several socioeconomic measures (e.g., median income, years of schooling attained, mortality rate, employment rate, poverty rate, etc.). Interpretive analyses of racial subjectivity – analyses akin to those Critical Media Studies scholars conduct on texts and audiences – typically receive marginal consideration in these studies. Interpretive analyses, it seems, do not generate the kind of "hard data" popularly associated with the positivist enterprise.

Different styles

Differences in reason and method, of course, generally go hand in hand with differences in the look of manuscripts, in *style*. Works within the Critical Media Studies tradition are characterized by lengthy narratives interspersed with pockets of theoretical reflection and interpretation.

Researchers frequently employ verbatim quotations of text or audience discussion as sources of data to illustrate whatever argument they are advancing. Rarely do we find in these works the tables, graphs or other data presentation devices one would expect to find in "rigorous" positivist works. This stylistic practice, of course, is rooted in necessity: the nuances of signification and meaning that critical works target are frequently lost when reduced to numbers and summary tables.

Meanwhile, studies developed within the Sociology of Race tradition typically seek to uncover representative, quantifiable – replicable – social "facts." Concerns with replication, of course, signal static understandings of concepts, indicators and measures.[22] Accordingly, researchers devote much of the narrative to elaborating on method – defining concepts, operationalizing variables, defending measures. Tables anchor the discussion as researchers attempt to describe relevant social facts in shorthand. Interpretive studies of race (i.e., ethnographies and historical pieces that look more like works in the Critical Media Studies tradition) do exist, of course, but they are part of a small minority. The unstable meanings and significations implied by a concept such as "racial formation" (Omi and Winant 1986, 1994) lead to "messy" analyses, analyses that seem to defy quantification and replication.

Forcing the neighbors to meet

The researcher interested in truly understanding the interplay of media and race, I contend, desperately needs an innovative framework. S/he needs a framework that combines sociological considerations of race with a critical focus on hegemony and "what might be." S/he needs a framework that respects concerns for reliability and validity without reducing complex meanings to static concepts, to mere numbers. S/he needs a framework that appreciates the contribution of two houses of knowledge many treat as irreconcilable, or at best, inconsistent.[23] Above all, s/he needs a *balanced* framework, one that incorporates key insights and leaves unnecessary baggage behind.

This book was inspired by the search for such a framework – one that forces the neighbors to meet. "British Cultural Studies," as practiced by researchers identified with the Birmingham School in England,[24] serves as my theoretical and methodological starting point. This tradition has long recognized the empirical utility of sociological and anthropological tools. Important empirical studies within the tradition bring these tools to bear on slippery questions of culture, meaning and power (e.g., Willis 1977; Morley 1980). But consistent with critical approaches, this tradition has also sought to discover "what might be" – to couple its theoretical agenda to a more explicitly political one. The concept of hegemony, as articulated by Gramsci (1971), forms a theoretical stronghold for Cultural Studies (cf. Hall 1992). Because hegemony is viewed as an inherently unstable order, meaningful change becomes a possibility, instances of resistance worth documenting and understanding.[25] Cultural Studies scholars understand the context surrounding these acts of resistance to be key; for these researchers refuse to accept the validity of inflexible laws of social behavior. In short, Cultural Studies "rejects the application of a theory known in advance as much as it rejects the possibility of an empiricism without theory" (Grossberg 1993, p. 89).

In the following pages I employ a mixture of qualitative and quantitative techniques designed to *triangulate* in on an understanding of my object of analysis. At times, my use of verbatim quotations and interpretation give this study the look of a Critical Media Studies work; at other times, my use of quantitative measures and tables give the study a look more often associated with mainstream sociological projects. In this book, style follows function: I borrow key insights and methodologies from two houses of knowledge out of necessity, to chart the complex interplay of media and race. Following the Critical Media Studies tradition, I couple my theoretical agenda to a political one: How might we use the findings of this study to identify strategies for facilitating audience resistance in the future? True to the Sociology of Race tradition, I use a variety of measures to operationalize "race," to document its influence on the social relations under study. Finally, consistent with the Cultural Studies tradition, I present my analysis as one that is contextually specific, *not* as one that uncovers timeless laws about media power and audience reception. The case: the production and reception of local television news portrayals of the 1992 Los Angeles "riots." How much power do news media have to advance a hegemonic view of the events in the face of viewer alternatives? In what ways might race figure into viewer tendencies to resist media influence? How might media experiences contribute to the construction and reproduction of racial subjectivities?

Plan of the book

In pursuit of answers to these questions, this study exposed fifteen groups of friends and/or family members – five "Latino," five "African-American," and five "white"[26] – to a 17-minute extract from local television news coverage of the first day of the "riots." Same-race interviewers then instructed informants to discuss amongst themselves "what you just saw." That is, interviewers avoided directing/focusing the discussions or defining terms: informants were permitted to set the discussion agenda as an outgrowth of the group interaction process. The study targeted college-aged informants (although some groups were mixed in terms of age) because this age cohort had not yet been born when the bulk of the 1960s "riots" occurred. Moreover, roughly half of the groups originated from South Central Los Angeles, a relatively low socioeconomic status area identified by the media as the center of the events, while the balance of the groups were from the more affluent Westside. Group screenings and the subsequent discussions were videotaped, transcribed, and coded in order to identify patterns that might link viewing behavior, group discussions and race. I was particularly interested in examining the sources of knowledge informants referenced when discussing the selected news extract. (see appendix A for a detailed discussion of the data and methods).

Part 1 of the study – Context and text – sets the stage for this empirical analysis of audience reception. Chapter 2 develops the theoretical framework from which I examine the interaction of media and race in the meaning-making process. This framework synthesizes important insights from British Cultural Studies, the Sociology of Race, social psychology and ethnomethodology.

Chapter 3 presents my analysis of the selected news extract in order to provide a benchmark against which to compare informant responses in parts 2 and 3. I identify and discuss fourteen major assumptions that were embedded in this extract.

Part 2 – Audience – is largely descriptive, consisting of audience ethnographies for each of the fifteen study groups. Chapter 4 focuses on data from the Latino-identified groups, chapter 5 on data from the black-identified groups, and chapter 6 on data from the white-identified groups. These ethnographies suggest that the screenings and subsequent discussions served as a forum for informants to negotiate and affirm their racial subjectivities.

In part 3 – Analysis and conclusions – I consider ethnographic and experimental findings from the study in terms of concerns with racial subjectivity, and enduring debates about media power and audience resistance. Chapter 7 argues that "raced ways of seeing" indeed shaped the reception experience for informants. Chapter 8 concludes the study by considering the social significance of these findings, by analyzing the relationship between informant meaning-making and resistance.

When all is said and done, the goal of this book is *not* to make generalizations about "Latino," "black," or "white" populations. At the very least, such an exercise would require a larger, more representative sample; it would also require a rather static conceptualization of race, one that I am not inclined to accept as valid. *Neither* is my goal to reconstruct how real viewers likely received the selected news extract *when the events were unfolding*. The historical context in which informants were embedded during the study was quite different from the one surrounding the actual events. Finally, despite my use of positivist techniques, my goal is *not* to deny the intrusion of my own interpretations on the data. As several scholars have noted, this intrusion is inevitable (cf. Ang 1989; Geertz 1973).

My goal *is* to unpack the black box surrounding a contextually specific case of audience reception. This exercise, I believe, holds much promise for documenting some of the ways in which race shapes the reception experience, and how this experience, in turn, influences the construction and reproduction of racial subjectivities.

PART I

Context and text

2

Media, race and resistance

Mass media are everywhere. Race is elusive. Resistance is unclear.

For scholars who seek to study the interplay of mass media and race, these three assertions affirm the complexity of the enterprise. To begin with, mass media are so ubiquitous today that it is virtually impossible to distinguish the boundary of one medium from that of another.[1] Defining meaningful boundaries of specific mass media texts is even more perplexing.[2] Should we, then, just throw up our hands and theorize media influence on the basis of our paradigmatic allegiances? As relatively *powerful?* As relatively *powerless?*[3] How might we empirically explode the compacted *process* by which real people respond to media?

Which brings us to a consideration of race. Race has played, and continues to play, a particularly significant role in the history of United States economics, politics and culture. Indeed, one of the first things we notice about people today when meet them is their race (Omi and Winant 1986, 1994). The perennial subtext, race invariably slips into our discourses, quietly organizing our commonsense understandings of the world and our place in it (Prager 1982). But the meanings associated with race (and various racial groups) continue to shift about us – in the media and in our interactions with others. This uncertainty over meaning makes it rather difficult to specify, in any given instance, the degree to which race (as opposed to other factors) shapes our thoughts and actions. Similarly, it complicates efforts to understand how and to what degree race intervenes when people respond to media.

Finally, whatever our responses to media, how are we to understand the significance of these responses in the overall scheme of things? Scholars interested in empirically exploring the balance of power between mass media and audiences eventually find themselves *evaluating* audience responses to media. For some of these scholars, audience "opposition" to the ideologies[4] inscribed in media – critical interpretations, lack of interest, and so on – constitutes a form of resistance against ruling power. For others, ruling power ultimately contains this opposition, transforming it into little more than *pseudo*-resistance, a vicarious venting of frustration that leaves the status quo unscathed. Which position is more valid? How would we recognize *real* resistance if we saw it?

Beneath these methodological problems, of course, lie questions of definition, of conceptualization, of theory. In order to successfully trace the interplay of mass media and race, we must first come to terms with this subterranean region.

The television experience

In the contemporary United States, *mass media*[5] have become a taken-for-granted necessity. As a society-wide process, they probably occupy more people, more of the time, than any other (McQuail 1987). Indeed, if we conceive of *culture*[6] as a vast array of playing fields, one where common-sense meanings and explanations for social questions are contested – where people come to negotiate a sense of themselves, their day-to-day lives in the overall scheme of things – then we must recognize mass media as the pre-eminent playing field. In recent years, television has dominated this field.[7] Its contests are becoming increasingly integrated into our daily routines, blending vicarious experiences with lived ones, helping us construct on a daily basis who we are, who we are not, who we ought to be.

Thus, in contrast to scholars who distinguish between the television experience and *lived* experience – between "fiction" and "reality" – I do *not* conceptualize the two as mutually exclusive spheres. Television images confront us continually, during our waking hours and as we dream (cf. Ewen and Ewen 1992). Furthermore, these images routinely reference one another, creating for us a hypermediated world, one composed of signifiers that often seem more *real* than the signifieds (cf. Baudrillard 1988). In short, the television experience has become an integral part of contemporary lived experience.[8]

On the one hand, this experience depends on what we might label the television *apparatus*. This ubiquitous, always-available field of discourses forever strives for an "assembly" of the masses (Heath 1990, p. 270). A continuous *flow* (cf. Williams 1975, pp. 78–118; Fiske 1987, pp. 99–105; Mellencamp 1990, pp. 240–241), it lures its audiences to the screen with a multitude of texts that are spread across many channels.[9] Each of these texts works to *interpellate* its viewers, to cause them to recognize that they are being spoken to, to urge them to adopt subject positions favored by the inscribed ideologies (Althusser 1971; Fiske 1987, 1987a; Morley 1992; Strinati 1995).

But the process of interpellation is an uncertain one (Morley 1992). The television experience – the outcome of audiences *receiving* the texts that *hail* them[10] – is also shaped by the audiences themselves and the social contexts in which they are embedded (Morley 1974, 1980, 1992; Fiske 1987). True, the producers of television texts *encode* certain ideological positions (Althusser 1971) and intended meanings (Hall 1973) into them. But these texts are necessarily polysemic because contradictory semantic fields exist within cultures (Eco 1979).[11] That is, television texts inevitably activate particular, socially situated ways of seeing, memories capable of generating differential audience interpretations or *decodings* (cf. Morley 1974, 1980; Fiske 1987; Lipsitz 1990).[12] Often these memories are of other specific media texts, texts that somehow position audience members in social space (Lipsitz 1990). Alternatively, these memories may be more diffuse, constituting an *intertextual* store of knowledge that seems to bear on the text in question (Fiske 1987). In short, the television experience is a *dialogic* one, an ongoing dialogue between immediate texts and the intertextual memories of audiences (Newcomb 1984). Media-powerful perspectives that ignore this empirical fact (e.g., Althusser 1971), that assume a priori that audiences are doomed to succumb to the influences of a particular media text, inevitably treat audience members as "judgmental dopes."[13] Meanwhile, audience-powerful perspectives that too readily celebrate textual polysemy (e.g., Fiske 1987), that fail to acknowledge patterns in (and limits on) the domain of possible meanings (cf. Hall 1973), essentially write off the possibility that mass media might influence lived experience. Surely there must be a more reasonable middle-ground.

Hegemony theory seems to define this middle ground (Gramsci 1971).[14] This framework recognizes that media texts work to interpellate and influence (i.e., position) audience members; but it also recognizes that the process is inherently unstable and unpredictable. That is, cultural struggle is *ongoing*; it is *not* decided in advance. Although opposition may be momentarily contained on one front in the struggle, it inevitably surfaces again on other fronts. Meaningful change is thus a theoretical possibility, empirical studies of resistance worth the undertaking.

Race-as-representation

When and where it exists, media influence on lived experience necessarily flows through the conduit of consciousness, through some awareness of self or *subjectivity*.[15] But the consciousness of human actors is composed of multiple subjectivities, each waxing and waning in salience with changes in the situations actors face (Hall 1988). In the contemporary United States, "race" defines particularly salient subjectivities, locations from which actors construct and/or receive media texts and make sense of the world. At the same time, what it *means* to belong to a "race" is continuously created intertextually (Hall 1988, 1989; Gray 1995), suggesting that an important interdependence exists between race and media.

When we consider how race exerts its influence in society, it quickly becomes rather obvious why race still matters. Indeed, despite a long-standing recognition in the sociological literature that "race" is not some biological or cultural essence,[16] and despite recent scholarly efforts to deconstruct racist discourses,[17] "race" continues to shape lived experience in society. Two recent scholarly works – Prager (1982) and Omi and Winant (1986, 1994) – offer insightful theoretical models for explaining the intractable nature of "race" in US economics, politics and culture.

Prager (1982) posits a model that argues the following: the inequality inherent in the material world activates the collective need for explanation and understanding; this need for understanding motivates the construction of collective *representations*,[18] commonsense, public understandings and explanations for inequality; race-as-representation serves this need (e.g., blacks are biologically inferior, whites are biologically superior, and so on); race-as- representation spawns future representations and over the long run influences behavior (e.g., interaction patterns, cultural styles, voting choices, and so on); this cycle repeats itself ad infinitum. While the model acknowledges the importance of material factors, it shuns "behavioralist" conceptualizations of racial processes "where different factors and situations predictably influence specific individual responses to racial differences" (p. 106). Instead, this model treats race-as-representation as a relatively autonomous, "transcendent outlook," one that "stands above any particular sub-group" and permeates the whole of society.

In contrast, the model posited by Omi and Winant (1986, 1994) seems to find somewhat less *play* between "race" and material conditions. That is, while Prager (1982) focuses on exposing the *function* of race-as-representation in society, this latter model actually attempts to trace the process by which economic, political and cultural factors continually shape the phenomenon. Toward this end, Omi and Winant (1986, 1994) review US history from the 1960s to the 1990s, specifying the trajectory of "racial formation" – the "sociohistorical process by which categories are created, inhabited, transformed and destroyed" (1994, p. 55). The scholars find that this process operates through "racial projects" (e.g., colonization, slavery, the civil rights movement, affirmative action, etc.), ideological vehicles (i.e., popular interpretations, representations, explanations) by which societal resources are redistributed along particular racial lines (1994, p. 56). In other words, race has everything to do with competing interests *and* the shifting meanings associated with them – with a "link between structure and representation" (1994, p. 56). And because these meanings shift, Omi and Winant define race in rather open terms, as "a concept which signifies and symbolizes social conflicts and interests by referring to different types of human bodies" (1994, p. 55).

As Omi and Winant illustrate, the "racial state" is a major player in the racial formation process. That is, in periods of "unstable equilibrium," the state enforces the current racial order; but when dissatisfaction with racial inequality sparks oppressed groups to mount social movements, a "crisis" point is reached; at this point, the state responds with policies of "absorption" (i.e., appeasement and co-optation) and "insulation" (i.e., relegating demands to symbolic areas rather than substantive ones) (pp. 84–87). This model, of course, is heavily influenced by Gramsci's (1971) notion of hegemony.

Despite differing over the amount of autonomy race exhibits from material conditions, Prager (1982) and Omi and Winant (1986, 1994) share the important insight that the phenomenon is a social construction that exerts its force *as representation*.[19] Indeed, both models depart from typical sociological treatments of race, approaches that conceptualize race (and associated meanings) in rather static terms. That is, both works convincingly demonstrate that what we *know* about race at any given point in time is composed of commonsense ideologies, expectations, rules of etiquette – representations. And these representations are linked to important economic, political and cultural forces – forces which shape, *and are shaped by*, the shifting meanings undergirding racial categories.

In the final analysis, this *race-as-representation* perspective provides a rather insightful articulation of the tide of racial meanings currently flowing through US society, particularly of the process by which racial categories are produced and reproduced. Elites, for example, "invented" the "white" pan-ethnic racial category as an effective means for dividing the laboring class (i.e., between "whites" and "non-whites") in early America (Allen 1994). That is, "It was in the interest of the slave-labor system to maintain the white-skin privilege differential in favor of the European-American workers" (p. 198).[20] Elite exploitation of this representation continued after Emancipation, limiting the emergent class struggles of the late nineteenth century (Omi and Winant 1986, 1994). By the end of World War II, "people from every corner of Europe were considered fully 'white'" (Hacker 1992, p. 9). Today, "white" continues to define the pinnacle of the US racial order (cf. Farley and Allen 1989; Hacker 1992).

In contrast, the category "black" has historically been associated with the very bottom of the US racial order (Baldwin 1961; Franklin 1965; Hacker 1992).[21] The category debuted in the US context when Africans from various tribes were grouped together and designated "black." This representation, of course, functioned primarily as an ideology of exploitation based on assumptions of black racial inferiority (Omi and Winant 1986, 1994). Today, the legacy of slavery in the US (and associated meanings) continues to distinguish "blacks" from other racial groups in the nation, effectively barring them from attainment of "white" status in the racial order (cf. Hacker 1992).[22]

Finally, "Native American," "Latino" and "Asian" might be viewed as "'intermediate'" categories in the US racial order (Hacker 1992, p. 16), a sort of buffer class that in the best of times is allowed to *approach* "white" status, that in the worst of times is at least *not* "black." In the contemporary US context, these racial categories represent relatively recent consolidations of previously distinct groups (Omi and Winant 1986, 1994);[23] all three represent responses to the distribution of rewards by the state (e.g., those based on census classifications), and adaptations to threats from the racial order (e.g., discriminatory immigration laws, racial violence, economic oppression, and so on) (cf. Omi and Winant 1986, 1994; Espiritu 1992; Hacker 1992).

Thus far, I have employed the race-as-representation perspective to suggest how racial meanings are produced, reproduced and transformed at the macro level. Before the insights of this perspective might be applied to questions of subjectivity construction and viewer decoding, however, the *mechanisms* behind how race-as-representation influences thought and action at the *micro level* need to be fleshed out in more detail. To this task I now turn.

Race-as-representation and norms

Despite criticisms that studies in the *ethnomethodology* tradition typically adopt non-political stands (cf. Jankowski and Wester 1991), this tradition – with its focus on the rules that govern everyday interaction – seems to provide important insights for understanding the mechanisms linking thought and action. Garfinkel (1967), for example, contends that the problem with conventional analyses of social action boils down to one central flaw: they ignore the actor's understanding of his or her own situation and actions. Thus regardless of the analyst's professed intentions –

perhaps he or she seeks to illustrate the existence of human choice, of volition in his or her model – the end result is the same: the actor's motives are portrayed as being conditioned by normative structures, his or her actions determined accordingly. Free will, if it is claimed to exist, becomes an analytical non sequitur as actors are treated as if they are really just "judgmental dopes" (p. 66).

The relationship between action and norms – i.e., the micro–macro link – is thus more realistically stated as follows: norms are *used* by actors on an act-by-act basis to *share* understandings of their "empirical circumstances" (Heritage 1984, p. 131). That is, "commonsense" explanations of action serve the necessary function of "accounting" for such actions to others, thereby bringing order to what would otherwise be perceived as chaos. These explanations rely upon norms and other background expectancies as reference points, as bases for common understanding. In other words, norms serve a necessary function in society because actors have a stake in the "perceived normality" of events, their "typicality," their "comparability with past or future events" (p. 188). Consequently, norms tend to be maintained rather than eroded over time. As Garfinkel (1967) puts it, "Not only does common sense knowledge portray a real society for members, but in the manner of a self-fulfilling prophecy the features of the real society are produced by persons' motivated compliance with these background expectancies" (p. 53). In other words, Garfinkel (1967) postulates an *interdependence* between actions at the micro level and norms at the macro level: norms are used by actors as frames of reference to interpret one another's action; as bases for "common-sense knowledge" norms exert a "moral force" (Heritage 1984, p. 102), demanding that actors account for their transgressions of them;[24] over time, due to continual use, norms tend to persist. Indeed, this particular insight seems to distinguish ethnomethodology from *symbolic interactionism* (e.g., Blumer 1969), two approaches that underscore the centrality of interpretation to human action. That is, while Garfinkel offers a reasonable model for explaining why norms tend to persist (despite the precariousness of interpretation), symbolic interactionism downplays the significance of norms, fixating, instead, on the role that interpretation plays at every turn in the micro-level interaction process.[25] Garfinkel's model, in the end, at least provides openings for considering the influence of macro-level structures on action.

In many respects, "representation"[26] as employed by Prager (1982) and Omi and Winant (1986, 1994) is quite similar to "norm" as conceptualized by Garfinkel (1967). In other words, what I have thus far referred to as race-as-representation operates very much like Garfinkel's conceptualization of "norm." That is, there does appear to exist an interdependence between individual actions at the micro level and race-as-representation at the macro level: race-as-representation is used by actors as frames of reference to interpret one another's action (e.g., prejudice, discrimination, raced solidarity), to share a common view of "empirical circumstances" (e.g., raced inequality and oppression); as bases for commonsense knowledge about these circumstances, race-as-representation exerts a moral force on actors, demanding that they account for their transgressions of raced expectations (e.g., those regarding interraced dating, attitudes toward affirmative action, and so on); over time, due to constant use, race-as-representation tends to persist as an important frame for understanding.

In short, neither norms nor representations need be "internalized" in the Parsonian sense for them to structure action (cf. Heritage 1984). From time to time, we all recognize the shortcomings of "race" as a frame for understanding ourselves and others, but we continue to use it anyway.

In the end, it seems, a synthesis of Garfinkel (1967), Prager (1982) and Omi and Winant (1986, 1994) provides us with insights for going beyond the static understandings of raced subjectivity so prevalent in mainstream works on race, and for overcoming the dupe/not dupe impasse characterizing debates over media power (cf. Heath 1990). That is, this synthesis provides us with a useful articulation of the link between micro-level action and structure. In the context of the present study, it provides us with the beginnings of a theoretical framework for exploring the role that race-as-representation plays in how viewers both negotiate their raced subjectivities *and* make sense of television texts: race-as-representation, as normative order, provides *prescriptions* for how viewers from different raced groups *ought* to think about themselves, and how they *ought* to decode what they see on television; when viewers fail to conform to these prescribed patterns they must somehow account for their deviations.

But an important question remains: Assuming that race-as-representation is constantly adapting to changes in society (cf. Prager 1982; Omi and Winant 1986, 1994), how do viewers determine on a day-to-day basis what decoding behaviors are expected of them as members of a raced group?

Race-as-representation, viewer networks and decoding

Network analysis, as a methodological tool, holds much promise for tracing the effects of social relations and structures on individual behavior (Fine and Kleinman 1983). Underlying this approach is the argument that individual behavior (e.g., viewer decoding) is poorly explained by focusing solely on personal attributes or abstract categories (e.g., "race"). Rather, behavior is seen as a function of *concrete* social relationships, relationships that are identified in terms of real ties to important others (Wellman and Berkowitz 1988). A social *network* might be defined as "a specific type of relation linking a defined set of persons, objects, or events" (Knoke and Kuklinski 1982, p. 12). If we identify *television viewing and discussion* as one such relation, then we might apply network analytic concepts in order to understand the *process* at work behind viewers' decoding behaviors. That is, we might apply network analytic concepts to better understand how viewers determine on a day-to-day basis what decoding behaviors are expected of them as members of a raced group.

One such concept is the *clique*. Cliques are generally defined as close-knit groups in which the social tie of interest exists between every group member (Erickson 1988). At the micro level, the social environment in which individuals view and make sense of television might be reasonably cast in terms of this concept. If we could identify the processes behind clique decoding behaviors, we might find ourselves one step closer to understanding *how* the discourses and institutions in which viewers are situated exert their influence. Other studies have foreshadowed this approach (e.g., Morley 1980; Liebes and Katz 1988, 1993), but they generally fail to explicate the social processes implied by their rather crude, *a priori* classification of viewers into meaningful groups. In the end, these studies cannot explain decoding differences in terms of micro-level *process*. Network analysis, in contrast, is nicely situated to zero-in on process. For example, network studies have found that members of cliques are more likely than those of loose-knit groups to share the same attitudes (cf. Bienenstock *et al.* 1990). This tendency might be explained by a key tenet of group theory: members of close-knit groups find it easier to determine what the group norm is and to sanction wayward members (cf. Festinger *et al.* 1965; Collier *et al.* 1991). And this explanation suggests that those who regularly view and/or discuss television together should feel pressured to decode it in similar ways.

Decoding and small-group theory

Contrary to popular media-powerful arguments, empirical research has long suggested that television audiences should not be conceptualized as a mass of socially isolated viewers (cf. Katz and Lazarsfeld 1955; Wright 1975). Even when we watch alone, our decodings are filtered through the lens of our prior interactions with important others.[27] Indeed, our decodings are in a perpetual state of negotiation and renegotiation as we interact with important others in the future. Because these social network interactions likely occur in an unpredictable array of forms (e.g., through multiple telephone conversations, multiple one-on-one meetings, group gatherings, and so on), tracing process for real viewers becomes immensely complex. A useful, but admittedly imperfect proxy[28] for this process is the group discussion (i.e., network discussion). By understanding how these discussions influence individual behavior, the decoding process may be brought into sharper focus.

An important tenet of small-group theory maintains that group discussion leads to attitude *polarization* (Moscovici and Zavalloni 1969; Myers and Lamm 1975; Erickson 1988). That is, "response tendencies generally favored by the subject population [e.g., a clique] tend to be strengthened by group interaction" (Myers and Lamm 1975, p. 299) and discussion. Two explanations for this tendency have been supported in various small-group experiments: "interpersonal comparison theory" (p. 300) and "informational influence theory" (p. 301).

Interpersonal comparison theory suggests that people desire to present themselves favorably relative to others. Thus, when a person finds in group discussion that others share his or her position on an issue (as is likely to happen in clique situations), he or she may feel free to become an even stronger advocate of this position. If each person's pre- and post-discussion positions on the issue could be measured on a Likert-type scale, then the post-discussion group average, this theory predicts, should move farther along in the direction of the initially dominant point of view (i.e., the pre-discussion group average).

Informational influence theory, it seems, complements interpersonal comparison theory. During group discussions, this theory suggests, "arguments are generated which predominantly favor the initially preferred alternative" (Myers and Lamm 1975, p. 301).[29] Some of these arguments, the theory continues, may not have been considered before (or may have been forgotten) by certain members of the group, thereby leading to a strengthening of these members' original positions, to a hardening of the initially dominant point of view for the group as a whole.

In short, it seems reasonable to assume that decoding behaviors are influenced at the micro level by social network interaction. That is, individual viewers likely *use* network discussions as a means of positioning themselves and their decodings *vis-à-vis* societal expectations. These discussions – in a Garfinkelian (1967) sense – serve as frames of reference, as cues for understanding one's "empirical circumstances" (Heritage 1984, p. 131). Thus, category membership does not *directly* determine decoding behavior, rather the discourses and institutions to which individuals are privy do (Morley 1980). And the *process* by which this influence is exerted operates through social ties to important others.

Figure 2.1 (appendix B) summarizes the proposed relationship between texts, discourses, representations, and ideology. This relationship is best described as a pyramid where (a) texts represent the apex, (b) discourses and representations the intermediate levels, and (c) ideology (i.e., background assumptions, common-sense definitions, and taken-for-granted justifications) the base. In other words, I conceptualize texts as relatively bounded constructions of images, written words and/or sound arranged by their creators in order to convey certain privileged discourses. And I conceptualize these discourses, in turn, as networks of ideas and statements constructed out of key representations, the normative expressions of underlying ideology.[30] In short, the process of textual *decoding*, whereby actors derive meanings from texts, necessarily depends upon the lower levels of the pyramid.

But real actors greatly expand the boundaries of these lower levels. When real actors receive a text, they consider not only the discourses and representations privileged by the text, but also those privileged by other texts to which they have been exposed. Thus, no text is ever self-contained: *intertextuality* is a given.[31] Indeed, when actors negotiate the meaning(s) of a text in network discussion, I propose, they often refer to privileged (or memorable) discourses from other texts. This activity necessarily involves establishing the situational meaning(s) of key representations, facilitating, by default, "a common view of [the actors'] empirical circumstances which are treated as 'morally required matters of fact'" (Heritage 1984, p. 131). In other words, when actors decode a text, they use systems of representation (discourses) in order to make sense of other systems of representation (other discourses).

In the end, the question relevant to the present study is whether certain representations – certain ideological configurations of assumption, definition and justification – are *more likely* to be activated by one raced group rather than another in the television decoding process. In the case of the Los Angeles events, where the language of race dominated related discourses, it seems likely (in an intertextual sense) that race-as-representation may play an important role in actors' decoding of a given text about the events. Moreover, it seems reasonable to propose that patterns may exist in how differently raced actors employ race-as-representation (and related discourses) in this meaning-making process.

Social ties, race and viewer opposition

The relationship between social ties and race might be summarized as follows: individuals use their social ties as frames of reference for understanding what is expected of them in the situations they confront; and

because race continues to cast such a heavy shadow on US politics, economics and culture, it is likely that these ties and the corresponding set of
expectations are raced; over time, through an infinite succession of interactions (i.e., through the activation of raced ties and expectations, through the
reception and negotiation of texts), raced subjectivities are constructed and
reproduced.

Opposition, of course, implies that something is being actively contested.
In the US context, where race has functioned as a central axis of social relations (Omi and Winant 1986, 1994), racial meanings are perpetually contested. Much of this contestation has stormed over media representations,
representations that either challenge or reinforce dominant racial ideologies. Indeed, media depictions of race invariably result in blustery contro-
versies as members of the dominant and subordinate groups sense that
much is at stake.[32] That is, the racial ideologies supported/challenged in the
media matter because they work to support and reproduce the status quo.
While members of subordinate raced groups in the US have much to gain
from a reworking of this status quo, members of the dominant raced group
often do not see change as being in their best interest (Feagin and Vera
1995). Media scholars have argued that such tendencies/interests do not
directly translate into viewer decoding differences (cf. Morley 1980). But
under the right conditions, I hypothesize, raced patterns may be discern-
able. That is, in cases such as the Los Angeles events, where the language of
race dominated media discourses, we should expect to find a patterning of
any opposition as viewers activate their social ties, the corresponding set of
raced expectations, and intertextual memories.

While media-powerful perspectives generally discount the significance of
viewer opposition, in-between perspectives view opposition as possible,
and audience-powerful perspectives treat it as routine. Concerns with
reworking the encoding-decoding model aside (cf. Morley 1992), if our goal
is to evaluate the validity of media-powerful, audience-powerful and in-
between perspectives, then at some point we must come to terms with active
viewer opposition – opposition toward *something* we can somehow
measure. Indeed, the empirical studies likely to have an impact on the
debate are those that target specific meanings encoded in specific texts
(despite the difficulties inherent in defining textual boundaries).

With this said, the dominant/negotiated/oppositional typology of viewer
decoding seems to retain much analytical utility (cf. Hall 1973).
Accordingly, viewer "opposition" is defined as decodings that deconstruct
textual messages in "the preferred code (dominant) in order to retotalize the
message[s] within some alternative framework or reference" (Hall 1973, p.
18). In contrast, viewers who decode a text according to the "dominant"

code exhibit no opposition toward (and/or no awareness of) the ideologies embedded in the text. That is, their interpretations of a text are based on the intended meanings encased in representations, meanings that tend to carry with them "the stamp of legitimacy" and "appear coterminous with what is 'natural', 'inevitable', 'taken for granted' about the social order" (Hall 1973, p. 17). Finally, some viewers might occupy a rather ambiguous region *vis-à-vis* the question of opposition. That is, these viewers make "negotiated" decodings of a text, decodings based on a mixture of adaptive and oppositional stances regarding the local legitimacy of the dominant code.

In our attempts to conceptualize viewer opposition, we might also classify decodings along another dimension: discussion mode. Empirical studies suggest that viewers of television drama tend to either discuss these texts in a "referential" mode or shift back in forth between "referential" and "metalinguistic" modes (Liebes and Katz 1988, 1993). Metalinguistic or critical decodings of texts are characterized by discussions in which viewers display an unprompted awareness and appraisal of the techniques used in the text's construction. In contrast, referential decodings are characterized by discussions in which viewers simply refer to media texts in terms of their own personal experiences or the text's narrative. In other words, referential decodings do not deconstruct the text *as-construction*. Similar practices, I propose, may be observable when viewers receive television news texts.

In the final analysis, the referential/metalinguistic dichotomy and dominant/negotiated/oppositional trichotomy are ideal types. That is, these two dimensions do not represent a *discrete* set of options for viewers, rather they represent a *continuous* range of potential practices. Figure 2.2 (appendix B) illustrates these possibilities along two dimensions. The first dimension is labeled "ideological position;" it plots viewer stances from "dominant" to "oppositional," with Hall's (1973) "negotiated" representing the large gray area in the middle. The second dimension is labeled "analytical mode;" it plots viewer analysis practices from "referential" to "metalinguistic," with hybrid practices again in the middle. In short, I propose that the degree to which viewers oppose the ideologies inscribed in a text, and the mode in which they accomplish this activity, may be empirically observed. Moreover, I propose that these observations may be plotted along the two continua.

From opposition to resistance

If our goal is to shed some light on debates concerning the balance of power between mass media and audiences, at some point we must come to terms with the *social significance* of audience opposition. Defining opposition as "resistance" necessarily involves making value judgments. The analyst must somehow distinguish elements in society that contribute to hegemony from those that are counter-hegemonic. Such an exercise involves taking a stand on controversial issues and treating this stand as a body of presuppostions in one's work. But this stand, of course, cuts across the grain of the value-neutral precepts of positivist social science (cf. Weber 1958, p. 145; Hare 1973, p. 74). Here, the insights of critical approaches become indispensable.

For some critical media scholars, audience opposition to media constitutes a form of resistance against ruling power. These scholars assume that ruling ideas are encoded in media texts, and that any opposition directed toward these ideas potentially threatens the status quo (cf. Fiske 1989a). For others, audience opposition to ruling ideas amounts to little more than pseudo-resistance, a vicarious venting of frustration that fails to alter the status quo in any significant way. That is, these scholars view audience opposition as a private sphere activity that has minimal effect on the structures of domination that order the public sphere (cf. Althusser 1971; Foster 1985; Dahlgren 1988).

A juxtaposition of Althusserian and Gramscian views of resistance, it seems, plots theoretical strongholds for these competing critical perspectives (i.e., "real" versus "pseudo"-resistance) and suggests important considerations for assessing their relative merit. For Althusser (1990), every social formation constitutes an organic totality composed of economy, politics and ideology, where the economic level is "determinant in the last instance" (p. 6). From this vantage point, resistance necessarily becomes pseudo-resistance. For resistance is always expressed "within the very structure of the dominant bourgeois ideology, within its system, and in large part with its representations and terms of reference" (p. 30). In other words, our very way of defining our situation and reacting to it – no matter how oppositional we may believe it is – fails to transform society because it is ultimately dependent upon bourgeois assumptions, definitions and discourses. That is, bourgeois "ideology has always-already interpellated individuals as subjects" (Althusser 1971, p. 175). And for Althusser, this ideology is the social "cement" that holds society together; it is "indistinguishable from lived experience" and assures our domination (Althusser 1990, p. 25). Consequently, we are caught in a cage that we cannot escape on our own. Our only hope for real change comes from without – from a "scientific" understanding of society.

Gramsci, in contrast, assumes no definite correspondence between economic, political and ideological realms (Hall 1986, p. 25). Social formations are complex structures in which the constitutive elements are relatively autonomous. For Gramsci, "hegemony" is the unstable, temporary, historically specific process that holds these formations together, that extracts consent from the masses (Gramsci 1971, p. 12). Order cannot be maintained by coercion (the threat of force) alone. In this model, societal change is always possible because shifts often occur in the balance of social forces (Hall 1986, p. 11). In other words, rather than being caught in Althusser's (1990) cage, the masses are parties to a "war of position," one waged on many fronts – economic, political and ideological – one that produces no decisive victories. For unlike Althusser, Gramsci sees no single dominant ideology; ideologies indeed serve to coerce, but they are not always coherent. Consequently, Gramsci is interested in "organic ideology," in practical everyday consciousness, in the structures of popular thought. This ideology is key to the war of position continually being waged in society.

In the final analysis, Althusser's (1990) prescription for a "war of maneuver," his belief that scientific knowledge can produce a decisive victory over the forces of bourgeois control, seems hopelessly utopian. Throughout history science-as-ideology has masqueraded as "subjectless" science. Furthermore, the position that social actors are judgmental dopes unable to transcend ideological control is theoretically untenable. Who, then, will be able to produce and apply "scientific knowledge" in order to transform society? What is the nature of these actors' special status? Gramsci's vision of society – of endless struggle, of hegemony, and of periodic progress through a war of position – seems much more realistic.[33] In fact, when we consider a primary function of media – news construction – we are able to identify specific ways in which hegemony may be destabilized by audience opposition (i.e., resistance).

News construction, hegemony and resistance

Most media scholars agree that "news" is the result of a complex process, not simply the product of professional newsworkers who objectively report on some reality out there (Lippmann 1922; Epstein 1973; Tuchman 1978; Altheide and Snow 1979; Fishman 1980). Indeed, many studies illustrate how the news construction process in the US has worked to reinforce a preferred vision of reality – a hegemonic one (e.g., Gans 1979; Parenti 1986; Herman and Chomsky 1988). Several factors order this process: *journalistic values, newswork routines, entertainment value, and the socio-political climate.*

Journalistic values. These values feature the central journalistic ideal of *objectivity*, which came into prominence early in the twentieth century – precisely when the inevitability of subjectivity was demonstrated by science

(Schudson 1978, 1982). That is, objectivity today is a "practice" for news-workers rather than an actual "belief" or achievement (Schudson 1978, p. 186); it is a "strategic ritual" used by newsworkers to legitimate their profession in a time when the line between "news" and propaganda appears fuzzy (Tuchman 1978). This value has important effects on the form and content of television news reports. For example, newsworkers use videotape footage in an attempt to create for viewers the illusion that they are wit-nessing events as they actually occurred, not as they were interpreted by newsworkers. "Newsworkers," as one study put it, "have simply carried to its logical end a widespread belief among readers that 'a picture is worth a thousand words'" (Altheide and Snow 1979, p. 98). These workers attempt to hide "the grammar" of videotape shooting and editing in an effort to "perpetuate the audience's assumption that what they are seeing is what happened" (p. 97).

Thus, when viewers oppose "what they are seeing" in a news text, they potentially subvert the journalistic enterprise. Indeed, when this opposition is metalinguistic in mode (cf. Liebes and Katz 1988, 1993), when it chal-lenges the news text *as-construction*, it effectively questions the reality of the objectivity ideal itself. By default, it also necessarily pecks away at common-sense assumptions about the role of journalism in US society, assumptions that generally contribute to the hegemony process (Parenti 1986; Herman and Chomsky 1988). In this sense, metalinguistic decodings may lay important textual ideologies bare, making opposition to them pos-sible. Such opposition, by definition, would constitute an act of resistance.[34]

Journalistic routines. These routines facilitate newsworkers' recognition of "news" as "news" in an otherwise overcrowded event-space. For example, news organizations cannot afford to assign reporters everywhere events of import are likely to occur; therefore, they tend to rely on centralized infor-mation outlets for the announcement of news. Most notably, news organi-zations assign certain reporters to regular beats (such as key sites in the governmental bureaucracy) and monitor other news media for their cover-age of events (Epstein 1973; Gans 1979; Altheide and Snow 1979; Herman and Chomsky 1988; McManus 1990). A long-run consequence of these rou-tines is what has been described as "pack journalism" (Parenti 1986, p. 36) or the "momentum of news" (Altheide and Snow 1979, p. 170): that is, there is a tendency for news media to select from an infinity of potential news items those items that have already been selected – deemed "newsworthy" – by other news media. Over time, this practice tends to produce the appear-ance of a jump-on-the-bandwagon effect in news selection that culminates in a rather standard news agenda from news medium to news medium.

When audience members oppose the selection of stories in a news text, they demonstrate an awareness of the constructed nature of newsworthiness. That is, audience members reveal that they are conscious of the fact that "news" does not assert itself, that newsworkers actively select some events over others for coverage. Moreover, when audience members understand this selection process in terms of pre-existing newsworker practices (i.e., routines), and when their critique of the text goes beyond explanations of poor journalistic *execution*,[35] then opposition to news selection detracts from the legitimacy of journalism as an institution. Given the role this institution plays in the maintenance of hegemony (Parenti 1986; Herman and Chomsky 1988), such audience opposition represents a potential act of resistance.

Entertainment value. News (and television news in particular) is a business dependent not only on the timely coverage of "newsworthy" events, but also on the *attraction* of audiences and advertisers (Altheide and Snow 1979; Gans 1979; Gitlin 1980; McQuail 1987). The program content of the television apparatus – news programming included – serves as commercials for the commercials. As such, this content must maintain the interest of the audience, whose eyeballs advertisers "rent" for the purposes of persuasion (Gitlin 1985, p. 254). Accordingly, the content of local news broadcasts is often teased throughout the course of the day, while sports, weather and other items within the broadcast are typically saved for the end of the broadcast in order to keep the viewer "hooked" – so that he or she will be available to watch the intervening commercials. This news-as-business reality has definite consequences for the format of news narratives. News stories tend to conform to formulas which stress action, a quick pace, completeness, clarity with parsimony and high esthetic and technical standards (Gans 1979). Indeed, real-time events are typically "decontextualized" and then "recontextualized" within some preferred news format (Altheide and Snow 1979, p. 90). In the end, the entertainment imperative leads television newsworkers to produce "shallow and brief reports about selected items" (p. 80).

Accordingly, when audience opposition critiques the *form* of a news text in terms of the business imperative, such opposition constitutes a potential act of resistance. That is, this activity serves to demystify the news construction process, to reveal how what common sense depicts as a clear window onto the world is, in actuality, a commercial product designed to garner ratings.[36]

Socio-political climate. The socio-political climate is important to news selection and construction because newsworkers tend to favor "legitimate" sources in the news gathering process. That is, newsworkers typically favor government officials or other elites as sources of "news." This practice, however, does provide for the coverage of conflicting views concerning socio-political issues. For when elite consensus on policy and tactics dissolves as it does from time to time, this debate is reflected in the media's coverage (Schudson 1978; Alexander 1981; Hallin 1984; Parenti 1986; Iyengar and Kinder 1987; Herman and Chomsky 1988; Kellner 1990). But rarely do newsworkers venture beyond the confines of "official" debates and ask questions that challenge status quo visions of reality (Gans 1979). At best, newsworkers might apply a "dialectical" model of reporting controversial issues (Epstein 1973). According to this model, the ideal of "balanced" news coverage often prompts newsworkers to present two sides of a controversial issue and suggest, in simple fashion, that the truth lies somewhere in between (pp. 66–7). In addition to the legacy of Federal Communication Commission policy concerning "fairness" in broadcast news coverage (Kellner 1990), television news – especially local operations – are likely to adopt this dialectical approach for purely economic reasons: because offended viewers are free to switch channels, it may appear safer (in terms of audience share) for news operations to avoid extreme positions on any issue (McManus 1990, p. 680). In short, how journalists frame potentially controversial issues – and how they organize the content of their news narratives – is dependent upon their perceptions of the socio-political climate surrounding these issues. By avoiding risky, or extreme positions and relying heavily upon legitimate sources, newsworkers tend to reproduce status quo understandings of events.

Accordingly, audience opposition that critiques newsworkers' exclusive reliance on official sources, that calls for the inclusion of alternative sources/viewpoints in the text, draws attention to the possibility that other interpretations of the news event may exist. This opposition, of course, is counter-hegemonic when it seriously challenges commonsense notions of the situation. In this sense, it constitutes a potential act of resistance.

In the final analysis, audience opposition to the ideologies embedded in any news text represents a potential act of resistance. This is because opposition flows from and shapes consciousness, and consciousness is a prerequisite of meaningful action. Given the hegemonic role of news media in society, audience opposition (as a precursor to action) necessarily has progressive potential in the on-going war of position. But the realization of this potential, of course, is ultimately dependent upon the content of audience opposition, how well it demystifies the process of hegemony in society.

Conceptual model

Figure 2.3 (appendix B) presents a conceptual model highlighting the proposed micro-level *process* behind the television experience. My focus, of course, is on local television news coverage of the Los Angeles events, and how viewers from different raced groups make sense of this coverage.

Congruent with Gramsci's (1971) notion of "hegemony," this model proposes that television is a vast cultural field that *tends* to validate (i.e., make irresistible) status quo, common-sense versions of reality. Race-as-representation is an integral part of this normative order. Many theorists (e.g., Durkheim 1965; Durkheim and Mauss 1903; Garfinkel 1967) have pointed to the human need to find order in chaos, to derive meaning from lived experience. As an interpretive norm, race-as-representation serves this purpose; it is a central frame of reference in the US context (cf. Prager 1982; Omi and Winant 1986, 1994). But the widespread acceptance of status quo frames – ideological "consent" – tends to facilitate the continued dominance of elite groups, groups who exploit representations in order to legitimate and reproduce their own power and privilege in society. Nonetheless, this consent is always unstable as the experiences and intertextual memories of individuals pose a constant challenge to status quo conceptualizations (cf. Gramsci 1971; Lipsitz 1990; Gabriel 1993).

In terms of the television experience, race-as-representation (1) tends to structure the treatment of "race" in television texts (2). That is, race-as-representation sets normative parameters for the types of assumptions, definitions and justifications about "race" generally considered "valid," "appropriate," or "acceptable" in a given period; accordingly, it shapes the consciousness and colors the work of those who create television texts. But viewers do not always decode television texts as intended (i.e., "encoded") by the creators (cf. Hall 1973; Morley 1980); intervening between television texts and individual decoding behavior (4) lies the intertextual memory (3) of viewers. This memory is the fluid product of prior negotiated decodings (6), outcomes which are themselves a product of viewers' discussions (and experiences) with the members of their social networks (5). This memory is also directly influenced by race-as-representation through other cultural, economic and political experiences. The model is interactive in the sense that negotiated decoding (6) informs intertextual memory (3), which intervenes between race-as-representation (1) and individual decoding (4), and between television texts (2) and individual decoding (4).

Conclusions

This book seeks to capture a slippery micro-macro link. It focuses on (1) the role that race-as-representation plays in the micro-level process of meaning negotiation and construction, and (2) the role that the television experience plays in the construction and reproduction of raced subjectivities. Furthermore, it generically conceptualizes the television viewing and discussion environment in terms of the network analytic concept of clique, employing insights from Garfinkel (1967) and small-groups research in order to trace the meaning-making process in action. The case study I employ, of course, is the Los Angeles events of 1992 and surrounding news coverage. Should one expect to find important raced differences in how viewers make sense of these texts? If so, what are the implications for debates concerning the power of media to influence versus the ability/tendency of viewers to resist? How is the construction and reproduction of raced subjectivities inscribed in the process?

By the time informants were interviewed for this study, the Los Angeles events had been "over" for months. But media discourses surrounding the events continued to circulate throughout the interview phase of the study. Indeed, the events had been hypermediated, continually represented and reconstructed in the print and broadcast media. The television viewing and discussion networks to which most informants belonged thus had ample opportunity to receive and discuss other event-related texts prior to the study interviews. Should one expect to encounter polarization effects given these conditions?[37] If so, why? If not, why not? Given the self-referential nature of today's television representations (see Baudrillard 1988), these appear to be important empirical questions. In today's media environment, where viewers are constantly exposed to representations of representations, identifying the boundaries of any given television experience becomes increasingly problematic. The proposed theoretical framework acknowledges this reality; it aims only to take snapshots – in mid-chain – of the ongoing, interactive process behind the production and consumption of raced representations.

In the next chapter, chapter 3, I establish a benchmark against which to compare informant decodings in this case study. That is, I identify key assumptions embedded in the news text that was screened for the fifteen study groups. By comparing this analysis of the text's "base" to informant decodings in later chapters (see figure 2.1), I explore enduring questions of viewer opposition and resistance.

3

Establishing a meaningful benchmark: the KTTV text and its assumptions

The year 1963 was a landmark for television in the United States. In that year, the major television networks instituted their half-hour news programs, and a majority of people for the first time reported in a Roper poll that their chief source of news was television (Barnouw 1982). Ever since, television has reigned supreme as the people's source of news in the US. Indeed, informants for the present study are living testaments to this assertion: while about 43 percent reported *never* reading Los Angeles' major daily newspaper over the course of the events, only 3 percent of the sample reported *not* watching television news coverage of the events the first night (see table A.2, appendix A). This latter finding echoes viewership figures for the city as whole. Following initial reports of the verdicts, viewer levels were not much above normal across the stations in the city. But by prime-time hours (i.e., by 8 pm), news of the police acquittals had spread throughout the city, as had reports of "violence," "looting," and other events of "protest." By this time, 77 percent of the households in the city were tuned to local news coverage of the events (*Los Angeles Times*, May 1, 1992).

If, as I advocated in the previous chapter, we conceptualize the television experience as a continuous meaning-making process shaped by texts, viewers and their intertextual memories, then the present chapter focuses on the first of these factors. From what position or positions did the news media speak? What encoded meanings did study informants have to work with or struggle against as they made sense of the selected news text?

Determining what the encoders of a news text intended, of course, is a tricky exercise fraught with uncertainty. The most the analyst usually has going for him or her in this endeavor is his or her own enlightened decoding of the text, which is presumably conducted in accordance with the dominant code (cf. Hall 1973). In this chapter, I attempt such a risky exercise.

35

Recognizing that any analyst's decoding of a text necessarily reflects at least some of his or her biases, I tried to bracket my own understanding of the events and guide my analysis of the text with a single question: What assumption(s) directly underlie textual propositions? In other words, keeping my analysis as apolitical as possible,[1] I treated identified assumptions as raw textual elements, *not* as valid or invalid claims in some extratextual sense. To facilitate this exercise, I relied upon argument analysis (cf. Toulmin 1958; Rottenberg 1985), semiotic analysis (cf. Eco 1979) and an analysis of the textual devices used in the construction of the chosen news text (cf. Brunsdon and Morley 1978). Once key textual assumptions were identified, I reasoned, exploration of what real viewers *did* with them could begin. What kind of ideological work was being performed by these assumptions? Did study informants tend to uncritically accept or reject the identified textual assumptions in their post-screening group discussions? What factors were associated with the acceptance or rejection of textual assumptions? The remaining chapters address these questions. This chapter merely aims to establish key textual assumptions by analyzing the devices that bind the news text together.

In the end, my analysis in this chapter presupposes a particular conceptualization of "text." That is, contrary to works that, in effect, define media "texts" as the creation of audiences, this analysis treats the selected news extract as a catalyst that *pre-exists* given instances of audience reception.[2] As such, this text has certain qualities that can be analyzed independent of audience reception, and later compared to audience interpretations. Indeed, this conceptualization seems absolutely necessary if one seeks to understand the so-called struggle between texts and audiences. That is, to blur the distinction between text and audience is to confound causes and effects, to mystify the meaning-making *process.* Thus, despite questions about the ultimate boundaries of texts (see Fiske 1987; Mellencamp 1990; Morley 1992), my analysis focuses on a discrete 17-minute extract from one news operation's coverage of the first night of the events. This choice facilitates my ability to relate specific textual assumptions to concrete instances of audience reception that directly relate to them. In this sense, I can more rigorously evaluate the cause-and-effect claims that ultimately underlie notions of media influence and audience resistance.

Summary of the text

It is, ah, now ten o'clock and, ah, tonight a community is venting its fury over the verdicts in the Rodney King beating trial.   (KTTV news anchor)

The selected text was extracted from news coverage of the events provided by KTTV-TV in Los Angeles.[3] Appendix C presents a verbatim transcript of the audio portion of this 17-minute text; it also describes the accompanying video. The text begins with images of burning buildings from above a darkened Los Angeles. A helicopter reporter compares the evening's developments to what occurred in Watts twenty-seven years earlier – "this part of the city just destroying itself, burning itself up." We move from these images to the anchor desk where KTTV anchor Chris Harris discusses with the helicopter reporter the fate of an Asian-raced man who had been beaten up by the "thugs in the intersections." We learn that a black-raced man, "who appeared to be a minister," had attempted to shield the man with his body.

From more aerial shots of burning property, we next move to a reporter on the scene at First African Methodist Episcopal church (First AME) in South Central Los Angeles. Several structures in the neighborhood surrounding the church are in flames. The reporter questions four young, black-raced interviewees who participated in a recently ended, church-sponsored rally to promote "peace and calm." All of the interviewees express their frustrations with the rally, its failure to offer residents any real plan of action for coping with the crisis. From these interviews we move to more footage of burning buildings and reports of how news crews were being attacked by people in the streets. "These people mean business," we are told.

We then move back to the anchor desk, where Harris and Patti Suarez – a second anchor – interview a young black-raced clergyman concerning his church's efforts to restore peace and calm. Suarez likens the clergyman to a noble fighter pilot who says, "I've tried A, I've tried B, I've tried C. They go through the list and they can't figure out what's wrong." The minister is asked by the anchors to "[p]lease stay with us. We need your voice, ah, tonight."

Finally, the anchors summarize the events of the day against the video backdrop of more burning buildings, black-raced youth attacking cars in an intersection, sidewalks filled with debris from "looting," men attacking a white-raced trucker[4] who lays beside his rig, and the eruption of "chaos" at police headquarters (Parker Center) in downtown Los Angeles. "Tonight," the anchors tell us, "a community is venting its fury over the verdicts in the Rodney King beating trial" and "Los Angeles is under a state of emergency." The text concludes with the Fox 11 News theme music, logo and announcer: "From KTTV Los Angeles, this is Fox News."

Identifying the textual assumptions

I identified what I feel are key assumptions embedded in the KTTV text by viewing the 17-minute videotape and analyzing the verbatim transcript. Insights from (1) argument analysis, (2) semiotic analysis and (3) an analysis of the devices used to construct the text proved to be particularly revealing when considered in tandem.

Argument analysis

If argumentation is the road to influence, then common sense is the pavement. As Geertz (1983) reminds us: "Common sense is not what the mind cleared of cant spontaneously apprehends; it is what the mind filled with presuppositions . . . concludes" (p. 84). Common sense is popular consciousness, constantly evolving, forever adapting to changes in systems of knowledge; it is "the terrain of conceptions and categories on which the practical consciousness of the masses of the people is actually formed" (Hall 1986, p. 20). As such, common sense underlies all forms of argumentation.

Rottenberg (1985) offers a simple, but informative definition of argument: "an argument is a statement or statements offering support for a claim (p. 10)." As such, arguments are composed of three primary elements – (1) the claim, (2) the support and (3) the warrant. The claim or proposition is what the communicator is attempting to prove; the support includes evidence or motivational appeals that might convince audiences to accept the claim; and the warrant is a stated or unstated assumption, "a principle or a belief that is taken for granted and that the [communicator] and audience must share for the [communicator's] argument to be accepted (p. 108)." In short, warrants are the presuppositions produced by common-sense understandings of the world.

In this chapter, I conceptualize the KTTV text as a tapestry of discourses, an interconnected network of ideas and statements – arguments – in which are encoded key explanations and expectations. These encoded explanations and expectations, as I argued in chapter 2, are the underpinnings of ideology. As such, they are assembled throughout the text into structures of common-sense, taken-for-granted knowledge about the world – representations. In the analysis of the KTTV text that follows, I seek to identify the explanations and expectations that compose key representations;[5] accordingly, I focus my attention on the latter component of argumentation – the warrant. For at base, the struggle between the KTTV text and its viewers is played out in the realm of warrant; that is, before the KTTV text can persuade viewers to accept the validity of its representations, viewers must accept (or at least not reject) important underlying assumptions (Toulmin 1958; Rottenberg 1985). Accordingly, my analysis of the KTTV text began by dissecting it into its constitutive arguments and then deriving key assumptions from these arguments.

Semiotic analysis

In this chapter, I employ semiotic analysis to identify textual assumptions that a conventional analysis of argumentation might overlook. In the simplest of terms, the goal of semiotic analysis is to chronicle *how* – within texts – meaning is produced. The "sign" is a central concept enlisted in this endeavor, one that I rely on in my analysis of the KTTV text. Because the meaning of a particular sign is ultimately *not* a product of the sign itself, but of the social context in which the sign arises, the semiotic enterprise is somewhat problematic (Strinati 1995). Nonetheless, I maintain that researchers may learn much by exploring *how* texts themselves work to communicate meaning(s) through a given sign.[6] Indeed, I find Eco's (1979) definition of "sign" particularly useful: . . . "everything that, on the grounds of a previously established social convention, can be taken as something standing for something else" (p. 16). Building on the work of Saussure and Peirce before him, Eco (1979) conceptualizes the sign as a composite of both *signifier* (i.e., "something standing for") and *signified* (i.e., "something else"). Examples of signs may include items as disparate as sounds, written words, images, and colors. Moreover, signs may function through metaphor (i.e., communication by analogy), metonymy (i.e., communication by association), paradigmatic structure (i.e., the assignment of textual items into mutually exclusive categories/oppositions), and syntagmatic structure (i.e., the structuring of paradigms into a narrative) (Berger 1990, pp. 143–149). Metaphors tend to work paradigmatically, while metonyms work to express meaning syntagmatically.

Given the contextual nature of signs, the proper way to conceive of the relation between signifier and signified is that it is one of probability, of correlation. In other words, the readers of signs are *likely* to link certain signifiers with certain signifieds on the basis of social convention. But as Eco (1979) points out, differential readings are possible because "in a given culture there can exist contradictory semantic fields" (p. 80), contradictory ways of seeing.[7] For example, by structuring news texts around key signifiers, news workers have in mind particular signifieds. The intended relationships between the signifiers used and the corresponding signifieds are *encoded* into texts on the basis of news and other societal conventions (i.e., established codes). Readers of news texts may *decode* these signs according to the intended codes; on the other hand, they may employ alternative codes that subvert the intended meanings (Hall 1973). The resulting struggle for meaning, between the "forces of production and modes of reception" (Fiske 1987), is what I aim to preface in this chapter with a semiotic analysis of the KTTV text.

Textual devices

In addition to arguments and signs, important textual devices also point to the centrality of certain assumptions embedded in the KTTV text. In their study of the *Nationwide* text, Brunsdon and Morley (1978) identify several such devices employed by the producers of the British news magazine to structure its text, devices that shed light on the text's underlying assumptions. These rather generic devices include *linking, framing, focusing, nominating* and *summing-up*. Each seems to play a rather critical role in the structuring of the KTTV text.

Linking. This device serves the textual function of guiding the viewer through the discourse(s) (Brunsdon and Morley 1978). Including such acts as the introduction of reporters and/or segments by anchors ("now over to . . ."), linking is the taken-for-granted glue that binds the different segments of the text together, helping to "naturalize" (White 1987, p. 147) them into a coherent narrative. As we shall see below, linking devices are used extensively by KTTV newsworkers to structure the text.

Framing. This device represents attempts to establish the preferred textual topics and explain or defend their relevance in terms of the audience's concerns – real or imagined. Brunsdon and Morley (1978) argue that linking and framing together define the "meta-language" of the text – "that which comments on and places the other discourses in a hierarchy of significance, and which therefore actively constitutes the programme as a 'structure in dominance'" (p. 61). In other words, linking and framing devices help reconstitute and simplify the "divergent realities" of the various program items "in terms of their reality-for-the-programme" (p. 61). An important characteristic of the *Nationwide* text – and the KTTV text – is that extra-program participants (i.e., those other than anchors and reporters) only have access to "lower levels of the discourse" (p. 61). In short, these participants' "contributions are always framed by the presenters' [anchors' and reporters'] statements" (p. 61).

Focusing. This device consists of attempts to establish the angle a narrative will take on a particular topic; that is, focusing involves highlighting certain aspects of the topic while pushing others to the background

(Brunsdon and Morley 1978). Focusing is routinely evident in the efforts of news reporters to ignore certain elements of an interviewee's statement while following up on others. In conjunction with linking and framing, focusing work in the KTTV text channels interviews and other potentially divergent textual elements into the flow of the emerging narrative.

Nominating. This device works to signal the audience regarding the identity and status of extra-program participants (Brunsdon and Morley 1978). This work typically includes brief references to a participant's social/organizational affiliations, experiences, expertise and so on, cluing the audience in as to his or her competency to speak on the issue at hand. Nominating work, as we shall see below, is an important feature of the KTTV text.

Summing-up. This device constitutes the final pass at drawing together the main threads of the text into a cogent, coherent narrative. Typically, each item in a news narrative is summed up before moving on to the next item (Brunsdon and Morley 1978). Choices, of course, must be made concerning which topics or themes touched on in the item will be highlighted and which will be relegated to the background. A news worker is typically assigned by his or her news desk to construct a particular story, one which generally fits into a pre-established news frame (see Tuchman 1978). Newsworkers tend to make summing-up choices concerning topics and themes in accordance with this frame. Summing-up work is also a prominent feature of the KTTV text.

Findings

My close analysis of the KTTV text revealed that at least fourteen major assumptions are embedded in it.[8] Below, I discuss each assumption in terms of the arguments, signs or devices linked with it in the text.

1. *The events are undesirable.* Throughout the text, KTTV newsworkers talked about the events as if they were undesirable, unfortunate, ill-fated. That is, statements concerning event-related activity were frequently prefaced or qualified with expressions of regret:

. . . The scene here again . . . *I hate to draw the comparison*, but it is the same thing that we saw twenty-seven years ago in Watts . . . this, part of the city just destroying itself, burning itself up (1).[9]

. . . *I hate to tell you this Patti*, but we feel guilty for this man [Asian man who was attacked], for having left him here (3).

Ah, ah, the fire department, *unfortunately*, in too many instances, can do nothing (5).

What you're looking at right now – and I don't have a monitor here, but I believe what you're looking at right now are two fires burning simultaneously on the corner of Western and Slauson. This, *unfortunately*, despite the calls for peace, ah, despite the calls for, ah, ah, lack of action . . . (20).

Ah, it, it is a serious situation out there *we're very sorry to report* (20).

The First AME church has been the site tonight of a, ah, of a huge rally in terms of numbers of people – several thousand. Ah, city officials, religious leaders, all praying and pushing and working as best they can for everyone to remain calm, and *unfortunately not all of us are listening to that* (21).

Ah, *it's totally disgusting*, ah, I had never thought that I would see another time like this in history. Ah, but history was made today when the verdicts came in (26).

Nowhere in the text is the argument (or counter-assumption) entertained that the events might be desirable, or even instrumental in some way.

2. *The events are centered in South Central Los Angeles.* Early in the text, KTTV newsworkers located the events firmly in South Central Los Angeles by discussing boundaries in terms of streets and freeways. The events were essentially confined to "this part of the city," "where all of the problems are:"

. . . The scene here again . . . I hate to draw the comparison, but it is the same thing that we saw twenty-seven years ago in Watt . . . *this, part of the city just destroying itself, burning itself up* (1).

Using his parameters, again, of the geography. That explains why the Harbor Freeway, we've had the report that the Harbor Freeway, both ways, has been closed between Century Boulevard on the South and the Santa Monica Freeway on the North because that would traverse right directly through *the area that Tony was telling us about where all the problems are* (9).

Indeed, a graphic is used to identify the location of event-related activity "taped earlier" as "South Central LA"

Throughout the remainder of the text, KTTV newsworkers used the term "South Central" four times in their discussion of the events. At only one point in the text do newsworkers mention possible event-related activity that was not centered in South Central Los Angeles. This brief reference concerned the "chaos" that erupted in downtown Los Angeles, outside police headquarters (Parker Center); newsworkers offered this reference toward the end of the text as part of their summing-up efforts, efforts to tie together the main threads of the text into a cogent, coherent narrative (Brunsdon and Morley 1978). But earlier in these same summing-up efforts, newsworkers had explicitly identified South Central Los Angeles as *the* site of the events, and "many residents" of the area (syntagmatically), it seems, as *the* event participants:

Fires are raging *in South Central Los Angeles* at this hour – a testament to the anger and frustration felt by many residents tonight (34).

3. *Elected officials/community leaders could/should say something to event participants that would influence them one way or another.* Throughout the text, KTTV newsworkers and interviewees talked about elected officials and community "leaders" as if they expected these "leaders" to take charge in the crisis. There existed the unspoken assumption in these statements that elected officials and community "leaders" had the ability to influence event participants, to either make statements that would persuade them to remain calm or to organize them in some other way:

But I have to admit I'm very disappointed in the rally. I thought that the black leaders had all congregated here – and it was a safe haven for people to come and talk – *but they didn't say anything.* When they should have been out there in the streets with the people who were really angry and venting their frustrations like the fires we're seeing across the street. There are people shooting – *they should be out in the streets with people, and telling them what we should be doing, what is our next step* (12).

Okay that's the reaction from some of the people who are attending this rally here that started at seven o'clock and ended about nine fifteen. A few minutes ago there was a prayer over here. I know downstairs some of *the male leaders of the church are meeting, trying to again call for calm* (19).

The First AME church has been the site tonight of a, ah, huge rally in terms of numbers of people – several thousand. Ah, *city officials, religious leaders, all praying and pushing and working as best they can for everyone to remain calm . . .* (21).

You've been particularly, ah, articulate the last, *ah, few days in this message.* I, I keep getting the image of, of a fighter pilot who says, "I've tried 'A,' I've tried 'B,' I've tried 'C.'" They go through the list and they can't figure out what's wrong. But, you, that must be what you're feeling. You've tried everything you know how to try . . . *Is there anything left . . . for you to say?* (23 to 25).

In short, the possibility that elected officials and community "leaders" may have had little credibility and/or clout with event participants – that they were not really "leaders" in this sense – was not considered by newsworkers or interviewees. Instead, these speakers seemed to argue that the events persisted due to a lack of communication by "leaders," or due to communication of the wrong message(s).

4. *The events were caused by the Rodney King beating verdicts.* Framing work in the KTTV text situated each textual topic in narrative space, establishing its relevance in terms of implied audience concerns. This work combined with linking work to complete the meta-language of the text, to

structure the array of potentially divergent textual topics into a coherent, unified narrative (see Brunsdon and Morley 1978). A graphic, which appears twice in the KTTV text, connected these potentially divergent textual topics, thereby establishing the master frame:

Cops On Trial: The Rodney King Case. (10, 21)

That is, this graphic frame ultimately worked to limit the domain of possible relations between each textual topic to one root relation: the Rodney King beating verdicts. Serving as the root common denominator, this frame syntagmatically established *the* logical association between each textual topic. KTTV newsworkers and interviewees buttressed this frame throughout the text with eight explicit references to the "verdicts" or "Rodney King," references that worked to identify the trial outcome as *the* cause of the events. The following are just two examples:

Ah, it's totally disgusting, ah, I had never thought that I would see another time like this in history. Ah, *but history was made today when the verdicts came in* (26).

It is, ah, now ten o'clock and, ah, tonight *a community is venting its fury over the verdicts in the Rodney King beating trial* (34).

Nowhere in the text are other possible causes of the events explicitly discussed by newsworkers or interviewees.

5. *The events are "riots."* The term "riot[s][ing][ers]" was used five times in the text to describe the events and event-related activity (7, 20, 22, 22, 35). Nowhere in the text was the use of this term questioned by newsworkers or interviewees. Furthermore, other terms that might describe the events – such as "rebellion," "insurrection," "uprising," "revolt," and so on – do not appear in the text. In short, the text paradigmatically works to link all of the characteristics/meanings associated with past "riots" ("known") to the emerging events ("unknown").

6. *Race is a central factor in the events.* As I discussed in chapter 1, race is an important representation in the United States, the central axis of social relations (see Prager 1982; Omi and Winant 1986, 1994). In this society, "one of the first things we notice about people when we meet them (along with their sex) is their race. We utilize race to provide clues about who a person is" (Omi and Winant 1986, p. 62) and why s/he might think and act in a particular way. In short, race-as-representation is a salient feature of the social landscape in the US, a feature chock full of meanings and interpretive codes. Journalistic convention seems to respect this feature, to acknowledge the potency of raced meanings in the US. For the "bible" of journalistic convention and writing practice, *The Associated Press Stylebook and Libel Manual* (Goldstein 1994), explicitly defines two situa-

tions in which the use of raced labels is appropriate in the construction of news texts (p. 167):

1. In biographical and announcement stories, particularly when they involve a feat or appointment that has not routinely been associated with members of a particular race.
2. When it provides the reader with a substantial insight into conflicting emotions known or likely to be involved in a demonstration or similar event.[10]

KTTV actually subscribes to about six different journalistic stylebooks, including the AP stylebook. But according to the station's news director, the rule of thumb concerning raced labels is as follows: "If pertinent to the story, we use them. If not, we don't."[11] This "pertinence," of course, is a socially constructed artifact of the current racial order, one that is reflected in journalistic conventions and stylebooks. It is not some absolute measure.

In light of this discussion, it seems that an undercurrent of raced representations indeed flows strongly throughout the KTTV text. Although the term "race" does not appear in the text, raced *labels* are used eight times to refer to event participants or victims (3, 3, 12, 16, 16, 18, 20, 28). While interviewees accounted for the majority of these uses, newsworkers nonetheless seemed to imply (syntagmatically) that race was "pertinent" to the story. For example, one newsworker prefaced his report of an event victim who was "drenched in blood" by noting that the victim "appeared to be an Asian man." The newsworker also noted that the victim was being helped by an "African-American man" (3). Another newsworker reported attacks on a KTTV photographer by noting that the photographer "happens to be white" (20). As I argue below, the importance of race-as-representation was further inscribed in the text by the designation of blacks as "event insiders."

7. *Blacks are "event insiders."* In the KTTV text, all of the interviewees were visibly "black" (i.e., those at the First AME rally and Reverend Washington). The interviewers, in contrast, were visibly "non-black" (i.e., KTTV newsworkers).[12] Non-black-raced interviewers posed questions about violence and efforts to restore order; they were outsiders to the events. Black-raced interviewees, as if they were uniquely positioned to do so, were singled out to respond to these questions; they were insiders to the events. In short, a syntagmatic line was structured into the text separating black-raced subjects (signifier) and event insiders (signified), from non-black-raced subjects (signifier) and event outsiders (signified).[13]

Furthermore, throughout the text, the choice of terminology by both interviewers and interviewees echoed this raced dividing line. The events were metaphorically compared to "Watts" (1, 7), a signature black "riot" of the turbulent 1960s (e.g., see Bullock 1969; Horne 1995); they were confined to South Central Los Angeles, "this part of the city" (1), and assumed to be initiated by "many residents" (34), "people" (1, 12, 14, 20, 22, 34), "crowds" (20), "my brothers and sisters" (16), and "thugs" (4) who live there. Before the recent influx of Latino-raced residents into the area, South Central Los Angeles was recognized as an overwhelmingly "black" community; today the population of the area is about half Latino-raced and half black-raced (Johnson *et al.* 1992). But there were no explicit references to "Latinos," "Mexicans," or "Hispanics" in the text. Instead, five of the eight raced labels appearing in the text – 62.5 percent – referenced "blacks" or "African Americans."

In the KTTV text, outsiders were often presented as the victims of insiders. For example, Reginald Denny – "the man there by that truck" (34) – was "severely beaten" (34) by insiders. Likewise, a news photographer who "happens to be white . . . got a lot of abuse" (20) from insiders.

8. *Ministers have a special responsibility to help restore calm.* Consistent with the text's syntagmatic establishment of the black-raced community as event insiders, newsworkers assumed that some of these subjects – i.e., black-raced ministers – occupied a special position in efforts to help restore peace. For example, an "African American man who appeared to be a minister" (3, 28), an insider, reportedly came to the aide of an "Asian man" (3) who was being beaten by "thugs" (4), an outsider and victim. Likewise, Reverend Washington was among the insiders who had been "disgraced" (28) by the events, who favored the restoration of peace. With the vigilance of a "fighter pilot" (23), he labored to convince his "communities" (28) to remain calm. In fact, as a testament to the assumed role of black-raced ministers in the crisis, their unique qualification to speak on the issues, Reverend Washington was nominated five times by KTTV newsworkers (Brunsdon and Morley 1978):

. . . But Reverend Washington, I think your view of what we've seen in terms of the video, of parts of South Central Los Angeles burning to the ground [is important for our audience to hear] (21).

You've been particularly, ah, articulate the last, ah, few days in this message. I, I keep getting the image of, of a fighter pilot who says, "I've tried 'A,' I've tried 'B,' I've tried 'C.'" They go through the list and they can't figure out what's wrong. But, you, that must be what you're feeling. You've tried everything you know how to try. Is there anything left . . . for you to say (23 to 25)?

Reverend Washington, thank you. Please stay with us. We need your voice, ah, tonight (29).

Stay with us (31).

If you have a few minutes we'd appreciate it (32).

In short, black-raced ministers (signifier) were syntagmatically linked in the text with efforts to restore calm, to restore order (signifieds).

9. *Voting is the appropriate outlet for change.* As I argued above, textual assumptions defined the events as an undesirable strategy for addressing the anger and frustration attributed to the Rodney King beating verdicts. In an attempt to frame video footage of burning buildings, to establish the relevance of this footage in terms of perceived audience concerns (Brunsdon and Morley 1978), a KTTV newsworker suggests that voting – as opposed to the events – is the appropriate outlet for social change:

What you're looking at right now – and I don't have a monitor here, but I believe what you're looking at right now are two fires burning simultaneously on the corner of Western and Slauson. This, unfortunately, despite the calls for peace, ah, despite the calls for, ah, ah, lack of action, and, ah, *taking action at the polls instead of out on the streets* . . . (20).

10. *Police ought to have a significant presence at the site(s) of the events.* Early in the text, newsworkers noted that it would be "unfair" of them to suggest that police were not present at key sites of event-related activity if, in fact, they were present. Underlying this perception, of course, is the assumption that police *ought* to have a significant presence at these sites, that this presence is expected as a part of proper, effective law enforcement procedure:

And, and, that's good information about the police officers being in presence. *Perhaps, perhaps we've been a little bit unfair through the evening, by, by continuing, continually saying, "No police presence. No police presence."* Now Tony Valdez tells us they are in the area and, ah, especially right on that intersection where it first began (8).

Later in the text, a KTTV newsworker reinforced this assumption by discounting the argument that a police presence might actually incite more event-related activity:

I believe primarily, and this is the sense we got from the command post at Van Ness and Fifty-fourth, that, ah, the police feel at this point that by going into these areas they simply will incite more, ah, just more rioting, ah, more trouble, more anxiety on the community's part. Ah, I can understand people's feelings here at First AME that they, *they need the police into these areas* (20).

This newsworker call for a police presence concludes textual discussion of the issue.

11. *The events are similar to the Watts riots.* According to one KTTV newsworker, event-related activities were identical to what happened during the Watts riots:

. . . The scene here again . . . I hate to draw the comparison, *but it is the same thing that we saw twenty-seven years ago in Watts . . .* this, part of the city just destroying itself, burning itself up (1).

Furthermore, later in the text, this newsworker identified the boundaries of the events as "basically the same" ones that defined the Watts riots:

We are hearing activity, we have seen some activity as far East as, ah, Avalon, ah, well, even going beyond that, ah, to Central and beyond that. Probably going all the way out to, ah, I would guess, Alameda, ah, eastern boundaries. *Curiously, these are basically the same boundaries, ah, we saw during the Watts Riots in August of 1965* (7).

In short, these events were paradigmatically compared to the Watts "riots," and nowhere in the text is this assessment questioned or qualified by other KTTV newsworkers or interviewees.

12. *The First AME "rally" was a reasonable response to the events.* First, KTTV newsworkers treated the First AME gathering as a significant event-related development, one that deserved intermittent news coverage throughout the evening. The coverage featured in the text was but one of several installments:

We want to go back now to the AME church where people are raising their voices in protest, in song, and in prayer (10).

Second, KTTV newsworkers described the First AME gathering as a "rally," a term that carries with it less negative connotations than "protest," "demonstration," or "chaos" – other terms that might have been used to describe the gathering. Moreover, KTTV newsworkers depicted this "rally" as an extremely large gathering, suggesting, perhaps, that they considered size an index of importance (see Gitlin 1980). Finally, these newsworkers noted that the "rally" was dedicated to maintaining order, a concern implicit in the first textual assumption:

Hi Patti. The *rally* wrapped up about 30 minutes ago. *This place, if you recall, was packed. There were three thousand people inside the building. I'm told just as many outside. The main message was, "Stay calm, remain calm. Let's take out our frustrations at the, the polling place* (11)."

One of the black-raced interviewees at First AME, however, noted that she was "very disappointed in the rally," that the "leaders didn't say anything" (12). But in their summing-up of the coverage – their attempts to draw together the main threads of the text into a cogent, coherent narrative (Brunsdon and Morley 1978) – KTTV newsworkers glossed over this complaint, concluding that leaders were trying to call for calm "as best they can:"

Okay that's the reaction from some of the people who are attending this rally here that started at seven o'clock and ended about nine fifteen. A few minutes ago there was a prayer over here. I know downstairs some of the male leaders of the church are meeting, *trying to again call for calm* (19).

The First AME church has been the site tonight of a, ah, *huge rally in terms of numbers of people – several thousand.* Ah, city officials, religious leaders, all praying and pushing and *working as best they can for everyone to remain calm* . . . (21).

13. *Prayer is a reasonable strategy for addressing the events.* The previous textual assumption depicted the First AME rally as a reasonable response to the events. An integral part of this gathering, as KTTV newsworkers noted in their framing of the KTTV coverage, was prayer:

We want to go back now to the AME church where people are raising their voices in protest, in song, *and in prayer* (10).

Moreover, Reverend Washington – whose special status in the crisis was highlighted by five newsworker nominations – twice advocated prayer as an important strategy:

Again, ah, to say there's really nothing left to say, but, ah, *now it's our job as ministers to go down on our knees in prayer and ask for a higher resource to intervene in this matter* (26).

We're not going to play Superman. But there are some people we can reach. And that's the message we want to say Chris, ah, Chris and Patti, *that we will continue to look for the higher resources* – even in the dilemma of this matter that's at hand right now (28).

Nowhere in the text do KTTV newsworkers or interviewees question the appropriateness of prayer as a strategy for addressing the events.

14. *The role of news media is to serve their viewers by providing them with fair and factual coverage of the events.* This assumption, it seems, defines a default position in U.S culture. The notion that the press has a special responsibility to disseminate news and information – that it constitutes the "Fourth Estate" in the US – has its origins in the first article of the Bill of Rights (see Emery and Emery 1978). Here, of course, we find the constitutional basis for the freedom of speech and of the press. Today, journalists understand this article to mean that the press has the right – as well as the duty – to provide fair and factual coverage of important societal events, "to dig out and interpret news and to offer intelligent opinion in the marketplace of ideas" (see Emery and Emery 1978, p. xv). As the Journalists' Code

of Ethics puts it, "We believe the agencies of mass communication are carriers of public discussion and information, acting on their Constitutional mandate and freedom to learn and report the facts" (Mencher 1981, p. 422).

Regardless of how well the press, as Fourth Estate, has exercised its rights or lived up to its duties over the years, journalists have had to present themselves to the world as if they *are* objective reporters of news, of "the facts." For as their code of ethics implies – and as Schudson (1978) argues in his social history of newspapers – journalists are interested in being *recognized* as professionals. Today, the objectivity ideal has become the very symbol of professionalism for journalists, a claim to credibility (Schudson 1978). Thus, implicit in news texts that are constructed by professional journalists (e.g., the KTTV text) is the assumption that the coverage is as fair and factual as possible.

Conclusions

The fourteen major assumptions embedded in the KTTV text are listed in table 3.1. In the preceding analysis, you will recall, I attempted to bracket my understanding of the events – to keep my analysis as "apolitical" as possible. That is, my goal was simply to employ argument analysis, semiotic analysis, and an analysis of textual devices in order to identify key assumptions embedded in the KTTV text. Indeed, my goal was to establish these assumptions as raw textual elements, not to comment on their validity or social significance in some extra-textual sense. (This latter project is undertaken in chapter 8, where I present an ideological analysis of the KTTV text.)

Given that I have conceptualized the television experience as a struggle for meaning between texts, viewers, and their intertextual memories (see chapter 2), I now turn to focusing my analysis on the latter two factors. What did study informants do with these textual assumptions? Did they tend to uncritically accept them in their group discussions? Did they reject them? Was the raced subjectivity of informants somehow associated with the acceptance or rejection of these textual assumptions? What role did intertextual memories play in informant understandings of the KTTV text? Part 2 (Audience) and Part 3 (Analysis and conclusions) focus on answering these questions, on exploring in more detail the interplay of media and race in the meaning-making process.

PART II

Audience

4

Stigmatized by association: Latino-raced informants and the KTTV text

[Latinos] just took advantage of it. Because they didn't even know what the hell was going on. It was none of their business what happened to Rodney King.   (Latino-raced informant)

According to the United States Census Bureau, "Latinos" do *not* constitute a racial group.[1] Instead, this rather heterogenous mix of people with Mexican, Cuban, Puerto Rican and other Central and South American backgrounds might be of any officially recognized "race," or some combination of two or more of them.[2] Indeed, in the last census these people were given the option of filling in a racial identification circle on the enumeration form. Mexican-Americans, for example, were evenly split between describing themselves as "white" or "other race" in 1990; virtually none considered themselves "black" (Skerry 1993).

In one sense, the term "Latino" suggests some type of panethnic solidarity across the various groups with Latin connections. Some scholars argue for the existence of this solidarity simply on the basis of these groups' shared experiences of discrimination and prejudice *as Latinos* – those who speak Spanish and/or exhibit other recognizable ties to a certain region of the world (Oboler 1992). At the same time, however, narrow nationalist sentiments do exist (e.g., "Chicano Power" versus "Latino Power"), sentiments that seem to invalidate notions of panethnic solidarity (Martinez 1990). Moreover, when particular groups within the "alliance" are singled out for analysis, it is often not clear whether they view themselves in *ethnic* terms (i.e., simply as culturally different) or *minority* terms (i.e., as systematically oppressed) (Skerry 1993). So what does it mean to speak of *Latino-raced* informants?

In another sense, "Latino" is a rejection of the term "Hispanic," a label imposed by the dominant society that makes explicit links to Europe, while submerging African and Native American roots (Martinez 1990). "Latino" appears to be more popular in Los Angeles, with its recent large influx of Central and South American immigrants, than in other US cities (Skerry 1993). But as we shall see below, few informants talked about themselves *as "Latinos."* Some informants even distanced themselves from other groups typically considered part of the panethnic group.

Nonetheless, I employ the term "Latino" in this study as an alternative to "Hispanic" because the dominant society *does* tend to lump Latino-raced people into a panethnic group and distribute rewards and punishments accordingly. As representation, this panethnic label becomes a racial one, attributing bodily and other characteristics to members of the group, explaining/justifying the group's relative position in the racial order (see Omi and Winant, 1986, 1994).

With this said, "Latinos" were largely invisible in the KTTV text (see chapter 3). This is an interesting observation given the demographics of the area identified in the text as "where all the problems are." That is, Latino-raced residents account for half of the population in South Central Los Angeles (Johnson *et al.* 1992), but none of the images/interviewees in the KTTV text. Indeed, figures on event-related arrests, deaths, and so on suggest that Latino-raced residents were greatly involved in the events (e.g., see Hazen 1992, p. 46). Accordingly, Latino-raced informants seemed to read between the images and project their group into the events depicted in the KTTV text. Even where panethnic solidarity was weak, many informants appeared to be stigmatized by association with Latino-raced event participants. From these informants' perspective, "It was none of their [Latino-raced participants] business what happened to Rodney King."

YOUTH

This interview was conducted in the word-processing instruction room of a South Central Los Angeles youth development center. The informants sat in swivel chairs and focused on a 19-inch color television set. Group members included Martha, female, 18; Carlos, male, 24; and Felix, male, 20.[3] Martha was a student studying for her high-school equivalency degree at the center; Carlos and Felix were both employed by the center as teaching assistants. All three informants identified themselves as "Latino" on the questionnaire. Martha, however, qualified this categorization by noting that she was also "Mexican." All of the informants described themselves as "somewhat religious." The socio-economic status of this group was rather low relative to other Latino-raced study groups (see table A.1).

Table 4.1 presents data on media consumption and previous event-related discussion for each of the Latino-raced groups. Two of the three informants in this group (YOUTH) reported that they watched more than three hours of television news on the first day of the events, while the third reported watching between one and three hours. At best informants reported reading the *Los Angeles Times* "sometimes." And although these informants frequently interacted at the youth center, they reported discussing the events with one another only about once per month since the events occurred.

Screening Highlights: This group approached the KTTV text rather solemnly, without much talk or animation. As the screening begins, informants sit quietly and fix their eyes on the screen. About two minutes into the text, intermittent talking begins over the helicopter reporters' remarks. This talking covers the segment in the text where one of the anchors, Harris, refers to people in the intersections as "thugs" and informants do not visibly react to the newsworker's comment. Intermittent talking continues until Angela – the first interviewee at First AME – begins to criticize the rally. At that point, informants devote their attention to the screen and each interviewee's views regarding the rally.

Informants also pay complete attention to Reverend Washington, who appears at the anchor desk for an interview by Suarez and Harris. Informants do not visibly react when Suarez compares the young black-raced minister – the vigilance with which he attempts to restore peace and calm – to a "fighter pilot." Talking begins again over the anchors' concluding summary. Informants audibly gasp, however, when summary footage of the attacks in the Florence and Normandie intersection appears on the screen. But informants sit rather quietly during the summary footage of the Denny beating and the unrest at police headquarters. In short, informants exhibited little visible opposition to the text as-construction during the screening.

Discussion Highlights: Table 4.2 presents the emergence of key arguments in the group's discussion. This group generally opted to focus on the implications of the events, not the media's *construction* of them. That is, this group received the text in a referential mode. Table 4.2 reveals that there were no arguments offered in the 19 minutes of discussion prior to prompt 2 (which asks specifically about the video and reporters) regarding news construction. When specifically asked "what was good" and "what was bad" about the video (prompt 2), informants again responded in terms of *events*, not in terms of the text's construction:

MARTHA: Nothing was good. I didn't see nothing good. Everything was bad to me. Some people talked consensus. I mean, there were riot –

FELIX: Maybe it was the only good part when the Reverend came out talking.

CARLOS: Ummhmmm, yeah.

The one criticism of the text as-construction followed this discussion and described the coverage as "sensationalistic." But this charge was quickly balanced by the argument that the media were trying to alert people, for their own good, to what was happening in their community:

CARLOS: And the communicators, the communicators, you could actually see them kind of putting, ah, sensationalistic –

FELIX: They had to.

CARLOS: They came up and try and kind of give a sense of what happened.

(several turns later)

FELIX: Because see, if it wasn't for them [the media], nobody would have known what was going on and a lot of people could have gotten hurt.

The group's referential decoding of the text is consistent with the behavior of group members during the screening: that is, they sat still and did not directly challenge the text as-construction.

Furthermore, as group means on the attitudinal scales suggest (see table 4.3),[4] this group discussed the outbreak of the events in terms congruent with the assumptions embedded in the KTTV text. That is, this group discussed the events in terms of the King beating verdicts (assumption 4) and associated raced tensions in society (assumption 6).[5] Informants also lamented the lack of leadership during the crisis – a void, they felt, that resulted in residents "destroying our own community." In other words, the group felt that the events constituted an inappropriate vehicle for change (assumption 1):

FELIX: I mean, protesting would be okay. I got nothing against that because we got freedom of speech.

MARTHA: That's true.

FELIX: But the looting and the burning of buildings . . . that got out of hand.

MARTHA: I mean, by solving a problem, it's not like we have to act all crazy, not like we have to react by beating other people, not going to react by burning peoples' places just because you have a problem! That's not right.

Despite acknowledging "Latino" involvement in the events, informants in this group seemed to accept the KTTV assumption that the black-raced community owned the events, that its members constituted the event insiders (assumption 7). Latino-raced looters, from their perspective, just took advantage of the situation following the King beating verdicts. This involvement clearly bothered the informants, who, as Latino-raced subjects, felt that they were actually targeted by the events:

FELIX: But nah, but the thing was . . . It's . . . I don't know. It's not about that though. It was all about . . . I think that the way we're telling it, it's not about Rodney King or race.

CARLOS: No –

FELIX: It's about people trying to come up with money, with things, freeloading. Because that's what it's really all about. I mean, *our race* [emphasis added] –

MARTHA: Yeah, but look. How would you tell him [your child] how it started? It started with Rodney King, right?

FELIX: But where did it end up, though? I mean, Rodney King had nothing to do with everybody going into a store and stealing.

MARTHA: Well that's true.

FELIX: Burning the store's . . .

MARTHA: But it got, it had, ah, some kind of part of it.

FELIX: Well, let's put it this way. Of all the cops there, that beat Rodney King, I didn't see no Hispanic cops there.

CARLOS: Yeah, there were a couple.

FELIX: Nah, I didn't see none.

(several turns later)

FELIX: It wasn't about that. All the anger that had built up for whatever reason. You know, cause up there by my house there were a lot of things happening for a while. You know, I was scared for my family to go out . . . Because they had started rioting . . . It wasn't only against whites. It was against Mexicans, too.

CARLOS: Ummhmmm.

FELIX: You can't do nothing but protect yourself and your family.

In the end, perhaps, these informants' belief that their Latino-raced status placed them at risk during the events resulted in them finding little fault with the KTTV text, its negative depiction of the events.

But this group's reception of the KTTV text also seemed to be inflected by intertextual memories from informants' television viewing on the first night of the events. During the group's discussion, for example, Carlos recalled another local television station's (KABC) coverage of the First A.M.E gathering. Rather than interview those who were "singing peacefully," he complained, a KABC reporter "started interviewing the people that were the most loud." One of these interviewees started talking like he "was some bum in the streets . . . just looking like a wino, you know. He started, 'Let's go to Westwood! . . . No peace, no justice!'" This memory clearly reflected Carlos' understanding of the events, that "sensationalistic" media coverage and a lack of community leadership allowed things to get out of hand. Indeed, this memory may also have shaped his reception of the KTTV text (and the other informants with whom he negotiated the text's meanings), facilitating his (their) acceptance of the assumption that the events were undesirable.

FAMILY

This interview was conducted in South Central Los Angeles, in the informants' living room. The informants sat on a sectional sofa and directed their attention to a large-screen, projection television set. The group was composed of the following informants: Irene, female, 21; Victor, male, 24; Marta, female, 24; Jilda, female, 26; and Jose, male, 20. Irene, a student at Freemont High School in Los Angeles, was the center of this network; Marta was her sister, Jose her brother, Victor her brother-in-law, and Jilda her cousin. All of the informants lived together at the site of the interview and identified themselves as "Latino" on the questionnaire. Marta, however, qualified this categorization by noting that she was also "Mexican." All of the informants described themselves as "somewhat religious." The socio-economic status of this group was quite low relative to other Latino-raced study groups (see table A.1).

The majority of the informants in this group reported watching television news "all evening" during the first day of the events (see table 4.1). In contrast, only one of the group members reported reading the *Los Angeles Times* every day throughout the course of the events. Despite living together as family members, most of the informants reported discussing the events quite infrequently in the months following the outbreak.

Screening Highlights: Compared to the previous Latino-raced group (YOUTH), this group received the KTTV text rather actively: the screening was filled with laughter, conversation, and frequent pointing at the screen. About 12 seconds into the screening the helicopter reporter mentions "looting" and the group immediately bursts into laughter. The mood of the group appears rather somber, however, when the reporter describes the plight of the Asian-raced man who was "drenched in blood." One of the informants, Marta, shakes her head at this point. Informants do not visibly react to the "thug" comment, although about four seconds later laughter again breaks out and Marta points at the television set. Marta shakes her head intermittently throughout the remainder of the reporter's remarks.

All of the informants pay close attention to the first interviewee at First AME, but begin laughing when she mentions the term "black leaders." "Black leaders!" Jose laughs. Informants alternate between talking and listening to the remaining First AME interviewees. They point to and discuss the various landmarks appearing on the screen during the Asian-raced reporter's remarks. Initially, informants pay close attention to Reverend Washington, showing no visible reaction to Suarez's "fighter pilot" comparison. But about 14 minutes into the text, Victor begins to read a magazine and the other informants start talking over the minister's interview.

When summary footage of the unrest in the intersections appears, however, all eyes again focus on the screen. "Oh, I hate that, I hate that!" Marta says. Victor puts down his magazine when one of the anchors mentions the phrase, "beating people up." Throughout the remainder of the summary, informants shake their heads at various points. One of the informants points out that a protester was carrying the Mexican flag during the police headquarters footage. In short, informants were quite animated during the screening, but this activity did not appear to signify any group opposition to the text as-construction – except in the case of interviewee comments.

Discussion highlights. Table 4.4 presents the emergence of key arguments in the group's discussion. The first inclination of informants in this group was to discuss the events reported in the text, *not* the text's construction of the events. That is, like the previous group (YOUTH), this group decoded the text in a referential mode. Table 4.4 reveals that arguments concerning news construction do *not* emerge in the first 7 minutes and 33 seconds of the discussion (i.e., prior to prompt 2). Only after the discussion stalled – after informants were prompted with questions specifically pertaining to the text, reporters and interviewees (i.e., prompt 2) – did arguments regarding news coverage emerge in the discussion. But none of this discussion questioned the text as-construction. Instead, informants debated what they thought was the most important news in the text, generally agreeing that news coverage of fires and looting incited more violence. While informants tended to question the courage and motivation of KTTV reporters, they also seemed to agree that the reporters did "a good job" in their reporting on the events:

VICTOR: They [reporters] were scared because they thought they were going to get hurt too.

MARTA: But I think they did a good job!

VICTOR: They did their job.

MARTA: I think they did a great job!

VICTOR: They did their job but they also got hurt.

MARTA: But, but, but didn't they do a good job?

IRENE: They let the whole world know what was going on.

VICTOR: That's what they get paid for, right?

As was the case with the previous group (YOUTH), this group's referential decoding of the text was also consistent with the behavior of members during the screening. That is, although informants in this group were more animated than those in the YOUTH group, their activity was *not* oriented toward challenging the text as-construction.

Furthermore, as group means on the scales might suggest (see table 4.3),[6] the arguments that emerged in this group's discussion were congruent with most of the assumptions embedded in the KTTV text. First and foremost, this group discussed the events as undesirable acts of self-destruction (assumption 1):

MARTA: I would tell him [her son] that there's a lot of angry people out there and they're, they're real upset about what happened and, and, that the way they're reacting is the wrong way, but, and, and, most of the people are just taking advantage of it.

JOSE: Right.

VICTOR: And the way they're reacting is wrong.

MARTA: Yeah, that's not the right way.

Informants attributed these acts to the King beating verdicts and other raced tensions (assumptions 4 and 6). They also appeared to accept the raced dividing line established in the KTTV text, discussing the events as if black-raced subjects constituted the only group whose participation was in any way reasonable (assumption 7). Latino-raced participants just exploited the situation, shaming their community:

MARTA: They [Latinos] just took advantage of it. Because they didn't even know what the hell was going on. It was none of their business what happened to Rodney King.

In the end, group members embraced a "Mexican" identity to the exclusion of a broader, Latino-raced one and essentially blamed the events on "blacks" and "Salvadorans":

JOSE:	But hold on! Hold on! No. No. It was all . . . okay . . . If you think about it, it was all Salvadoran people, right?
VICTOR:	Sal –
JOSE:	It's because Salvadoran people are full of shit, right. YYYYYYYYYYYYYYYYYYYYYYYYYYYYYYYY[7]
JOSE:	It was a higher percentage, it was a higher percentage of Salvadoran people being in the Pen than there was Mexican.
MARTA:	Well –
JOSE:	During the riots – YYYYyyyy
VICTOR:	They got deported, though.
JOSE:	Yeah, oh yeah.
MARTA:	They should deport every single one of them – everybody back to El Salvador.
VICTOR:	The Salvadorans to El Salvador. Blacks to Africa.

Furthermore, informants seemed to bring these feelings toward other groups with them to the interview. Intertextual memories emerged several times in group discussion, echoing informants' disparaging characterizations and appraisals of event participants and insiders. For example, Victor's contempt for "blacks" was vehemently expressed by one such memory. In the middle of the group's discussion, but seemingly unconnected to the flow of the dialogue, he suddenly recalled and then condemned all of the media attention that had recently been given a film about a controversial black leader:[8]

VICTOR:	And then they bring up that shit about Malcolm X. Who the fuck is Malcolm X?

LATINA

This interview was also conducted in South Central Los Angeles, in the living room of one of the informants. The informants sat on a large sofa, their gaze fixed on a 19-inch color television across the room. This group was composed of the following members: Carla, female, 18; Bette, female, 18; Nina, female, 16; and Vicki, female, 18. Carla, a student at Freemont High School in Los Angeles, was the center of this network; Bette and Nina – who were sisters – were Carla's cousins, and Vicki was their close friend. All of the informants identified themselves as "Latino" on the questionnaire. Three of the four informants described themselves as "somewhat religious." The socioeconomic status of this group was quite low relative to other Latino-raced study groups (see table A.1).

As was the case with the previous group (FAMILY), most informants in this group reported watching television news "all evening" during the first day of the events (see table 4.1). But unlike the previous group, most informants in the group also reported reading the *Los Angeles Times* "sometimes" over the course of the events. Finally, despite maintaining close ties, group members reported discussing the events among themselves only about once per month or less in the months following the outbreak.

Screening highlights After a somewhat quiet start, this group became rather animated during the screening, frequently talking back to the screen at key points. Near the beginning of the text, over portions of the helicopter reporter's comments, group members engage in intermittent, unintelligible talk. When the plight of the Asian-raced man who was "drenched in blood" is described, a worried look develops on Carla's face and she shakes her head. The group begins to discuss the ethnicity of the beaten man about 2 minutes and 40 seconds into the screening. When the news anchor refers to event participants as "thugs," Bette mocks him and his use of the term. There is much talk and laughter among group members during the remainder of the helicopter reporter's comments. They criticize the reporter for what they see as his obsession with event boundaries.

About 4 minutes and 41 seconds into the screening, the group members start discussing what night of the events is being covered by the text. But when coverage turns to First AME and the black-raced interviewees who attended the rally, informants stop talking and pay strict attention to the screen. When one of the interviewees argues that "If we go to Beverly Hills, they'll probably drop tear gas on us," Bette nods her head in agreement.

The moment the First AME interviews stop, and reporter commentary begins, talking resumes in the group. Carla laughs when a reporter mentions that event participants were "carrying whatever they could, large tv sets, shoes . . ." When the Reverend Washington interview starts, however, talking again ceases and the group fixes its attention on the screen. "You know what was good about the burning though," Nina interjects into the silence, "that they burned down a lot of old buildings." Informants do not visibly react when one of the anchors compares the reverend to a fighter pilot. But when the reverend pleads with viewers to stay calm amidst the events, Bette remarks, "How can you stay calm when your house is about to get burnt?"

Group members sit quietly during the beginning of the anchors' summary. But when footage appears depicting the activity in the intersection of Florence and Normandie, informants audibly gasp. "Damn!" Nina exclaims. "Are those Hispanics?" During the footage of the protests at police headquarters, Nina again interjects: "Damn! Look at that! Look at that! They want respect but they don't deserve it." In short, informants in this group were quite animated during the screening, and some of this activity appeared to challenge the text as-construction; other screening activity seemed to be directed at the events depicted on the screen, as if the text was a clear window onto them.

Discussion highlights Table 4.5 presents the emergence of key arguments in the group's discussion. The table shows that discussion stalled in this group quite early, after about 4 minutes and 48 seconds. During this initial discussion period, none of the arguments offered by informants concerned the KTTV text as-construction. That is, the first inclination of informants in this group was *not* to decode the text in a metalinguistic mode. Instead, they decoded the text in a referential mode, focusing on the events as-events and their feelings about them.

However, following prompt 2 (which specifically asked group members about media coverage), informants launched into a rather scathing critique of the KTTV text, blaming the media for, among other things, inciting the events. Informants were also particularly annoyed by one of the anchors' reference to event participants as "thugs." This term, informants felt, stereotyped the residents of South Central Los Angeles:

NINA: They said "thugs." They said "thugs."
BETTE: Thugs.
NINA: Not everybody was thugs. Yeah, there were gangsters out there, I mean shooting and stuff.
BETTE: Yup.
NINA: Not all of us were thugs. (mumbled something) That has nothing to do with it! But, you know, last year, I mean, they just, everybody in South Central, they're thugs. We're gangsters. We're . . .
VICKI: Low lifes.
NINA: We're low lifes.

In many respects, the stance this group adopted regarding the events differed from that of the two previous Latino-raced groups from South Central Los Angeles (YOUTH and FAMILY). First, the post-discussion group average on the looting and fires scales were nearly a full point below that of the previous Latino-raced groups – indicating that this group, while it viewed the events as "wrong," was somewhat less condemning of the events than the other Latino-raced groups (see table 4.3). Second, this group, unlike the previous Latino-raced groups, felt rather ambivalent toward event-related arrests. The previous groups clearly supported these arrests. Perhaps a key exchange between the informants regarding the nature of the events sheds some light on the group's stance. In this exchange, informants seem to agree that event participants took advantage of the situation, but ultimately blame this activity on the low level of education in the area,[9] residents' lack of exposure to other options for responding to the verdicts:

BETTE: They totally . . . You know what . . . this whole thing, this whole thing, was just taking advantage.

NINA: It wasn't taking –

BETTE: And it started with anger and it ended up with taking advantage. yyyyyyy

BETTE: And the anger was just, I would say, for the first hour.

CARLA: For the first hour.

BETTE: The first hours. The first hours. The first hours. The next, the next day you see, nobody even knew why. There were some people out there and they'd say, "Oh, this is open, so let's get some." You know, "This is, this, you now, it's free. Let's get it." You know, people out there, they didn't know what the hell was going on.

NINA: But that's what's wrong with us. Because why were they angry? They were not educated. We don't know how to take –

BETTE: We are educated!

NINA: I'm talking about in the whole area. I'm not saying you personally, okay. You know that we are not. Because if we were, this would have never happened.

In one important respect, however, this group's stance regarding the events was very similar to that of the other Latino-raced groups from South Central Los Angeles: this group also accepted the raced dividing line embedded in the KTTV text. That is, informants viewed "race" as "the main issue" surrounding the events (assumption 6), and talked as if the black-raced community owned them, as if its members were the event insiders (assumption 7). From the informants' perspective as "Hispanics," members of their "own race" had no business being involved:

BETTE: Didn't, didn't you notice how, how the majority of people that came out were black? And not to put my own race down, but, ah . . . [reacts to look of another group member] . . . You were out there too! You were out there! You were the first one in that store! lllllll[10]

BETTE: No, I'm just playing.

NINA: It's true. It's true.

BETTE: I don't understand either . . . you know –

NINA: I mean, that's bad, you know. But you have to admit –

BETTE: And I'm kind of mad with Hispanics. I mean, like . . . they had nothing to do with it.

Underlying this group's concern with "Hispanic" involvement in the events, were a host of intertextual memories about negative media representations of their "own race." In an extended exchange, informants recalled and lamented past media representations of Latino-raced residents from South Central Los Angeles, how they were frequently depicted as "low lifes." Bette understood these portrayals in terms of racism, noting that news in the US is always biased, always presented from a "white" perspective. But Nina, who often debated fine points with her older sister during the discussion, countered with an intertextual memory of her own. This memory was of a popular, black-raced talk-show host (and former news reporter):

NINA: Oprah? Oprah's, you know, she's level-headed.

MARIA

This interview was conducted on Los Angeles' affluent Westside, in the off-campus (University of California, Los Angeles) apartment of two of the informants. The informants sat on a sofa in the living room and fixed their attention on a 19-inch color television on the other side of the room. The group was composed of the following members: Maria, female, 19; Nora, female, 18; Karen, female, 19; and Julie, female, 19. Maria, a history major at UCLA, was the center of this network; Nora, a biology major, was her "new roommate." Karen, a civil engineering major, and Julie, an art history major, were her close friends. Maria and Nora identified themselves as "Latino" on the questionnaire. Julie identified herself as "half-Japanese" and "half-Mexican," while Karen identified herself as "white or Caucasian." Two of the informants described themselves as "somewhat" religious, while the other two described themselves as "not at all" religious. The socioeconomic status of this group was quite high relative to other Latino-raced study groups (see table A.1).

As in the previous two Latino-raced groups (FAMILY and LATINA), most informants in this group reported watching television news "all evening" during the first day of the events (see table 4.1). Informants were evenly split in their readership of the *Los Angeles Times* over the course of the events: half reported "never" reading the newspaper, while half reported reading at least "sometimes." Despite daily interaction, most informants reported discussing the events amongst themselves "less than once per month" in the months following the outbreak.

Screening highlights This group sat quietly throughout most of the screening, exchanging glances from time to time, offering few comments. Informants offer no visible reactions to the report of the Asian-raced man "drenched in blood" or the description of event participants as "thugs." Julie and Karen, however, exchange smiles during the helicopter reporters' discussion of event boundaries, and when coverage first moves to First AME. A brief episode of talking begins over the reporter's description of the rally but abruptly halts at the beginning of the interviews. During Denver's interview, Maria asks aloud, "It happened that night?" For the next 12 seconds or so, group members discuss what period of the events the text covers. Julie and Karen exchange smiles when another interviewee, Shelly, warns event participants that they will be "destroyed" when troops are called in. Maria claps at the end of Shelly's interview and exclaims, "Go, Girl!"

When the Asian-raced reporter, Carol Lin, begins her report, Julie – who identified herself as "half-Japanese" and "half-Latino" – points at the screen and Nora mumbles something to her. Lin attempts to explain the lack of police presence by suggesting that this presence would have led to "more anxiety on the community's part." Maria responds by saying, "That's fucked up." When the reporter mentions that event participants were throwing rocks and bottles, Nora and Julie exchange a few words. Karen and Maria join in on this discussion and the group begins to reminisce about the period surrounding the events. "Yeah," Maria points out, "My mom picked me up that Thursday, and school was canceled Friday."

Quiet resumes at the beginning of the Reverend Washington interview. "What does AME stand for?" Maria asks over the silence. But no one answers. When one of the anchors compares the reverend to a fighter pilot, informants do not visibly react. Maria, however, asks aloud whether the reverend was the person who "spoke the BS at the AME rally." The group discusses this question over the remainder of the reverend's interview.

When footage of the activity in the Florence and Normandie intersection appears during the anchors' summary, Julie exclaims, "My God!" When one of the anchors reports that people were pulled from their vehicles and beaten up, Nora adds, "I saw that stuff live . . . Reginald Denny. I saw that live." "I remember this," Julie says in reference to the police headquarters protest footage. "I watched tv for like hours," Nora adds. Julie – who identified herself as "half-Japanese" and "half-Mexican" – remarks that it is a "disgrace" to see people waving the Mexican flag during the protest. "Why is it a disgrace to see them waving the Mexican flag?" Maria, who described herself as "Latino," asks. "Destroying property, waving the country's flag," Julie replies. With the exception of this late flurry of conversation, this group was somewhat quiet during the screening compared to the previous group (LATINA). Moreover, none of this late activity seemed to question the KTTV text as-construction.

Discussion highlights Table 4.6 presents the emergence of key arguments in the group's discussion. The table reveals that in the 14 minutes and 29 seconds before discussion initially stalled, informants offered no arguments concerning the KTTV text as-construction. That is, like the previous Latino-raced groups, members of this group did *not* decode the text in a metalinguistic mode. Instead, informants decoded the text in a referential mode, discussing the events as-events and debating the issues surrounding them in terms of the KTTV narrative or their own experiences.

Following prompt 2 (which specifically asked about the news coverage), informants turned their attention to the text as-construction, but were not nearly as critical of it as informants from the previous group (LATINA) were. First, despite acknowledging that much of the news coverage of the events was poor, informants generally thought that the KTTV reporters did a "good" job in their reporting on the events:

MARIA: It's, it's kind of sad because remember the day when the riots happened? And all the, there were newscasters who didn't even know what they were saying. They were just, first of all, news-casters –

           yyy

KAREN: These newscasters were pretty good.

MARIA: I know, they were pretty good, but the day of the riots?

KAREN: That was the day of the riots.

JULIE: That was the day of the riots.

Second, despite arguing that media coverage incited people to participate in the events, informants seemed to agree that the coverage provided a service for people who wanted to avoid the activity areas:

JULIE: I keep wondering . . . I don't know . . . I remember when it was going on and someone said, "Do you think that it's more harm than good?" You know, showing everything that was going on. Do you know what I mean?

MARIA: Yeah.

JULIE: And like me, I don't know. I guess it's good so if people are like what . . . if you're somewhere and you see it, it says that, that's where it is, you know –

MARIA: You want –

JULIE: And you're not going to leave and go over there.

MARIA: Exactly. No. Or another thing you can –
JULIE: But then it also made people go –
MARIA: Oh, no. Or another thing . . . yeah, exactly. Or another thing, it's
           like also, my aunt lives like, like, like two blocks from where
           everything was happening. So, I mean, I, as soon as I heard it
           on the news like what was going on, I just like ran to the phone
           to call and say, "Hey," you know, "You okay? What's up." You
           know what I'm saying? Because, I mean, it did that too. But,
           umm, it probably did make a lot of people go out there.

As for this group's stance toward the events, its scale scores were quite
similar to those of the previous Latino-raced group, LATINA (see table 4.3).
That is, while this group ultimately considered the looting and fires
"wrong," its scale scores suggest group members were less condemning of
this activity than informants in the first two Latino-raced groups (YOUTH
and FAMILY). And like informants in the previous group (LATINA), informants in this group appeared to be quite ambivalent concerning event-
related arrests.

But underlying these group scale *averages,* it seems, was a rather interesting discussion dynamic. Maria, who identified herself as "Latino," frequently found herself pitted against Nora and Julie, who identified
themselves as "Latino" and "half- Japanese"/"half-Mexican," respectively.
Maria felt somewhat sympathetic toward event participants, arguing that
the events represented participants' only option for addressing the injustice
of the verdicts. In contrast, Nora and Julie lamented participants' "lack of
regard for property," arguing that the events were not "justified" and would
just cause more problems in the long run:

JULIE: Look at the complete lack of regard for property –
MARIA: They don't have property to begin with! Yet they're, I think it's
           more like, okay –
JULIE: That's just a personal opinion. Personally, I'm just saying it's a
           complete lack of respect, lack of regard for property.

(several turns later)

NORA: Well, I was pissed off when it was first happening, thinking,
           "God, this is so, so stupid." You know, everything. And I still
           feel that now. I don't think that it was justified. I understand
           they were very angry and I don't think that justifies anything
           that they did. I don't think that, that type of anger should have
           been vented in that way at all.
MARIA: How, how would, how way? In what way, other way?

NORA: Well, well, what did it gain them? It hasn't gotten them anywhere. Except that they lost a lot of money, lost a lot of property. They lost their, their community. It just, it just caused them
more problems. They just caused themselves a lot more problems and it, and, and in the long run it just hurt them more.

Ultimately, it seems, these opposing arguments failed to persuade either
side: Neither Maria, on the one hand, nor Nora and Julie, on the other,
changed their responses on any of the scales following group discussion.
Reflecting this lack of group consensus, the responses of the lone white-
raced informant – Karen – remained in the "ambivalent" range on the
looting and fires scales following discussion.

   Finally, this group differed from the previous Latino-raced groups in one
important respect: "race" was not an explicit item on its discussion agenda.
That is, informants made no *overt* references to "blacks," "whites" or
"Latinos" in their discussion, and made only one mention of "racism" in
passing. Group debate seemed to downplay the racial overtones embedded
in the KTTV text (assumption 6) in favor of more abstract issues of "right,"
"wrong," and "justice." Nonetheless, at least one of the informants, Maria,
may have received the KTTV text aware of these racial overtones, if not outspoken about them. That is, she chose to express her ambivalence about the
events – as against the KTTV text's negative depiction of them (assumption
1) – by recalling a film about Malcolm X she had seen the previous day:

MARIA: I didn't feel like they [event participants] were idiots. Yesterday
I just saw *Malcolm X* – how having a leader or having someone
work together as something and organize them. I mean, I think
they just went about the whole thing wrong, ah, the wrong way.
They just didn't have anyone to lead them.

While it may be reading too much into this memory to claim that it indicates
Maria agreed with the textual assumption that blacks were *the* event insiders
(assumption 7), her decision to express it – given that the film is essentially a
narrative about black-raced oppression and empowerment in the US – does
seem to suggest that race-as-representation intertextually informed (if only
by analogy) her understanding of the Los Angeles events and participants.

JULIO

This interview was also conducted near UCLA, in the living room of one
of the informants. The informants sat on a sectional sofa and focused on a
19-inch color television set across the room. The group was composed of

the following members: Julio, male, 19; Marc, male, 21; Tom, male, 24; and Donna, female, 20.[11] Julio, a "world arts and cultures" major at UCLA, was the center of this network; Donna, was a roommate, but "not someone I [Julio] know well." Marc, a political science major at UCLA, and Tom were close friends of Julio. Tom and Donna were not students at UCLA. Julio identified himself as "Latino" on the questionnaire, while Tom, Donna, and Marc identified themselves as "white or Caucasian."[12] Two of the informants in this group described themselves as "somewhat" religious, while the other two described themselves as "very" religious and "not at all" religious, respectively. The socioeconomic status of this group was quite high relative to other Latino-raced study groups (see table A.1).

As with the previous Latino-raced groups, informants in this group reported watching more than one hour of television news the first day of the events (see table 4.1). Most of the informants, however, reported "never" reading the *Los Angeles Times* over the course of the events. And despite maintaining close ties, informants reported discussing the events quite infrequently amongst themselves in the months since the outbreak – about "once per month" or less.

Screening highlights This group was rather animated during the screening, frequently pointing at the screen and commenting on reporter statements. Less than six seconds into the screening, Julio points to the screen and exclaims, "Look what's happening!" Talk continues over most of the helicopter reporter's description of the events as group members reminisce about where they were at the time. When the reporter mentions that the Asian-raced man was "drenched in blood," Julio shakes his head and Donna winces. Informants do not visibly react when the anchor refers to event participants as "thugs."

When one of the anchors, Patti Suarez, begins to discuss the lack of police presence in the area, Julio rises from his seat and exits the frame. Marc points at the screen and says, "That's an awful jacket." Marc, Tom and Donna laugh. Julio reenters the frame and takes his seat again.

When coverage moves to the First AME interviewees, Julio is talking, while the other group members focus on the screen. Julio stops talking as Angela, the first interviewee, begins to speak; he nods his head in agreement when she says that she is "disappointed in the rally," that black-raced leaders "should have been out in the streets," and that black-raced leaders should have been telling people "what is our next step." When Kevin begins to talk, Julio turns to Tom and says, "He's cute." Marc and Donna question the interviewees' suggestion that community leaders should walk the streets. The leaders may get shot, they agree. Informants do not pay much attention to the final interviewee, Shelly. They continue to talk and laugh with one another over most of the Lin report. When Reverend Washington begins to speak, Julio averts his attention back to the screen. Tom, doing his impression of a Southern preacher, shouts, "Oh, Lord!" Marc mocks Suarez's comparison of Reverend Washington to a fighter pilot. During the remainder of the reverend's interview, group members ignore the screen and discuss news coverage surrounding a recent San Francisco earthquake.

As the anchors' summary begins, talking ceases and group members again turn their attention to the screen. "This isn't as interesting the second time around," Marc says. When footage of the activity in the intersection of Florence and Normandie is shown, Donna shouts, "God! Shit!" while other group members gasp in response to the Denny beating footage. All of the group members point to the screen or otherwise indicate that they recognize the police headquarters footage. "The press were just having a field day," Julio remarks. In short, informants in this group were quite animated during the screening, and much of this activity seemed directed at the text as-construction.

Discussion highlights Table 4.7 presents the emergence of key arguments in this group's discussion. The table shows that in the 13 minutes and seven seconds before the discussion stalled, informants offered no arguments concerning the KTTV text as-construction. In other words, like the previous Latino-raced groups (YOUTH, FAMILY, LATINA, and MARIA), informants in this group did not decode the KTTV text in a metalinguistic mode (despite their screening behaviors). Instead, they decoded the text in a referential mode, discussing the events as-events and offering their own perceptions of the implications.

However, following the second prompt (which specifically asked about the news coverage), informants displayed an awareness (at least) of the media effects discourse by noting that hypermediation of the events had "desensitized" them to the news coverage:

MARC: I don't know, I feel that I'm kind of desensitized by the news.
DONNA: Oh, really?
MARC: Watching it, I was just like, "Ehhhh." Well, maybe it's because
          I had seen it before, but –
JULIO: Yeah –
DONNA: Yeah –
          YYYYYYY
DONNA: Yeah, but I didn't see all of these, though.
TOM: But you know, when it came on the first time I was like, "Okay,
          nothing's happening . . . click."

But this awareness of the media effects discourse did not lead to a scathing critique of the text as-construction like that found in the LATINA discussion. Aside from the above criticism, and the questioning of KTTV's choice of Reverend Washington to speak as an authority on the events,[13] the informants' comments regarding the text as-construction were reserved for making fun of KTTV's style and its reporters' dress:

MARC: The newscast was boring because it was the second time I've
        seen it and they were stalling for time and they, I wasn't –
TOM: Plus Fox News is tacky.
        LLLLLLLLLLLLLLLLLL
MARC: We ought to give her a jacket.
JULIO: We should have been watching Tom Brokaw.
TOM: Exactly.

In other words, informants in this group offered no appraisals of the text's validity, fairness or ideological slant.

Despite its essentially referential decoding of the KTTV text, the group's scale scores (see table 4.3) suggest that its members questioned a central textual assumption – that the events were undesirable (assumption 1). That is, although the informants generally felt that event-related looting was "wrong," they were significantly less entrenched in this position than three of the other four Latino-raced groups (YOUTH, FAMILY, LATINA). Furthermore, among Latino-raced groups, this group was the most tolerant of event-related fires. In fact, the group averages for this latter scale barely locate the group out of the ambivalent range regarding this issue. Finally, following discussion, the group was somewhat ambivalent regarding event-related arrests.

Underlying these scale scores was an interesting discussion dynamic, pitting Julio, the center of the network and its lone Latino-raced member, against two white-raced group members, Donna and Marc. Julio argued that event participants were justified in their actions, while Donna and Marc seemed to accept the textual assumption that the events were undesirable (assumption 1):

MARC: Well, what would you tell your kid? Would you say that what
        some of those people are doing was okay or not?
(pause)
JULIO: Yeah, I think what they were doing was okay.
DONNA: Is okay?
MARC: I, I would not tell my kid that.
DONNA: You think rioting is the answer to, to disagreeing –
MARC: I would tell him . . .

TOM: No, but it happened. If it happened then it's got to be doing
          something right, you know. I think I, like that's how I see it . . .
          YYYYY
DONNA: And you thought it was right just because it happened?
JULIO: I'm not saying it was right because it happened. I don't, I mean,
          I don't think violence is the solution, but –
DONNA: Well, you're wrong.

Julio attempted to explicate his position by arguing that the events were an
opportunity for people "who are not heard" to express themselves. But
Donna and Marc countered, in essence, that the ends did not justify the
means:

JULIO: These people . . . I think that that community that was rebelling
          are people who are not heard and that was their way of express-
          ing themselves and their, their, their –
DONNA: Well, well I agree that that made them heard around the world,
          and that like really made an effect, but, so you think that they
          would have been able to have like better, umm, well like have less
          people injured and like just have them heard? I don't know –
JULIO: That was the loss. And that's the travesty of it all, but –
MARC: I would tell my kid that this is an awful thing that's happened.

In the end, this debate seems to have had little effect on the stances of Julio,
Donna and Marc. These group members seemed entrenched in their particular stances regarding the events and did not change their views after
encountering alternative arguments in group discussion. But the third
white-raced member of the group, Tom, moved into the ambivalent range
on the looting and arrests scales following the discussion. This ambivalence, you may recall, is similar to that noted for a white-raced informant
in the MARIA group – another group characterized by debate between two
opposing points of view regarding the events.

   Finally, "race" was not a salient topic on this group's discussion agenda.
That is, the consideration of "race" was dispensed with rather quickly after
Julio first raised it:

JULIO: So what about all the racial stuff that was happening, I mean,
          what were you, your concerns about that?
MARC: What!
JULIO: Well, I was like, I mean, because they're going to see, see this,
          this white man, this white man get beat –
TOM: Oh, fuck! We almost had black –
          llllll

JULIO: This white man get beat up on the on tv, I mean, are they going to be, going to be scared? I mean, what do you tell your kids about like the racial issue?

DONNA: Well, they see people getting like beat up all the time. Sometimes they're black, sometimes they're white. This time the reason is the, the color of their skin. So then you have to explain that. Because, I mean, when they watch movies white people and black people get beat up all the time.

JULIO: Umm, you can't get into the technical stuff with a twelve-year-old. I mean –

MARC: I would just explain to my kid –

DONNA: Yeah, you can!

(several turns later)

TOM: I would try to explain to, just the beginning of, you know, this is just like rudimentary ways of expressing our, you know, our angers toward –

JULIO: No, but just getting into like institutionalized racism and how, you know, how the country acts certain ways toward Rodney King and how the police treat people and, you know, stuff like that.

TOM: Yeah.

JULIO: But getting into the like the depth of how we have these laws that we just, like the whole institutional part and how the government, you know, is like doing all of it.

Note that white-raced group members did not seem terribly interested in discussing "race," despite Julio's efforts to consider "institutional" racism. As Donna put it, people get beat up all the time: "Sometimes they're black, sometimes they're white." From here, the discussion quickly turned into a discussion of whether the events were "right" or "wrong," and the drawing of the battle lines outlined above.

While race-as-representation was clearly not the basis for commonality among group members, sexual orientation it seems, was. This was the only group in the sample in which the majority of members openly embraced a gay identity during discussion. Numerous exchanges suggested that this identity was a primary bond among group members. For example:

MARC: Okay, let's go one by one. What would you tell your child?
(pause)

MARC: Julio?
          llLLll

TOM: I'd say, "Put on some heels and make up and get over it!"
          YYLLYYLL

Moreover, informants also affirmed this identity through intertextual memories:

DONNA: You didn't see it ["The Crying Game"]?
JULIO: It's like "Basic Instinct."
DONNA: Oh. No.
TOM: No, no. It's good, but it's just like –
DONNA: It's not anti-gay.
          YYYYYYYYYYYYYYY
TOM: No, actually, it's perfect. It's perfect because it totally balances
          so much, like if you go just to watch how all the straight people
          in the audience react to it. Because they don't know what to do.

In the end, sexual orientation – much like race-as-representation or SES in
the other study groups – seemed to be an important coordinate of the location from which informants in this group engaged the KTTV text.
Unfortunately, this study was not designed to systematically examine the
influence of sexual orientation relative to other subjectivities.

Conclusions

In this chapter, I sought to explore in detail how each Latino-raced group
arrived at its particular decoding of the KTTV text. In other words, I
sought to identify what I felt were several critical elements of the meaning-
making process surrounding the text as these elements emerged in each
group's discussion. Several findings are worth summarizing:

First, the Latino-raced informants from South Central Los Angeles generally accepted the textual assumption that the black-raced community
owned the events, that its members were the event insiders (assumption 7).
From their perspectives as non-black-raced subjects, the events were indeed
"wrong;" event participants expressed their anger in ways that were inappropriate, too destructive (assumption 1). Many informants argued that the
Latino-raced subjects who "looted" during the events just took advantage
of the situation, shaming the larger Latino community.

Second, the two Latino-raced groups from UCLA (MARIA and JULIO)
were racially heterogenous and experienced interesting discussion dynamics. In both groups, the center of the network was a Latino-raced informant
who was somewhat sympathetic toward event participants, who viewed the
events as an opportunity for oppressed people to be heard by the power

structure. In each group, however, this individual found himself or herself defending the events against other white-raced and/or Latino-raced group members who viewed the events as too destructive.

The stances adopted by the informants at the center of the two UCLA groups, of course, were quite different than those adopted by most Latino-raced informants from South Central Los Angeles. It is not clear at this point whether these differences should be attributed to socio-economic status, the group dynamic, or some other factor or factors (I shall explore these issues in chapter 7). In the first instance, the Latino-raced informants from UCLA were relatively affluent and were geographically somewhat removed from the areas where much of the destruction occurred. Perhaps these informants understood the events in abstract terms, a luxury that South Central Los Angeles informants could not afford. In the second instance, race-as-representation was clearly not an important commonality among members of the UCLA groups: the groups consisted of racially heterogeneous mixtures of roommates and/or friends, and within the groups there was very little discussion of the raced implications of the KTTV text. Perhaps the dynamic that pitted the Latino-raced centers of each group against the other members was in actuality a racially motivated one; that is, the raced meanings surrounding the events may have been understood by group members but unspeakable, leading members to cast their racially motivated positions regarding the events in other, more acceptable terms.

Third, none of the Latino-raced groups decoded the KTTV text in a metalinguistic mode. Only one group – a group from South Central Los Angeles (LATINA) – offered a scathing critique of KTTV's news coverage. But this critique was offered only after the group was given a prompt that specifically asked about the news coverage. Several of the informants from the UCLA groups talked as if they were aware of discourses of media deconstruction. But informants seldom translated this awareness into unprompted metalinguistic decodings of the KTTV text.

Finally, in each group, intertextual memories seemed to shape how informants understood the events; these memories also affected informants' reception of the KTTV text, their reaction (or lack thereof) to its depiction of the events.

5

Ambivalent insiders: black-raced informants and the KTTV text

> I would just say that, to me, there's not a riot. It's a rebellion. It's not only
> a rebellion against the verdict that was handed down – the not guilty ver-
> dicts. But it was also a rebellion against the way black people are treated
> in this country.   (black-raced informant)

Unlike the term "Latino," "black" is an unambiguous racial label in the
United States. The US Census Bureau, for example, employs the label to
denote a specific raced group – African Americans.[1] Among members of
this group, the label is often an expression of solidarity, of shared heritage,
of the shared discrimination and oppression they experience at the bottom
of the US racial order (see Jaynes and Williams 1989). Indeed, the above
quote is a reflection of this understanding.

As we saw in chapter 3, "blacks" – unlike "Latinos" – *were* prominent in
the KTTV text as interviewees and event participants. In fact, they were
depicted as event insiders, those either responsible for the events or best
positioned to persuade event participants to "do the right thing" and cease
participation. At first glance, this insider status appears to be the natural
outgrowth of *the* cause of the events. These events did, after all, erupt
directly following media announcements of the not-guilty verdicts in a
high-profile police brutality case, one in which an "all-white" jury exonerated four white-raced police officers in the beating of a black-raced
motorist (i.e., see chapter 3, assumption 4). Furthermore, the events *were*
linked by many observers to a long history of injustices against the black-
raced community, including a white-raced judge's sentencing of a Asian-
raced (i.e., "Korean") woman to probation for the shooting death of an
unarmed, 15-year-old black-raced girl. But a more comprehensive analysis
reveals that the events were multi-faceted, exacerbated by a multitude of
causes (Johnson *et al.* 1992; Dentler 1992). That individuals from various

raced groups participated in the events, and that they offered a range of explanations for their participation, underscores this complexity.

Nonetheless, black-raced study informants generally accepted the textually inscribed role of event insider. Group discussions suggest that this acceptance was prompted by informant consciousness of what it means to be "black" in the US, to occupy the lowest stratum of the racial order. Recognizing flaws in the system and the need for change, these informants generally empathized with event participants. Ambivalence toward the events, however, was also evident. This ambivalence seemed rooted in a sense of loss surrounding resource destruction in the black-raced communities engulfed by the events.

GANG

This interview was conducted in a South Central Los Angeles gang-prevention/rehabilitation center. Many of the youths who worked at the center either belonged to gangs (some had criminal records) or were considered to be at-risk for gang involvement. In a rather cavernous room of the warehouse-like structure, four informants sat in chairs facing a 19-inch television screen.

The group was organized by a key on-site administrator of the program – a black-raced woman – who was asked to identify a group of youths who all knew each other well. In this case, the common bond between group members was that they all worked together at the center. Group members included James, male, 16; Deshon, male, 16; Hector, male, 18; Edward, male, 17. James and Deshon identified one another as good friends. Hector, reported that he and Edward had been friends for about two years; he said he had known James and Edward for about nine and six months, respectively. While Deshon identified himself as "African-American" on the questionnaire, James opted not to check this box; instead, he wrote in that he considered himself "black." Hector and Edward identified themselves as "Latino" on the questionnaire. This group was actually composed of two rather close-knit subgroups, one black-raced and one Latino-raced.[2] Three of the four informants in the group described themselves as "somewhat" religious. The socioeconomic status of this group was rather low relative to other black-raced study groups (see table A.1).

Table 5.1 presents data on media consumption and previous event-related discussion for each of the black-raced groups. The table reveals that most of the informants in this group reported watching television news for "more than three hours" on the first day of the events; in contrast, they reported reading the *Los Angeles Times* only "sometimes" over the course of the events. And despite daily interaction, informants in this group reported discussing the events with one another only "once per month" or less in the months following the outbreak.

Screening highlights During the screening, members of the black-raced subgroup constantly "clowned around," while members of the Latino-raced subgroup sat rather quietly, their attention affixed to the screen. Hector immediately recognizes the events when the first images of fires appear on the screen. "Oh!" he says, "The riots." The black-raced informants talk with one another over most of the helicopter reporter's comments, while the Latino-raced informants focus on the screen. When the helicopter reporter describes the plight of the Asian-raced man "drenched in blood," Latino-raced informants do not visibly react. The black-raced informants do not pay attention to the screen at this point; James fiddles with his beeper; Deshon pulls a skull cap over his head and partially covers his face. However, when one of the anchors refers to event participants as "thugs," James laughs and points out the comment to Deshon. They both laugh and talk over the rest of the helicopter reporter's narration. Hector and Edward, in contrast, continue to watch the screen quietly.

When coverage moves to the First AME rally, James and Deshon continue to talk, not paying much attention to most of the interviews. Hector and Edward continue to listen quietly. James and Deshon stop talking, however, when footage of fires reappears on the screen during the Lin report. But when the footage disappears and Lin herself returns to the screen, James and Deshon begin talking again. Deshon rises from his seat and exits the frame at about 12 minutes and 33 seconds into the screening.

James, Hector and Edward focus on the screen during the beginning of Reverend Washington's interview. But when Deshon re-enters the frame about 13 minutes and 8 seconds into the screening, he and Deshon begin to chat about something quietly. Hector and Edward continue to focus on the screen. Group members do not visibly react when one of the anchors compares Reverend Washington to a "fighter pilot." A few seconds later, James's beeper goes off and he and Deshon start laughing. The beeper goes off again about 45 seconds later and the two resume laughing. Hector and Edward continue to focus on the screen.

As the anchors begin their summary of KTTV coverage, Deshon and James talk with one another. Meanwhile, Hector and Edward sit quietly, their attention focused on the screen. Deshon and James start laughing when footage of the activity in the Florence and Normandie intersection appears. They start laughing again when the Denny beating footage appears. When footage of the Parker Center protest appears, however, James says something to Deshon and the two begin discussing the police headquarters activity with their eyes fixed on the screen. James laughs as the FOX news logo scrolls across the screen and the text ends.

In short, the black-raced group members were quite animated during the screening, paying only sporadic attention to the text, mocking it from time to time. The Latino-raced group members, in contrast, sat quietly throughout the screening, focusing their complete attention on the KTTV text.

Discussion highlights Table 5.2 presents the emergence of key arguments in the group's discussion. As was the case with the Latino-raced groups discussed in chapter 4, this group decoded the text in a referential mode, discussing the events in terms of their own experiences and the text's narrative. Prior to prompt 2, which specifically asked about the news coverage, there were no references to the text as-construction. However, when informants were specifically asked to identify "the most important news" in the text (prompt 2), one of the black-raced informants argued that the media coverage inflamed the situation at Florence and Normandie:

JAMES: . . . [I]f they would not have showed all that really on the news what happened on Florence and Normandie, if they had showed all that, you know, the, the, the news kind of hyped it up too. If they didn't show all that I don't think it would have really been that, that bad. Because people wouldn't have knew that, that was going on.

Nonetheless, informants seemed to place a great deal of faith in the media as a source of information. Media bias, fairness or accuracy, at least, never became an issue in the discussion. James, for example, recalled that he had no idea of what was happening as the events were erupting – even though he lived in the midst of event activity. One of the Latino-raced informants, Edward, teased that he needed to "turn on the tv:"

JAMES: When I got, got out of school I didn't know all that was going on. And I was right by there, I was going to Freemont. And that's like a couple of blocks, a couple of streets down.
EDWARD: Tell him to turn on the tv.
JAMES: And so I didn't know nothing about that [the verdicts] until I got home and, and they said, they asked me did I hear about it. And I was like, "Nah, I didn't hear about it." I just thought, you know, it was just a case like it always be. And, and I looked at the news and that, that was . . . they [event participants] was just acting a fool.

My observation that the Latino-raced informants sat still and intently focused their attention on the text during the screening is consistent with their referential decoding of the KTTV text. That is, just as the Latino-raced informants did not appear to question or challenge the text during the screening, they did not question or challenge the text as-construction during the discussion.

The incongruity between the screening and discussion behaviors of the black-raced informants, however, was rather interesting. These informants did not focus on the monitor during much of the screening. Instead, they spent a large portion of the time talking with one another, laughing, and fumbling with a beeper. When they did watch the screen, it was often to poke fun at what was being shown. For example, James and Deshon laughed when the KTTV anchor referred to event participants as "thugs," and when the Denny beating and other violence was summarized. Perhaps this apparent incongruity is resolved if the black-raced informants' actions during the screening are interpreted as being a product of both their relative lack of interest in the interview[3] and a culturally induced concern with appearing "cool."[4]

Both black-raced and Latino-raced informants in this group were less condemning of event-related looting than the Latino-raced informants discussed in chapter 4. Before and after discussion, the group mean for the looting scale remained in the ambivalent range (see table 5.3). Likewise, this group was somewhat less supportive of event-related arrests than the earlier groups; the group mean on this scale was also in the ambivalent range before and after discussion. Only on the event-related fires scales was there an apparent split between the black- and Latino-raced subgroups. Prior to discussion, Latino-raced group members viewed the fires as "wrong," while their black-raced counterparts were ambivalent toward them. After discussion, one of the Latino-raced informants continued to view the fires as "wrong," the other became more ambivalent, and both black-raced informants remained ambivalent.

While both the black-raced and Latino-raced informants in this group felt ambivalent about much of the event-related activity, they felt this way for different reasons. Black-raced informants viewed event-related activity in raced terms, as a "tragic" protest against raced injustice in the US:

DESHON: See, it was – to us, man, we wasn't just looting just to be getting free stuff.

JAMES: We was beating up on people and stuff.

DESHON: We was looting because – we thought about the Koreans – what happened to Latasha Harlins.[5]

JAMES: Yeah.

DESHON: We thought about that, too. So that was the reason we would have stole something anyway or started something with them anyway. It wasn't just because of that. And what happened to Rodney King, that was a whole different situation. To a lot of people, between the Koreans and the blacks and whites and the blacks. So it was different things going on between the Koreans and the blacks and the whites and the blacks. So we just put it all together and just tried to get them all at once.

Latino-raced informants, in contrast, viewed the events primarily in economic terms, as an opportunity to grab a larger piece of the socio-economic pie, to "come up:"

HECTOR: I'll say that when I was out there, it wasn't all about Rodney King. Ain't nobody care about no Rodney King. It was all about –
DESHON: We did care about Rodney King, man!
HECTOR: I didn't.
DESHON: You all didn't care about Rodney King –
HECTOR: For a lot of people it was just all about coming up. Ain't nobody care about Rodney King.

As the above exchange illustrates, black-raced group members challenged the economic explanation expressed by Latino-raced group members. Indeed, black-raced informants seemed to accept the textual assumption that the black-raced community owned the events, that its members constituted the event insiders (assumption 7); these same informants clearly received the argument that the verdicts were not important as an affront, a Latino-raced challenge to the black-raced community's ownership of the events. Accordingly, black-raced informants retaliated in raced terms, while Latino-raced informants stood fast:

JAMES: You all didn't care about Rodney King because you all just wanted some new furniture –
DESHON: New furniture and bags of oranges.
JAMES: Yeah, because in Mexico –
DESHON: We cared about Rodney King, man, because that was one of our brothers. If that was one –
HECTOR: Yeah, at first. And, and, at the end.
DESHON: If that, that, that was one of the Hispanic brothers you all would have cared about it, man.
HECTOR: Yeah, okay, but see –
DESHON: Because it hurts us to see the white man utilize one of our cousins –

HECTOR: Yeah, at first! When it first started, but after a while, people weren't doing it for Rodney King, man. They were doing it to come up.

EDWARD: To come up.

HECTOR: It's all about coming up.

In many respects, the early form and trajectory of this group's discussion, if not the content, was shaped by intertextual memories. For example, when informants were first instructed by the interviewer to discuss "what they had just seen . . . as a group," Deshon responded by recalling a popular television game show: "Ah, like the Family Feud." This show, you might recall, pits two groups (families) against one another in a contest to name the most common survey responses to a number of trivial questions. But the format of this show also features a host who interviews each group member about his or her background, occupation, and so on. Echoing this memory – as well as oppositional media formats in "black youth subculture" like rap (Kelley 1994, p. 213) – Deshon early on sought to structure group discussion by punctuating each member's statement with a single phrase: "Okay, pass the mic." Indeed, there seemed to be more of an awareness of the camera in this group than in any of the other study groups. Twice, Deshon reminded James that "You on camera man!" as if he was saying things that Deshon deemed somehow out of character for the (media) interview. In the end, informants in this group – particularly the black-raced informants – cast themselves in roles during the interview that they had seen enacted on television many times before.

CHURCH

This interview was conducted in the lobby of First African Methodist Episcopal Church (First AME), the South Central Los Angeles site of the rally featured in the KTTV text. The informants – three males and two females – sat in folding chairs around a small counter, their eyes raised to a 19-inch television screen suspended from the ceiling.

This group was composed of the following members: Tim, male, 22; Daryl, male, 19; Pamela, female, 16; Jamal, male, 18; and Dawn, female, 18. The group was organized by an administrator at the church who was asked to identify a group of youth who all knew each other well. Daryl was the center of the network, and the other members were connected to him as follows: Dawn was his cousin; Tim was his fraternity brother who "go[es] way back;" Jamal was another fraternity brother; and Pamela was his co-worker. All but one of the informants, Tim, identified themselves as

"African-American" on the questionnaire. Tim opted not to check the "African-American" box, writing in, instead, that he considered himself "black." Four of the five informants in this group described themselves as "very" religious. The socioeconomic status of this group was rather high relative to other black-raced study groups (see table A.1).

Most of the informants in this group reported watching television news for more than three hours on the first day of the events, but "never" reading the *Los Angeles Times* over the course of the events (see table 5.1). Responses varied among informants regarding the frequency with which they had discussed the events in the months following the outbreak; most of the informants reported having these discussions either "once per week" or "less than once per month."

Screening highlights Informants in this group sat rather quietly through-out most of the screening. At key points in the text, however, members exchanged sneers and grins. For example, about 14 seconds into the screening, the helicopter reporter mentions "looting" and Tim quickly glances over his shoulder at Jamal, who is sitting behind him. About 25 seconds later, the reporter compares the events to Watts and Tim again quickly glances over his shoulder at Jamal, who responds by grinning. About 1 minute and 15 seconds into the screening the reporter says that he and his colleagues have "seen at least three gas stations being held up." Following these words, Tim and Daryl exchange glances; Daryl grins. Tim looks back at Jamal yet again when the reporter mentions that the Asian-raced man was "drenched in blood." Informants do not visibly react when one of the anchors refers to people in the intersections as "thugs."

At about 3 minutes and 30 seconds into the screening, Tim yawns and looks at his watch. But all of the informants perk up about 2 minutes later when one of the anchors says, "We want to go now back to the AME church . . ." For the first time, informants exchange a few words with one another. As the first interviewee complains about the "rapper" at the rally, Daryl chuckles and Tim sits with his hand on his cheek, staring pensively at the screen. When the second interviewee argues that "putting another person [new police chief] in is not going to change anything," Tim turns and rolls his eyes. Dawn shakes her head. When the third interviewee accuses the ministers of "playing church," Daryl makes a face and Tim frowns. Finally, when the last interviewee says, "But if we go up to Beverly Hills, . . ." Daryl chuckles.

In the middle of the Asian-raced reporter's remarks – about 10 minutes and 15 seconds into the screening – Tim rises from his seat and walks out of the screen. About 1 minute later, Jamal picks up a book from the counter and starts to read. When the reporter concludes that "these people mean business," Daryl makes a face. With the exception of brief talking about 2 minutes later, the remaining four viewers sit quietly as Reverend Washington speaks. Informants do not visibly react when Suarez likens the reverend to a "fighter pilot."

At the appearance of the Florence and Normandie footage in the summary, Daryl exclaims, "Dag!" Dawn makes a comment over the Denny beating footage and the other viewers briefly respond. Talking resumes and covers most of the footage of the unrest at police headquarters. (Tim returns to his seat in time for the post-screening discussion). In short, despite sitting quietly throughout most of the screening, informants in this group seemed to receive the text somewhat skeptically. That is, the frequent exchange of sneers and grins suggests that members questioned the text's depiction of the events.

Discussion highlights Table 5.4 presents the emergence of key arguments in the group's discussion. Unlike the previous study groups, this group began to discuss news constructions of the events almost immediately – before specific prompting about the coverage (prompt 2). Furthermore, the informants were critical of the text:

TIM: Yeah. And I would, and I would tell my kid that it wasn't like that.
PAMELA: And I would, I would tell her how it actually happened.
TIM: It wasn't like that at all.
DARYL: Tell her [his child] what led up to it.
TIM: I would tell her also how tv, tv always manipulates the black person anyway.
DARYL & PAMELA: Ummhmm.
DAWN: Yes.
TIM: Always portrays us as the bad –

In other words, this group – unlike the groups discussed thus far – decoded the text in a metalinguistic mode from the very beginning.

Discussion in this group was dominated by Tim, who happened to be a youth minister at First AME; he was one of only seven informants in the sample (n = 65) to offer a critical analysis of the KTTV text in the pre-discussion questionnaire – where informants were asked to "describe what you just saw." He wrote simply: "I would describe it as being far from the truth." Tim initiated the group's discussion of media coverage, a topic that emerged three times in the 7 minutes and 38 seconds *before* the second prompt was issued (i.e, when informants were first questioned specifically about media coverage). This immediate deconstruction of the text by Tim is consistent with his actions during the screening: the glances over his shoulder, the sneers, and his exit midway through the Asian-raced reporter's remarks. He was clearly annoyed by the KTTV text.[6]

Unlike the previous black-raced group (GANG), this group seemed to accept the textual assumption that the events were undesirable (assumption 1). That is, group means on the attitude scales indicated that informants generally felt that the event-related looting and fires were "wrong" (see table 5.3). But informants had ambivalent feelings regarding event-related arrests. Perhaps the paradox between the group's views regarding looting and fires on the one hand, and arrests on the other, is resolved by the group's understanding of the events. This group did not accept the textual assumption that the King beating verdicts was *the* cause of the events (assumption 4). Instead, institutional racism was discussed by group members as the underlying cause.[7] Although the events, informants argued, were *triggered* by the King beating verdicts, they could actually be traced to a long series of socio-economic frustrations in the black-raced community. The system, informants argued, is stacked against black-raced subjects, and the police are an integral part of the system.[8] Thus, group members were not overly supportive of the whole-sale arrest of black-raced participants. In short, group members decoded the text first and foremost as black-raced subjects:

TIM: It's the system, period. It's the system's totally against the black person . . . period. They totally against us. That's it. I mean like the only way to, the only way to talk about it because where ever we go it's racist.

DAWN & DARYL: Ummmmhmmmm.

At the same time, however, the group maintained that the events were unproductive, that more progress could be made by working within the system:

TIM: . . . But when we understand how the white system works then we have to work within the white system. We can't just go out and tell the people, "Go ahead and loot, or go ahead and let's do this." We have to do it the white man's way. The only way we can beat, beat the game is to beat them at their own game.

In an interesting way, informants in this group managed to reconcile ultimate acceptance of important assumptions embedded in the KTTV text (e.g., the undesirability of the events) with an acute suspicion of official information (e.g., like that presented in the KTTV text). Intertextual memories seemed to fuel much of this suspicion. Tim, for example, repeatedly referenced narratives popular in the black community surrounding the assassinations of Martin Luther King, Jr., Malcolm X and John F. Kennedy (Turner 1993). Informants seemed to agree that these texts were directly connected to the KTTV text, that "white" conspiracy was the common denominator. "Black" resistance, these informants felt, had to be more savvy than the tactics employed by event participants. "The only way we can beat, beat the game is to beat them at their own game."

CORNER

This interview was conducted in South Central Los Angeles, a few blocks away from the infamous corner of Florence and Normandie,[9] in the living room of one of the informants. The informants – four women and two men – sat on a sectional sofa and focused their attention on a 25-inch color television set. Group members included: Detra, female, 20; Tanya, female, 21; Kalima, female, 20; Bell, female, 22; Marcus, male, 34; and Ronald, male, 36. Detra was the center of this network of viewers; Tanya was her sister; Kalima and Bell were good friends who grew up with her; Marcus and Ronald were her good friends. All of the informants identified themselves as "African-American" on the questionnaire. Three of the informants described themselves as "not at all" religious, two as "somewhat" religious, and one as "very" religious. The socioeconomic status of this group was quite low relative to other black-raced study groups (see table A.1).

Most of the informants in this group reported watching television news "between one and three hours" on the first day of the events (see table 5.1). Informants were evenly divided between "never" reading the *Los Angeles Times*, reading it "sometimes" and reading it "everyday" over the course of the events. Only one of the informants reported that she had "never" discussed the events with her fellow group members in the months after the outbreak; the other informants reported discussing the events with group members with frequencies ranging from a low of "once per month" to a high of "several times a day."

Screening highlights Throughout the screening informants talked with one another, identifying the locations of the events depicted in the footage and placing the events in what they perceived to be proper chronological order. During the helicopter reporter's opening remarks, for example, Detra says, "That was the first night." Likewise, during the reporter's description of the Asian-raced man as "drenched in blood," Detra points out, "That was on Normandie." When the reporter tells the anchor that he and his crew felt guilty for leaving the man, the informants start to laugh.

"They left him!" But informants do not visibly react when one of the anchors refers to the people in the intersections as "thugs" or when the helicopter reporter compares the events to "Watts."

Talking among informants abruptly ceases when the first of the First AME interviewees appears; all eyes are fixed on the screen. But when the second interviewee says, "I think the rally should have addressed more of . . .," Bell interjects, "the white community!" Detra and Kalima respond by giggling. During the Asian-raced reporter's remarks, Detra says, "Oh!" as she recognizes something depicted in the footage.

The informants listen closely to Reverend Washington's interview and do not visibly react to Suarez's characterization of him as a "fighter pilot." Finally, during the summary footage of the attacks in the intersection – which an anchor identifies as "Florence and Normandie" – Detra nods her head, "Yeah, yeah. That's Normandie right there." In short, although informants were quite animated during the screening, this activity was generally not aimed at challenging the KTTV text as-construction.

Discussion highlights Table 5.5 presents the emergence of key arguments in the group's discussion. After quickly dispensing with the question of what to tell their children about the events (i.e., prompt 1), informants in this group settled down into a discussion of their personal memories of the events and what these events meant to them at the time of the interview. Initially, informants did not opt to question the construction of news in the KTTV text. That is, this group began its discussion by decoding the text in a referential mode. Table 5.5 reveals that arguments concerning media coverage did *not* emerge prior to specific questions pertaining to news coverage (i.e., prompt 2). But when specifically asked about the KTTV reporters (i.e., prompt 4), informants in this group became quite critical:

RONALD: I didn't like them [the reporters].
MARCUS: They shouldn't have been out there.

(after a few seconds of giggling and talking over one another)

RONALD: They didn't talk right.
INTV: What do you mean?
RONALD: You know, they just didn't talk the way I want them to talk . . .
KALIMA: Really?
DETRA: They –
RONALD: You know, about the total situation.

Indeed, intertextual memories of other news coverage seemed to influence this group's reception and negotiation of the KTTV text:

KALIMA: Okay . . .

DETRA: But they're news people regardless. So whatever news come in, they going to tell it just like they get it, so –

KALIMA: No.

DETRA: That's how they work.

KALIMA: Excuse me!

DETRA: No, no, no, no. Here's how they do it.

KALIMA: Excuse me. Okay. During the Gulf War, okay. Wasn't they telling us to be strong, stick together, support your family? Okay, so why they wasn't doing that . . . even though it was a riot, but why they wasn't giving us moral support? From the media? You know, I mean they wasn't saying nothing.

Interestingly, however, group members' misgivings about KTTV reporters and coverage did not materialize during the screening. As the news images flowed across the screen, group members did become quite animated, identifying people, places and events. But consistent with the group's decoding of the text, this activity did not question or challenge the text as-construction.

The group means on the looting and arrests scales suggest that group members felt somewhat ambivalent about these event-related activities (see table 5.3). At the same time, however, informants were firmly opposed to the event-related fires, and this opposition increased following discussion:

DETRA: I don't feel the riots was . . . I'm not going to say the riots . . . It was wrong. But I feel by them taking it out on –

BELL: It just should have been –

DETRA: . . . by them looting –

MARCUS: It was alright looting, but –

DETRA: Looting's okay, but I hated the stuff they took. But when they started burning the buildings down.

MARCUS: Yeah. Now that's something that –

DETRA: It was like they was going to put them [burned buildings] back up the next day.

Although this group seemed to accept several of the assumptions embedded in the KTTV text, it challenged others in interesting ways. That is, like most of the groups discussed thus far, this group attributed the outbreak of the events directly to the King beating verdicts (assumption 4).[10] Furthermore, the circumstances leading up to the verdicts were talked about purely in terms of the raced dividing line inscribed in the text (assumptions 6 and 7). But as black-raced subjects, members of this group were hesitant to completely condemn the events, to accept the textual assumption that the events were undesirable (assumption 1). That is, despite the group's condemnation of the fires, there was the feeling among members that the events would somehow improve things for their community (i.e., the black-raced community):

MARCUS: We needed that [the events]!
KALIMA: We needed that to get stuff in our community.
MARCUS: Right.
KALIMA: You see how they building schools and all that over there where we at now.

KEISHA

This interview was conducted on Los Angeles' affluent Westside, in the off-campus (University of California, Los Angeles) apartment of several of the informants. Informants sat on a sectional sofa and focused their attention on a television screen on the other side of the living room. Group members included: Keisha, female, 21; Rene, female, 21; Billie, female, 22; Sandra, female, 20; and Kim, female, 21. Keisha, a communications and sociology major at UCLA, was the center of the network; Rene, a sociology and pre-medical major, was her cousin; Billie, a political science major, was her good friend; Sandra, a psychology major, and Kim, a psychobiology major, were also her good friends. All of the informants identified themselves as "African-American" on the questionnaire. Three of the informants described themselves as "very" religious, while the other two described themselves as "somewhat" and "not at all" religious, respectively. The socio-economic status of this group was quite high relative to other black-raced study groups (see table A.1).

Each member of this group reported that she watched television news "all evening" during the first day of the events (see table 5.1). In contrast, most informants reported that they "never" read the *Los Angeles Times* over the course of the events. Most informants also reported that they discussed the events with their fellow group members "less than once per month" in the months following the outbreak.

Screening highlights This group was extremely active during the screening, informants discussing their views on event-related issues, talking back to the screen. When the first images appear on the screen, Rene and Sandra giggle momentarily as they realize that the subject of the text is the events. Keisha tells the other group members that in one of her classes she was given an assignment to watch videotapes of several local television stations' news "to see what their coverage was like." When one of the anchors refers to event participants as "thugs," Sandra seems surprised. "The thugs?" she asks. "Is that what he said?" Rene responds. "Yeah," Sandra answers. As the helicopter reporter identifies the boundaries of the events, group members start discussing the various locations.

When KTTV coverage moves to First AME, Rene immediately recognizes the church. Talking ceases and everyone focuses on the screen as Angela, the first interviewee, begins to talk. But when Angela argues that black-raced leaders should have been out in the streets with event participants, Billie exclaims, "What they going to do?" Group members talk over the remainder of Angela's statements, questioning her assessment of the situation. When the next interviewee, Denver, appears on the screen, group members begin to laugh. "Look at his afro!" Rene says. As Denver offers his assessment of the situation, Sandra shakes her head and asks, "What are you talking about, brother?" "He doesn't know," Rene answers. Group members talk over the rest of Denver's comments, as well as most of the next interviewee's. But they begin to focus on the screen again when this interviewee describes how church leaders attempted to block an angry black-raced woman from speaking on the stage. "Oh yeah," Billie says, "remember that?" When the final interviewee says that she is "representing the Black Students' Association of Occidental College," Keisha commends her, yelling, "Ah, well go ahead!" Group members pay attention to the rest of her comments, expressing their agreement at several points.

As Lin gives her report of the events, group members focus on the screen quietly. Group members begin to giggle, however, when Lin describes the "people looting, carrying whatever they could, large tv sets." When she points out that "nobody was laughing out there. This wasn't a joke," group members appear annoyed. "Why would they be laughing?" Sandra asks. "You know? What's funny?" Rene adds. Finally, when Lin reports that event participants attacked a KTTV cameramen, and that he "happens to be white," at least one group member was again annoyed. "She said he 'happens to be,'" Kim exclaims.

The moment the Reverend Washington interview begins, Rene rolls her eyes and says, "If this is who I think it is, he is the biggest sellout." Keisha agrees with her. "Yeah, you know what? He was on everybody's station. Okay?" Sandra is particularly annoyed by the reverend's labelling of the events as "riots." "Rioting!" she exclaims. When one of the anchors commends the reverend for being "particularly articulate" in his assessment of the situation, Rene giggles and looks at Keisha. Keisha, in turn, glances over at the other group members. Rene mocks the reverend as he calls for viewers to "stay calm, stay in your houses." And when one of the anchors asks the reverend to stay with them, that "we need your voice tonight," Sandra says something that prompts the rest of the group to start laughing.

Group members focus on the screen as the anchors begin their summary of the KTTV coverage. When footage of the activity at the Florence and Normandie intersection appears, Sandra exclaims, "Oh, my goodness!" There is not much visible reaction among group members when the Denny beating footage appears. But group members talk with one another at the appearance of the police headquarters footage, trying to make sense of what is happening on the screen. In short, informants in this group were quite animated during the screening, and much of this activity seemed to challenge the text as-construction.

Discussion highlights Table 5.6 presents the emergence of key arguments in the group's discussion. This group opted to decode the KTTV text in a combination of referential and metalinguistic modes. That is, while the group did not deconstruct the text with the same vigor as the CHURCH group, it nonetheless critiqued the text as-construction a few times prior to prompt 2 (which specifically asked about news coverage). One of these criticisms, for example, centered around the media's treatment of "African Americans" as "scapegoats:"

BILLIE: You know what I mean? It's like, I mean, yeah, I think we should tell our kids that it's not just an, I mean, if, . . . they have focused primarily on African Americans, but everybody was down there –

RENE: Always on African Americans.

BILLIE: Yeah.

RENE: Always the scapegoat.

BILLIE: And, yup, we were the scapegoats.

RENE: That's how we always are, yup.

KEISHA: Yup.

However, following the second prompt (which specifically asked about news coverage), group members launched into a full-scale attack of the KTTV text. Consistent with informants' reaction during the screening when the anchor referred to event participants as "thugs," informants condemned the use of the term during their discussion, arguing that it symbolized the biased nature of the KTTV news coverage:

RENE: I mean, it was just, oh, God! They were just like, white people saying the "thugs" and then talking about how, um, what else did they say? Everything that they said, it just really, they had a chance to show their true feelings and it came out . . .

KEISHA: And, I mean, that's just really forcing it because as pervasive as
          it is, you know, everyone, I don't know, I don't know one person
          who was not glued to the tv that night. They're looking at that.
RENE: Ummhmm.
KEISHA: And especially if you're going to try to educate whites on social
          issues that happen to African Americans? And they're sitting
          there looking at news like that?

Among the black-raced groups, this group was the least supportive of the
textual assumption regarding the undesirability of the events (assumption
1). That is, the averages of group member scores on the fires and looting
scales were in the ambivalent range, while the average on the arrests scale
revealed that group members viewed the arrests as "wrong" (see table 5.3).
Furthermore, this was the only black-raced group that was *not* clearly
opposed to the fires.[11] Although all of the black-raced groups discussed
thus far agreed that the anger of event participants was justified, that event
participants were protesting economic and raced inequities in society, the
other groups generally felt that event participants went too far when they
set the fires – that these participants, to some degree, had unwittingly
destroyed their own neighborhoods. Perhaps this group's reluctance to
condemn the fires is explained by its unique conception of the events: it was
the only black-raced group that *spoke* of the events as a "rebellion," informants using this term five times during the discussion.[12] Sandra nicely
summed up the group's feeling regarding the nature of the events:

SANDRA: I would just say that, to me, there's not a riot. It's a rebellion.
          It's not only a rebellion against the, umm, verdict that was
          handed down – the not guilty verdicts. But it was also a rebel-
          lion against the way black people are treated in this country. We
          are not treated fairly. This is a, umm, white-dominated society
          and black people have no, no, no – you know, they don't fit in
          anywhere. And so, I think that, that's why we rebel. It's not
          because we're ignorant or anything like that.

As the quotes above suggest, race-as-representation figured prominently
in this group's discussion. But the group's consideration of "race" went far
beyond a mere elaboration of its role in the events. The screening and subsequent discussion, it seems, became a forum for informants to affirm and
enact their raced identities as "African Americans:"

RENE: So how would, what, what would you . . . I mean, the only thing
          I could tell my, my child is that it's okay to be African
          American because –

SANDRA: It's great to be African American!

RENE: . . . Yeah, I mean, it's, it's, that's, black is beautiful. And I know from the perception of tv and from the media and everything –

SANDRA: From America.

RENE: You will feel, you might have self-esteem because you will feel that, I mean, it's just been . . . You don't see when –

KEISHA: But at the same time you want to be careful not to instill in him those same racist values.

BILLIE: Yeah.

KEISHA: You see what I'm saying? Because you don't want him to take the negative energy from whites and have –

RENE: But you're not going to tell him that white is not right. I wouldn't tell them that. But I, just let them know –

SANDRA: Black pride.

Shortly after this exchange, one of the informants in the group, Kim, reluctantly revealed that she was racially "mixed." The following exchange demonstrates her struggle to reconcile the group's discussion of "race" with her own sense of raced identity:

RENE: . . . I would just tell [my child], we, you have to instill in them the, the preservation and unification of the African American race. That's the only way we're going to get anywhere. The only way.

KIM: I mean, I don't know. I really . . . I didn't grow up thinking, feeling that I was like not completely . . .

KEISHA: Say it!
    YyLLLLLLLlll

KIM: No, I mean, I don't know what I mean. I, of course I believe in the preservation of the race and stuff, but I mean I can't help that I'm not, you know, I mean, I'm mixed. I mean, I mean, most people can't tell anyway, so . . .
    lllll

KIM: I figure, hey, but any, I mean, what are you supposed, I mean, you grow up, you don't feel like, well . . . See, maybe it would be different if you, if you looked, if I looked different or something. I don't know. But –

KEISHA: Ummhmm.

KIM: But, but when you grow up and stuff, what, what are you supposed to tell your child? I mean, I guess that I would just tell him that . . . I mean, because my parents really didn't tell me much about anything and they . . .

KEISHA: Ummhmm.

KIM: I just had to go learn everything out for myself. And so, I mean, I would make those options available. I mean, let them know about their culture. And I also think, though, that I should be more interested in my other culture just because it's something I should know about and I really don't know anything about it and I feel bad about that part of it. But, I mean, when my mom came out here, I mean, they made an agreement that I was going to be American, so I didn't have any . . . I don't know the language or anything else about the other culture. And I, I guess they decided to make me American. But I don't know.

In short, the KTTV text ignited important raced meanings for informants in this group. But these meanings were clearly fueled over the course of the discussion by intertextual memories, memories that facilitated informants' affirmation of their own raced subjectivities. Indeed, informants seemed to collectively negotiate the meaning of the "black" condition – their condition – with references to media texts like *Roots, Jungle Fever*, and television news reports of the Rodney King beating verdicts.[13] Rene, for example, revealed that she first learned about the connection between slavery and the oppressed status of black-raced Americans when she saw *Roots* on television. She also referenced a controversial film about interracial relationships, *Jungle Fever*, to support her contention that "blacks must stick together." Finally, Keisha – the sociology and communications studies major who performed an analysis of news coverage for one of her classes – recalled that news reports of the King beating verdicts enraged her:

KEISHA: When I was sitting at home and I saw the television and I was, and I couldn't believe it. At, at that moment non-violence went out the window!

Indeed, throughout the group's discussion, she referenced her awareness of media deconstruction discourses to critique the KTTV text. In the end, as each of these intertextual memories shaped informants' understanding of themselves as raced-subjects, they also, by default, shaped informants' reception of the KTTV text.

NORTH

This interview was also conducted near UCLA, in the living room of the informants. Informants sat on the floor, in front of a small color television set. Group members included: Terri, female, 18; Lynell, female, 18; Ayesha, female, 17; Dara, female, 18; and Trina, female, 18. Terri, an undeclared social sciences major, was the center of this network; Lynell, a psychology major, and Dara, a communications major, were her good friends from high school; Ayesha, a history major, was also a good friend from high school; and Trina, an engineering major, was a good friend she met after arriving at UCLA. All of the informants were freshmen who had recently come to Los Angeles from Northern California. In other words, none of them lived in the Los Angeles area at the time of the events. With the exception of Dara, who wrote that she considered herself "Malaysian," the informants identified themselves as "African American" on the questionnaire. All of the informants described themselves as "somewhat" religious. The socioeconomic status of this group was quite high relative to other black-raced study groups (see table A.1).

Informants in this group reported watching television news from one hour to "all evening" on the first day of the events (see table 5.1). But none of the informants reported reading the *Los Angeles Times* over the course of the events – most likely due to the fact that none of them lived in Los Angeles at the time. For the same reason, perhaps, most informants reported discussing the events amongst themselves only about "once per month" in the months following the outbreak.

Screening highlights This group was quite animated during the screening, discussing their views on event-related issues over much of the text.[14] When one of the anchors refers to event participants as "thugs," group members visibly react by talking amongst themselves. Group members also perk up when they hear one of the anchors say that coverage would move to the First AME church. Group members focus on the screen at the beginning of this coverage. One group member says that the church is in a "nice part of the 'hood.'"

When coverage moved to Reverend Washington's interview, group members begin talking about "looting," not paying much attention to the screen. But when the anchors begin their summary of the KTTV coverage, and images of the fires return to the screen, group members revert their attention to the screen and reminisce about what had happened. In short, although informants were quite animated during the screening, this activity – with a few exceptions[15] – was not aimed at challenging the text as-construction.

Discussion highlights Table 5.7 presents the emergence of key arguments in the group's discussion. This group generally opted to discuss their reactions to the events, not KTTV's construction of them. That is, the inclination of this group was to decode the text in a referential mode. Table 5.7 reveals that there were no arguments offered in the eleven minutes of discussion prior to the second prompt (which specifically asked about news coverage) regarding the text as-construction.

After the second prompt, however, informants in this group offered several critiques of the text. First, following up on their reactions during the screening, informants complained during the discussion about the anchor's labelling of event participants as "thugs:"

TERRI: I think the worst news was when the guy called
                   them –
TERRI & AYESHA: Thugs.
TERRI: Racist. He might as well've said niggers.

Informants in this group also complained about the lack of black-raced reporters in the text and the text's failure to show white-raced event participants "making an ass of themselves."

Despite these criticisms, however, informants in this group seemed to agree with the textual assumption that the role of news media in society is to provide factual and unbiased coverage of important events (assumption 14). Informants discussed their complaints about KTTV coverage as if these complaints referred to *mistakes, anomalies,* incidents of poor *execution* in an otherwise noble journalistic enterprise. In fact, with the exception of the anchor who referred to event participants as "thugs," KTTV reporters were described as "okay" by group members. Near the end of the discussion, one informant actually became an apologist for the efforts of KTTV reporters, while another informant reiterated the assumption that reporters are "supposed" to remain objective:

LYNELL: I think that the, that it's a very tense situation and you, you
          know, you don't want to say anything wrong.
TERRI: Right.
LYNELL: And they're figuring, you know, maybe, maybe they don't
          understand the whole situation or whatever.
TERRI: Yeah.
LYNELL: But, and, you know, they're just kind of, you know what I
          mean, you hear, see people out on the corner beating each
          other's ass, you going to assume some thugs.
TERRI: Yeah, it's first instinct to say "thugs" but you're not supposed
          to use biased words like that in news. You're really supposed to
          say, "Such, such, such a," you know, you know, "height, weight,
          color," stuff like that.

Like most of the other black-raced groups, this group's scores on the attitudinal scales suggest that informants were opposed to event-related arrests and felt quite ambivalent toward event-related looting (see table 5.3). However, unlike the other black-raced group from UCLA (KEISHA), this group's score on the remaining scale suggests that informants were somewhat opposed to event-related fires. Underlying these scale scores was an important debate between Dara, the group member who identified herself as Malaysian, and other group members. Dara argued that event participants had a right to be angry, but that the events, in the end, were too self-destructive. In contrast, other group members argued that event participants had few other options to make their feelings heard, and that they also had "nothing to lose:"

DARA: But I justify that, you know, if that happens to you, don't just go and destruct your friend's house or something just because you're upset. You know, there are better ways to go about it. I don't think the looting was all that . . .

TERRI: You don't think it was necessary? What do you think they should have done?

DARA: I really don't know what they should have done, but that's just not . . . I don't have the answer really, but that, that did a lot of damage to the city and everything else. And, and a lot of people are going to be out of jobs because of that. And so it's not like helping anything.

TERRI: I don't think it helped anything but I think it was necessary to at least make a point . . .

AYESHA: I think they felt like they had nothing to lose anyway –

TRINA: Exactly.

AYESHA: So why, you know . . .

TERRI: So, like really, when you have no job, you're on welfare –

AYESHA: Right.

TERRI: Your house is in the projects . . .

AYESHA: Really, you don't own your house anyway, so why not burn it down?

TERRI: Thank you. And it's wrong, still, you know, to destroy anybody else's stuff, but, ah, I understand why people did it.

Nevertheless, informants seemed to agree that event-participants could have made *more* of an impact by concentrating events in the predominantly white-raced area where the King beating trial was held. Ayesha forcefully expressed this perspective by remembering the words of a popular black-raced rapper:[16] ". . . like Ice Cube said, surely somebody knows the addresses of the jury . . . Burn down the courthouse, you know. Go to Simi Valley." Indeed, intertextual memories worked in this group – as in each of

the previous black-raced groups – to center "race" in informants' understanding of the KTTV text. That is, informants clearly viewed themselves
as black-raced subjects and saw the text as further testimony to the persis-
tence of "black" oppression by the "white" power structure in the US. As
Terri put it:

TERRI: It's the whole structure because . . . it's the power structure.
AYESHA: Right.
TERRI: Every white man with any money in this country has the power
             to step on any of us in this conversation. So even by looting,
             you know, a rich store in Beverly Hills, that's not going to mean
             nothing.
             YYYYYYYYYYYYLLLLLlYYyyy
TERRI: Well, believe it or not, no matter how much money you have
             you're still a nigger to, to most white people.

Conclusions

In this chapter I sought to identify key elements of the meaning-making
processes within each black-raced group, so that we might better understand how each group arrived at its respective stance on the events. Several
findings are worth summarizing:

Firstly, all of the black-raced groups were somewhat sympathetic to the
events and/or event participants, agreeing with the KTTV text that the
black-raced community owned the events, that its members were the event
insiders (assumption 7). From the perspective of these groups, the KTTV
text was about injustice in the United States – raced and economic. Some
black-raced informants insisted that the events were a "rebellion," that the
term "riot" misrepresented the nature of the events. The one black-raced
group that strongly felt that event-related fires and looting were "wrong"
(CHURCH), felt this way *not* because it viewed the events as unjustified, but
because it thought that black-raced subjects had to be more savvy about
placing demands on the system. Nonetheless, because this group perceived
that the system is stacked against black-raced subjects, it – like the other
black-raced groups – did not support the arrest of event participants.

Secondly, there were few differences between the black-raced groups
from South Central Los Angeles and UCLA regarding how they received
the KTTV text. All of the groups were extremely active during the screening, visibly reacting at key points in the text, embracing, perhaps, their perceived status as event insiders.

Third, although only two of the black-raced groups offered unprompted metalinguistic decodings of the KTTV text (CHURCH and KEISHA), all of the groups managed to oppose key textual assumptions on the basis of member experiences and intertextual memories.

Fourth, rather than accept the textual assumption that the events were undesirable (assumption 1), black-raced informants appeared to feel some-what ambivalent toward event-related activities.[17] This ambivalence, I propose, may be the direct result of competing arguments that emerged in group discussions: the recognition and condemnation of raced oppression, on the one hand; the mourning of resource destruction in South Central Los Angeles, on the other.

Finally, the screening and discussion of the KTTV text became a forum for black-raced informants to enact their own raced subjectivities. More so than any of the Latino-raced groups, each of the black-raced study groups early on centered "race" as a topic of discussion. The KTTV text, in essence, became a lightening rod for raced meanings within the black-raced groups. These meanings surfaced again and again during group discus-sions, defining informants' understandings of who they were, who they were not, who they ought to be.

6

Innocent bystanders: white-raced informants and the KTTV text

> I think one thing I can start with is that the use of violence that was shown
> – I think that is totally wrong. It's like there are other, better ways of, more
> constructive ways of doing it [protesting] rather than going out and
> burning things. (white-raced informant)

Throughout United States history, "white" has been defined in contrast to
"black." That is, if something was said to be *white*, then it was necessarily
not-black; conversely, if something was said to be *black*, then it was also *not-white*. Indeed, "black" and "white" have come to represent the ultimate in
mutually exclusive categories, an essential binary opposition. Despite the
increasing raced complexity of US society, the terms retain a special social
meaning (see Baldwin 1961; Hacker 1992): while "black," describes the
lower-most depths of the racial order, "white" describes the uppermost
reaches; while "black," signifies primitive, inferior and soiled, "white" signifies civilized, superior and pure.

This black-white divide, as we saw in chapter 3, is inscribed in the KTTV
text. That is, "blacks" were presented as the event insiders (i.e., those who
participated in the events and/or were in a position to affect them one way
or another), while "whites" were depicted as event outsiders (i.e., those who
watched the events, reported on them, and from time to time, fell victim to
them). In short, "whites" were innocent bystanders to events that were
"black" in nature. This observation, of course, fits neatly with another: in
the white imagination, "black" is often associated with crime (Estrich 1989;
Omi and Winant 1994). Accordingly, the Los Angeles events were cloaked
in a discourse of criminality (Fiske 1994b; see chapter 8), a discourse that
worked to reinforce the racial divide of *black/thug/them/guilty* versus
white/citizen/us/innocent. White-raced informants, as in the above quote,
typically viewed the events as "wrong" and described the activity of event

participants as "crime." And because the system was absent in most media analyses of the events, there existed few *visible* links to implicate "white" responsibility. Not surprisingly, then, white-raced informants generally received the KTTV text with minimal dissonance, rarely finding it necessary to give voice to the racial assumptions submerged in the text, typically failing to consider the possibility of their own culpability.

MATES

This interview was conducted on Los Angeles' affluent Westside, in the off-campus (University of California, Los Angeles) apartment of the informants. The informants sat on a large sofa, their eyes focused on a color television set on the other side of the living room. Group members included Janet, female, 19; Yin, female, 19; Ellen, female, 19; and Marcia, female, 19. All of the informants were currently roommates and had lived together on the same dormitory floor the previous year, at the time of the events. Janet and Marcia were English majors; Ellen was a chemistry major; and Yin was an economics major. With the exception of Yin, who wrote in that she considered herself a "Taiwanese American," the informants identified themselves as "white or Caucasian" on the questionnaire. Two of the informants described themselves as "very" religious, while the other two described themselves as "not at all" religious. While all of the white-raced groups exhibited high socio-economic status relative to other-raced groups, this group was particularly privileged in this regard (see table A.1).

Table 6.1 presents data on media consumption and previous event-related discussion for the white-raced groups. Most of the informants in this group reported watching television news for "more than three hours" on the first day of the events. Two informants reported reading the *Los Angeles Times* "sometimes" over the course of the events, while the other two reported "never" reading the newspaper and reading it "everyday," respectively. Finally, informants discussed the events rather infrequently amongst themselves in the months following the outbreak; responses ranged from a high of "once per month" to "never."

Screening highlights This group, for the most part, sat quietly during the screening. For example, group members do not visibly react when the plight of the Asian-raced man "drenched in blood" is described or when one of the anchors refers to event participants as "thugs." Moreover, informants do not visibly react during the First AME interviews. But when Reverend Washington appears on the screen, Janet says that he "looks like he's twenty." Marcia chuckles. Informants do not visibly react when one of the anchors compares the reverend to a fighter pilot. However, when footage of the activity in the Florence and Normandie intersection appears during the anchors' summary, Marcia reaches for her drink and takes a sip. "Jesus!" Ellen exclaims, shaking her head. When the police headquarters (Parker Center) protest footage appears, Janet suddenly recognizes someone on the screen. "There's Sonny! Oh, my God!"

In short, with the exception of these late bits of activity, this group – unlike most of the Latino-raced and black-raced groups – sat quietly during most of the screening, failing to visibly challenge the KTTV text as-construction.

Discussion highlights Table 6.2 presents the emergence of key arguments in the group's discussion. Consistent with its screening behavior, this group decoded the KTTV text primarily in a referential mode; that is, informants generally talked about the KTTV text in terms of its narrative or informant feelings about the events. However, the group also displayed a few instances of metalinguistic decoding prior to the second prompt (when informants were specifically asked about news coverage). For example, group members recognized and discussed differences between viewing media representations of the events and seeing the events firsthand. That is, unlike some of the other study groups, this group acknowledged early on that the KTTV text was *not* a clear window onto the events:

JANET:	What's interesting about what we just watched is that it's so detached. It's so far away. I mean, just look at those aerial views of the fires.
YIN:	That's the media.
JANET:	Well, you know, that's, that's something that, there are other shots where they're just right there. You know, Reginald Denny[1] right there.
YIN:	You know, the media picks certain, selects . . .
JANET:	No, no . . . I'm not arguing with you, I'm not arguing with you. I'm just saying that everyone's sitting in their living room watching this stuff. They weren't, you know . . .
MARCIA:	Would you rather them be like Sylvia, you know, and go out there and head on down to Copelands [sporting goods store near UCLA] . . .
JANET:	No, no, I'm not, I'm not.
MARCIA:	. . . And break out some window?
JANET:	No, no, no, I don't want to do that. I'm just saying that so many people saw it on TV and it was like . . . I think, for a lot of people it was just like . . . I mean we looked out and saw the actual smoke clouds and stuff.

MARCIA: Yeah.

JANET: But a lot of people didn't see that.

Prior to the second prompt, one informant also challenged KTTV's representation of the events by pointing to a specific example of bias. As Yin put it, "the media portrayed it [the events] as a black thing." From her perspective, the events were "much more deep rooted."

As this group's scores on the looting, fires and arrests scales might suggest (see table 6.3),[2] informants generally accepted the textual assumption that the events were undesirable (assumption 1). But underlying these scale averages was an interesting discussion dynamic, pitting Janet – who identified herself as "white or Caucasian" – against the other two group members who identified as such. In essence, Janet played "Devil's advocate" in the group, questioning many textual assumptions, as well as those of her fellow group members. Although Janet's scale scores suggest that she condemned the events with nearly the same zest as her compatriots, she frequently contested other informants' depiction of event participants as "animals," and as "uneducated":

MARCIA: But you got to wonder, what makes a whole city act like a
           bunch of –
ELLEN: It wasn't a whole city. It was just an isolated group of people.
YIN: No.
ELLEN: Uneducated. Uneducated.
YIN: No. No. Very widespread.
ELLEN: Uneducated.
JANET: How can you say that?
ELLEN: It's just a small area.
JANET: You don't know everyone who's out there. You know, You
           really don't.

As the group discussion progressed, tensions between Janet and the other white-raced informants came to a head. For example, in another exchange, Ellen and Marcia argued that event participants were "taking advantage of a situation" and that the events had little to do with "race." Janet disagreed with their view, asking Yin – the lone Asian-raced informant – for validation of her own view:

MARCIA: Yeah, it was a racial thing at first and after that it
                     was a bunch of people taking advantage of a situa-
                     tion. It was free TVs, it was free food. It was all kind
                     of stuff. It was not, I mean, for the first hours it was
                     about Rodney King . . . maybe.

ELLEN:	Yeah.
ELLEN & MARCIA:	Maybe.
ELLEN:	Yeah, I agree.

(three turns later)

MARCIA:	. . . There's some tension but nothing like deserving rioting and looting and things like that, you know. If it had stayed centralized right there, then maybe. And you're totally disagreeing, so –
JANET:	No, I totally disagree. I'd like to hear what Yin has to say. She hasn't spoken in a while. But, umm, I, I, I really . . . I know that for a lot of people, like for Linda,[3] it was totally just an opportunity to go out and get whatever she wanted. And I think there were a lot of people like that but I cannot say it was purely economic.
YIN:	Yeah.

Soon thereafter – when Janet tried to convince Ellen and Marcia that it is hard for them as white-raced subjects to recognize raced tensions – Ellen had a sharp reply:

ELLEN: It's because we're not doing that. We're not discriminating.

Indeed, "race" developed into a hot topic of debate in this group. On one side, Ellen and Marcia talked about the text as being more about the disintegration of order, of people taking advantage, than about "race." On the other side, of course, Janet and Yin embraced the textual assumption that "race" was an integral element of the events (assumption 6). In the following exchange, Marcia and Ellen argue that the events had been blown out of proportion, that they were not that important to "most of society."[4] But Janet, once again, disagrees with their position and links it to their status as white-raced subjects:

MARCIA: I don't think it was very . . . as monumental as everybody thinks it was. Yeah, that's true.

ELLEN: Even, even, every once and a while people talk about the Watts riots that happened twenty years before. I mean, it's just, just, just kind of a memory that comes up occasionally. But it's not something that I take time, because I wasn't there and it didn't personally affect me. If it doesn't personally affect me, I just have a hard time relating to it. And I think that most of society is probably that way.

(pause)

JANET: White society.

Intertextual memories, of course, shaped informants' perspectives and helped fuel debate in the group. Informants often referenced other texts to support their positions on issues raised as they negotiated the KTTV text. Janet, for example, recalled her experience writing for the campus newspaper in order to challenge textual depictions of blacks as the event insiders (assumption 7). While writing a reaction story on the events for the newspaper, she discovered what she remembered as a "huge mistake" in a front-page article written by one of her friends:

JANET: She said something like the African Americans were looting, when in actuality, it was just a group of a lot of different people from different races.

Meanwhile, Marcia and Ellen referenced other texts to support their position that event participants – whom they seemed to define as "blacks" (assumption 7) – protested in the wrong way. Marcia, for example, argued that instead of "rioting," "they" need to vote (assumption 9):

MARCIA: And the bottom line is, you've seen Jesse Jackson yelling at, you know, everyone in the country, "Get off your butt and" – and he calls everyone "bumps on a log" – "and register to vote!"

By referencing another memory, Ellen concurred:

ELLEN: Martin Luther King is *their* biggest leader. He did it with peace. But why didn't *they*, why doesn't anyone protest peacefully? You know? [emphasis added]

DORM1

This interview was conducted on the UCLA campus, in a dormitory recreation room. Informants sat in chairs and on a sofa facing a 19-inch, color television. Group members included: John, male, 19; Brad, male, 18; Tom, male;[5] and Bill, male, 19. Tom was a biochemistry major at UCLA, and Bill was a film major; John and Brad reported that they had not declared majors. On the questionnaire, John and Tom identified themselves as "Korean American;" Brad identified himself as "Filipino," while Bill identified himself as "white or Caucasian."[6] Two of the informants described themselves as "somewhat" religious, while the other two informants described themselves as "very" religious and "not at all" religious, respectively. This group exhibited a socioeconomic status considerably lower than that of the previous white-raced group (MATES), but higher than that of the typical black-raced or Latino-raced group (see table A.1).

Most of the informants in this group reported watching television news for "more than three hours" on the first day of the events (see table 6.1). Informants were evenly split between reading the *Los Angeles Times* "sometimes" and "every day" over the course of the events. Finally, there was very little pre-interview discussion among informants regarding the events. That is, most of the informants reported "never" discussing the events amongst themselves in the months following the outbreak.[7]

Screening highlights Like the previous white-raced group (MATES), this group sat motionless and quietly throughout the screening of the KTTV text. Group members do not visibly react when the plight of the Asian-raced man "drenched in blood" is described or when one of the anchors refers to event participants as "thugs." They also do not visibly react during the First AME interviews, the Reverend Washington interview, or the anchors' summary. In short, informants offered no visible signs that they challenged the KTTV text as-construction during the screening.

Discussion highlights Table 6.4 presents the emergence of key arguments in the group's discussion. Unlike the previous white-raced group (MATES) – which alternated between referential and metalinguistic decoding modes – this group decoded the KTTV text solely in a referential mode. That is, prior to the second prompt (which specifically asked about news coverage) this group offered no arguments which challenged or questioned the text as-construction. Instead, informants simply offered arguments about their perceptions and feelings concerning the events; they seemed to treat the KTTV narrative as an unbiased account of the surrounding circumstances.

Following the second prompt, however, informants were a little more critical of the KTTV reporters and text. One criticism held that the media facilitated the events by providing too much coverage of them. Another criticism sprung from moments in the text when reporters and interviewees offered "platitudes" and "hackneyed" statements, "oversimplifications" of the issues surrounding the events. But rather than identify these "oversimplifications" as attempts to frame the events, as attempts to present a privileged understanding of them, group members recognized these statements as instances of poor performance resulting from the "confusing" nature of the events:

JOHN: I mean, okay, well the . . . in, in the newscasts, you, you have to take into consideration that, you know, it is in the midst of, you know, chaos. It is, you know, where violence is just literally going on out, outside the door. But, I mean, I still thought that, you know, the people who were being interviewed and, and as well as the newscasters, the, the reporters – they fell into this trap of throwing out platitudes, ah, you know, these kind of . . .

Lllllllllll

JOHN: These, these, you know, these hackneyed kind of statements like

. . .

LLllllllll

BRAD: "Hackneyed?" I'm sorry, I need a thesaurus.

JOHN: You, you know the reporters would say things like, "Oh, you know, it's something, something, something, and, ah, people should, you know, take their frustrations out in the voting booths instead of on the streets." Ummm, you know, it just, I mean, I found it, I found some kind of really oversimplifications. Ah, ah, one person said, "Oh, well now, it's all about the Rodney King, ah, incident."

BILL: I think those guys got the same problem we do. I mean, those newscasters – it's got to be hard for them.

JOHN: Right. I mean, right. I mean, I acknowledge that. I mean, I realize that. But, ah, I mean, what else is there. Ah, was it, ah, you know, just sweeping statements like, "Oh, you know, these people mean business." Ah, you know, ah, you know, "Oh, all these people are these, these kind of non-entity kind of people are, are venting out their frustrations and, and anger." You know, it's, it's kind of very assuming on the part of the reporters. And, ah, just kind of a lot of, ah, generalized statements like that.

BRAD: But then it was really confusing. I mean, there in the –

JOHN: Oh, yeah. Oh, yeah. Definitely so. You don't have time to kind of formulate these eloquent statements.

In many respects, the apology informants offered for newsworker and interviewee "oversimplifications" – their failure to consider that the text might be engaged in ideological work – was consistent with the group's failure to question a key textual assumption: that the events were undesirable (assumption 1). As was the case with the previous white-raced group (MATES), this group's scores on the looting and fires scales indicate that informants viewed these event-related activities as "wrong." Accordingly, informants viewed event-related arrests as "right" (see table 6.3). Informants in this group were particularly opposed to the use of violence by event participants, reasoning that more constructive means of protest could have been undertaken. Tom, for example, said he would explain the events to his children this way:

TOM: I think one thing I can start with is that the use of violence that was shown – I think that is totally wrong. I mean, I would explain to him as much anger as he might feel or whatever, you know, is justified in like feeling, you know, retaliating or whatever for him, I think. I'd make it clear to my, you know, kids that it's wrong. It's like there are other, better ways of, more constructive ways of doing it rather than going out there and burning things.

While informants were strident in the view that the events were undesirable, they appeared to be somewhat noncommittal as to the exact cause(s) of the events. One informant, Bill, seemed to question the textual assumption that the events were caused by "just outrage" over the King beating verdicts (assumption 4). He speculated that living in "raggedly conditions" may have prompted participants to act. Furthermore, unlike many of the other groups, this group did not seem to accept the textual assumptions that the black-raced community constituted the event insiders or that the events were a "racial thing" (assumptions 6 and 7). As Bill put it, the footage showing the protesters outside police headquarters suggests that "every race" was involved:

BILL: And then you had . . . another thing that, that stood out in that scene [at police headquarters] is that you just didn't have black guys, Mexican guys – you had black guys, Mexican guys and white guys. There's every, every . . . every race was, was, was in that scene. I mean, you had every, every race represented. So, is it really a racial thing then?

DORM2

This interview was conducted on the UCLA campus, in the same dormitory recreation room in which the previous interview (DORM1) was conducted. Informants sat in chairs and on a sofa facing a 19-inch, color television. Group members included: Gloria, female, 21; Paul, male, 18; Glenn, male, 19; and Ted, male, 18. Gloria, the resident assistant on the floor, was a history and political science major; Paul, was a biology major; Glenn was an electrical engineering major; and Ted was an art major. Two of the informants, Paul and Ted, were freshman who were not living in the Los Angeles area at the time of the events. With the exception of Gloria, who identified herself as "Latino," the informants uniformly identified themselves as "white or Caucasian" on the questionnaire. Informants were evenly split between describing themselves as "very" religious, "somewhat" religious, and "not at all" religious.[8] This group, like the previous group

(DORM 1), exhibited a socio-economic status considerably lower than that of the other white-raced groups, but higher than that of the typical black-raced or Latino-raced group (see table A.1).

Most of the informants in this group reported watching television news "more than three hours" on the first day of the events (see table 6.1). Informants reported that they were evenly split between "never" reading the *Los Angeles Times* over the course of the events and reading it "every day." Finally, as in the previous group (DORM 1), informants reported "never" discussing the events amongst themselves in the months following the outbreak.[9]

Screening highlights Like the previous white-raced groups (MATES and DORM 1), this group sat motionless and quietly throughout the screening of the text. About one minute into the screening, however, when the helicopter reporter notes that event participants were "firing shots rapidly into cars parked in the parking lot," Paul shakes his head and sighs. Group members do not visibly react when the plight of the Asian-raced man "drenched in blood" is described or when one of the anchors refers to event participants as "thugs." Similarly, informants do not visibly react during the First AME interviews, the Reverend Washington interview, or the anchors' summary. In short, informants exhibited no visible signs of challenging the text as-construction during the screening.

Discussion highlights Table 6.5 presents the emergence of key arguments in the group's discussion. Like the first white-raced group (MATES), this group decoded the KTTV text in a combination of referential and metalinguistic modes. That is, prior to the second prompt (which specifically asked about news coverage), informants in this group not only discussed the text in terms of their own experiences and memories, but they also questioned the text as-construction (despite a visible lack of such activity during the screening). For example, Gloria – the only non-white-raced informant – challenged newsworker "judgments" in the text, recognizing them as products of a racially and economically oppressive society:

GLORIA: What makes them say that? What draws it? They, they're already making judgments just based on these little small instances. They're just assuming that everyone out there is doing the same thing.

GLENN: Ummmmmmm.

GLORIA: And when I see that, I see just another form of this racist and economically stratified society that's the problem in the first place.

GLENN: Did you see when that –

GLORIA: It makes me sick.

GLENN: . . . when that reverend came on? And he was talking about, he would bring up the verdict and the guy goes, "No, no, beyond the verdict, talk about these people." And they are turning this into some kind of freak show that they just wanted to make us, oh, God –

Following the second prompt, informants continued their critique of KTTV's coverage of the events, identifying the media's preoccupation with ratings as a problem. While the continual coverage of fires might have been exciting, one informant argued, it did not "tell us anything." Informants, in short, generally criticized KTTV for providing images without context.

Despite these criticisms, however, even Gloria seemed to sympathize with KTTV newsworkers, arguing that they "were doing their best to respond to the situation." Furthermore, as Ted argued, any biased coverage in the text was not deliberate: the use of stereotypes and generalizations was subconscious. The reporters, he added, cannot help "the way they are."

Nonetheless, mirroring Gloria's earlier connection of newsworker judgment calls to societal oppression, this group was the least condemning of the events among the white-raced groups. That is, although group averages on the looting and fires scales suggest that group members found event-related looting and fires "wrong," the group as a whole was much less strident in these views than the other white-raced groups. Furthermore, like many of the black-raced and Latino-raced groups, this group actually felt somewhat ambivalent about event-related arrests (see table 6.3).

Underlying these group averages, however, was an interesting discussion dynamic. This dynamic pitted Gloria – the sole Latina-raced informant in the group – against two white-raced informants, Glenn and Paul. Gloria generally viewed the events as unfortunate, but felt somewhat sympathetic toward the plight of event participants. From her perspective, her understanding of an economically and racially stratified US, she could not simply place a "good" or "bad" label on event participants. Accordingly, her pre- and post-discussion scale scores were in the ambivalent range on the looting, fires and arrests scales. In contrast, Glenn and Paul were convinced that the events were "bad," little more than "mob" activity that lacked any plan.[10] The pre- and post-discussion scores for both informants were located at or near the farthest possible points on the looting and fires scales. The following exchange exemplifies the debate between Gloria on the one hand, and Glenn and Paul on the other:

GLORIA: I can't put a good or bad label on newscasters. Just as I can't put a good or bad label on the actions of the people in the community either.

GLENN: Ouch! You can't say that was bad? Just straight out?

GLORIA: I can't say that was bad.

PAUL: That was bad. Whether it was their fault or not is something different. But it was definitely bad. But would you – you, you can't categorize, would you categorize it as good?

GLORIA: No.

PAUL: Of course not. It's not good, then it's bad.

GLORIA: No, it's never that clear –

Interestingly, this debate seemed to influence the perceptions of the remaining group member, Ted, moving him closer to Gloria. Prior to discussion, Ted was somewhat opposed to event-related looting and fires. But after discussion, his scale scores indicate that he felt ambivalent toward these event-related activities.

Characteristic of the white-raced groups in general, there was little discussion of "race" in this group. In one of the few instances where "race" became the focus of discussion, informants debated whether the importance of "race" to the events was overemphasized by the media. According to Glenn, KTTV coverage implied that he would be harassed because of his "white" skin color if he decided to visit South Central Los Angeles. But he disagreed with this assessment, one he said suggested that "if you're white, you don't belong down here." Instead, he argued that "everybody's human" and that the people in South Central would treat him as such if he decided to visit. Gloria, however, argued that the residents of South Central are harassed when they visit "up here," and that white-raced visitors to South Central might provoke animosity in the area:

GLENN: Well, I think the bad part was the way the media showed the fires every single like, showed the fires over and over and over. And I thought that the, that the news lady had a good point in saying that this guy was white and he was being harassed. But it seemed like she focused on, if you're white, you don't belong down here kind of idea. And so, that again is –

PAUL: It's true, isn't it?

GLENN: Well, what you're saying there is that you're saying these people are a mob. I mean, guaranteed that night maybe wasn't a good idea, but now you're saying, I mean, "When I come back from that, I'm thinking, 'There's no way I'm ever going to walk down there because these people are going to shoot me on sight.'" And that's not true. I mean, everybody's human. You're not going to get shot down there just because you're white. At least I don't think so. yyy

GLENN: I can guarantee you that there's going to be groups that, you know, there might be a group of angry people, but –

GLORIA: Ummhmm.

GLENN: . . . guaranteed I'm not going to be turned down in a store because I'm white. I mean, it's not –

GLORIA: Yeah, it's not like, well, they have to face the fact everyday when they come up here, that they don't get adequate service in stores up here. And they are like the first people who are looked at when the shoplifting's been going on, "Oh! You did it! I know you did it!" So, umm, you know. It kind of comes down both ways.

In short, informants in this group seemed somewhat divided over the significance of "race" to the events. While white-raced informants generally seemed to discount the importance of "race," Gloria – the sole non-white-raced informant – agreed with the textual assumption that "race" was a central factor in the events (assumption 6). Indeed, Gloria referenced intertextual memories to express this point:

GLORIA: It was a couple of weeks after the riots and they said, "Ah, yeah! Now there's all these Mexicans running around in the city. And, let's call the INS! Because I know they all don't live here." And I said, "How do you know all those, all those people are not, ah citizens?"[11]

DORM3

As with the previous two interviews (DORM1 and DORM2), this interview was conducted on the UCLA campus, in a dormitory recreation room. Informants sat in chairs and on a sofa facing a 19-inch, color television. Group members included: Greg, male, 18; Margo, female, 18; Kathy, female, 21; and Rob, male, 20. Kathy and Greg were political science majors at UCLA; Margo was a civil engineering major; Rob was a biochemistry major. One of the informants, Greg, was a freshman from New York and was thus not living in the area at the time of the events. On the questionnaire, Greg and Margo identified themselves as "white or Caucasian," while Kathy and Rob identified themselves as "Chinese American."[12] Two of the informants described themselves as "somewhat" religious, while the other two described themselves as "very" religious and "not at all" religious, respectively. Relative to the previous two white-raced groups (DORM1 and DORM2), this group exhibited a rather high level of socioeconomic status (see table A.1).

Two of the informants in this group reported watching television news "all evening" on the first day of the events; the other two reported watching "one to three hours" and "none," respectively (see table 6.1). Informants were also divided over their reading of the *Los Angeles Times* during the events. Half of the informants reported reading the newspaper "sometimes," while the other informants were divided between reading it "never" and "every day." Finally, half of the informants in this group reported discussing the events amongst themselves about "once per month" in the months following the outbreak.[13]

Screening highlights Like the previous three groups, this group sat motionless and quietly throughout the screening of the text. Group members do not visibly react when the plight of the Asian-raced man "drenched in blood" is described, or when one of the anchors refers to event participants as "thugs." However, when the helicopter reporter notes that there is "no love lost out here for the media," Kathy nods her head in agreement. Informants do not visibly react during the First AME interviews, the Reverend Washington interview, or the anchors' summary. In short, informants exhibited no visible signs during the screening that they questioned the KTTV text as-construction.

Discussion highlights Table 6.6 presents the emergence of key arguments in this group's discussion. Unlike the MATES and DORM2 groups, this group decoded the KTTV text solely in a referential mode. That is, prior to the second prompt (which asked specifically about news coverage), informants in this group discussed the events in terms of the KTTV narrative and their past experiences. In other words, informants offered no unprompted challenges to the text as-construction.

Following the second prompt, however, informants began to consider the KTTV text as- construction. But unlike informants in the previous white-raced groups, these informants seemed to accept the KTTV text and its "direct footage" as a "realistic" rendering of events gone by:

ROB: One good thing about it, it was live.
MARGO: Yeah.
ROB: You can't really twist it. You know, show this part and not show this part.
MARGO: There's something to be said for seeing direct footage that's happening or that has just happened so recently. You know, umm, rather than just hearing about it over the radio. Personally, like, you know, if this would have happened, you know, sixty years ago, fifty years ago, and to read it in the newspaper the next day and see one or two pictures, you don't, you don't see what's

going on. You don't grasp what's going on. And even a tv is nothing compared to like if you're in an apartment building right across the street. But just the fact of seeing anything televised is, it's much more realistic and, I mean, that's better. It's, it keeps people from being so sheltered.

Despite this basic trust in pictures, informants were not without their criticisms of KTTV. Greg, for example, felt that KTTV was too preoccupied with ratings to emphasize what it should be emphasizing: the idea that event participants should "stop doing this." Consequently, he argued, KTTV did not make the events seem "as serious and life-threatening as [they] were." On balance, however, informants generally agreed that the KTTV coverage was "good," that the media's job is "basically just to report what's going on" (assumption 14).

Consistent with the dominant view among the white-raced groups, this group generally agreed with the textual assumption that the events were undesirable (assumption 1). That is, the group's scores on the fires and looting scales indicate that informants generally found this event-related activity "wrong," while the group's score on the arrests scale indicates that informants viewed the arrests as "right" (see table 6.3).

Informants in this group also agreed with the textual assumption that the King beating verdicts lay at the center of the events, that this injustice incited people to participate in violent protest (assumption 4). And this stance, of course, was expressed and reinforced through intertextual memories of the hypermediated King beating video:

ROB: You guys brought up a lot of points, but I think that, you know, violence is wrong – you got to tell them that. But, I mean, what do you tell a child that says, you know, when they showed the, the Rodney King beating?

MARGO: Yeah.

ROB: What do you say?

MARGO: What do you tell your kid when they say that or when they, when your kid asks why the officers, you know, if your child saw the, the taping of Rodney King being beat and then heard the decision. How do you explain that, I mean. There's, there's got to be some kind of reaction to it.

Despite their memory of this brutal beating, informants seemed to oppose the events simply because, as Greg put it, "violence is never the answer:"

GREG: I think it's important to realize that both sides – the police officers and the rioters were wrong. You know, they, the police

> officers were in no way right in beating him. And the rioters in
> no way were right for, ah, destroying their communities by . . .
> Yeah, you have to stress the fact that violence is never the
> answer.

Indeed, Greg compared the destruction resulting from the events to intertextual memories of a recent natural disaster, the 1989 San Francisco earthquake. Only this time, he argued, a "small community" chose "to destroy
itself."

Later in the discussion, however, Greg expanded the discussion agenda
by considering another possible motivation for the actions of event participants: the idea that "the system wasn't working for them." But almost
immediately he seemed to discount this motivation by noting that "things
were a lot worse" in the past. Another white-raced informant, Margo,
found hope for the future in this observation, but concluded that "a lot of
work" remains to be done:

GREG: Then again, I think the reason, the main reason why the vio-
         lence and all the looting that happened there and in other cities
         . . . people weren't going to stores and just saying, "I'm just
         stealing this tv, this stereo for Rodney King. Yeah, they were
         upset at a system, a society that, you know, they were working
         hard and it was just not paying off for them. And the verdict
         reinforced that to the point where they couldn't take any more
         and now they had a chance to vent their anger and get some of
         those material possessions that, you know, that they couldn't
         get because the system, the system wasn't working for them.

MARGO: Yeah. I mean, for every action there's going to be some reaction.
         And unfortunately so many people came out and, you know,
         decided to think, "Well, I'm going to benefit from all of the
         times that I've suffered, that I've lost – which wasn't the best
         reaction, but it's realistic when that happens, you know. And the
         way this society is now, maybe in a hundred years it won't be
         that way. But people should have seen it coming.

GREG: If you go back a hundred years things were a lot worse.

MARGO: ⟨Right, which gives hope for the next hundred years, but still at
         this point there's a lot of work to be done.

Of all the study groups – Latino-raced, black-raced or white-raced – this
group made the fewest overt references to "race" in its discussion. In fact,
no overt references were made to "whites" or "Asians," even though the
group was composed of two white-raced members and two Asian-raced

ones. Nonetheless, in the few instances where "race" was overtly mentioned, informants seemed to accept, implicitly, the textual assumption that "race" was an integral element of the events (assumption 6). For example, in response to the interviewer's question about what she saw in the KTTV text, Kathy said she would tell her child that there are "a lot of different races in our culture," and that "you have to respect other people and their differences."

In short, informants in this group accepted most of the assumptions embedded in the KTTV text – foremost, that the events were undesirable (assumption 1), that "blacks" were the event insiders (assumption 7), and that the events were similar to the Watts "riots" (assumption 11). But informants seemed divided over whether the King beating verdicts constituted *the* cause of the events (assumption 4). In one of the group's few explicit references to race, Greg linked the events to the "history" of racism and dashed expectations in the US, noting that media coverage of the verdicts merely presented black-raced participants with another reason and "chance to vent their anger:"

GREG: You know, it would take a day, lll, at the least, to explain to a child the history of racism in this country. When I heard on the video that, ah, these riots are the people's reaction to the Rodney King verdict. I said, it's, it's not just Rodney King. That just reinforced, ah, the, the oppression and, and of the country. They, they alluded to the, ah, 1965 riots in Watts. Well, that wasn't so much because of police brutality again. It was because as the black community was getting more rights and nothing was improving. They began to think that, you know, nothing's going to work. "We're hopeless." And then, they, they felt worse than they had to start with. And that's when they rioted. That's the reason why they rioted in '65. And maybe things had gotten to the point today where things aren't improving. They're just getting so much worse. I think that's a major part of the reason why they rioted. The Rodney King verdict just reinforced that. And being as, as, as, as high key, as much as the media covered the Rodney King case, that only helped them, maybe give them a chance to vent their anger.

JILL

This interview was conducted not far from the UCLA campus, in the living room of two of the informants. The informants sat on a sofa and fixed their attention on a 19-inch, color television set on the other side of the room.

Group members included: Jill, female, 19; Mike, male, 20; Joseph, male, 23; and Larry, male, 21. Jill, a sociology major at UCLA, was the center of this network; Joseph, a law student at another area university, was her boyfriend; Mike, an English major at UCLA, was her boyfriend's brother; and Larry was a friend from school. All of the informants identified themselves as "white or Caucasian" on the questionnaire. Half of the informants described themselves as "somewhat" religious, while the other half described themselves as "not at all" religious. Like the previous white-raced group (DORM3), this group exhibited a rather high level of socioeconomic status (see table A.1).

Informants in this group reported that they were evenly divided between watching television news "more than three hours" and "all evening" on the first day of the events (see table 6.1). They also reported being evenly divided in their reading of the *Los Angeles Times* over the course of the events: two informants reported reading the newspaper "sometimes," while the other two reported reading it "every day." Finally, informants reported discussing the events amongst themselves rather infrequently in the months following the outbreak.

Screening highlights As was the case with the other white-raced groups, members of this group sat quietly and motionless throughout the screening of the text. Informants do not visibly react when the plight of the Asian-raced man "drenched in blood" is described or when one of the anchors refers to event participants as "thugs." There are also no visible reactions during the First AME interviews, the Reverend Washington interview, or the anchors' summary. The first episode of talking among group members occurs 16 minutes and 40 seconds into the screening, as the Fox News logo appears on the screen at the end of the text: Jill mumbles something to Mike. In short, informants exhibited no visible signs that they questioned the KTTV text as-construction during the screening.

Discussion highlights Table 6.7 presents the emergence of key arguments in the group's discussion. As was the case with two of the other white-raced groups (DORM1 and DORM3), this group decoded the KTTV text solely in a referential mode. That is, prior to the second prompt (which specifically asked about news coverage), informants offered no arguments that challenged the KTTV text as-construction. Indeed, this decoding behavior seemed to echo the lack of informant activity during the screening.

Following the second prompt, however, informants offered a few criticisms of KTTV reporters that signalled their awareness of the techniques used in the text's construction. For example, Joseph and Mike were annoyed by the KTTV anchor's use of the fighter pilot analogy to describe

Reverend Washington. The informants viewed the analogy as "stupid," the result of anchors speaking without the benefit of a script:

JOSEPH: Yeah, that really stupid fighter pilot analogy. What the heck was that all about?
           lll
MIKE: That was a newscaster trying to make some cool, literary thing
           . . .
           lllll
MIKE: . . . Which was way above their heads . . .
           lllLll
MIKE: I had no idea what she was trying –
JOSEPH: I go, what is she babbling about?
MIKE: That's what happens when they get the stories like this, when they don't have time for someone to write all of the lines for them
           . . .

Informants were also annoyed by KTTV reporters who made a point of mentioning that covering the events had placed their lives in danger. The reporters, informants felt, should "just cover the news." Nonetheless, informants agreed that the KTTV reporters were "better than the anchor people" because they were not as "phoney" or "goofy." In short, media criticisms in this group focused on newsworker personality and reporting style. That is, informants seemed to have no problems with the validity, fairness or slant of the text as-construction.

Consistent with this group's apparent faith in the text's validity, informants – like those in each of the other white-raced groups – generally agreed with the textual assumption that the events were undesirable (assumption 1). That is, the group's scores on the looting and fires scales indicate that informants found these event-related activities "wrong," while its score on the arrests scale indicate that informants found this event-related activity "right" (see table 6.3).

Underlying these group averages was an interesting dynamic, pitting Mike against the other members of the group. Mike's score on the pre-discussion fires scale, like those of his fellow group members, indicates that he viewed the event-related fires as "wrong." But this stance seemed to be predicated on his observation that event participants burned their own community – that is, the fires would have been "right," he seems to have argued, if they had been started "somewhere else." Unlike others in the group, Mike did not find the looting "wrong." Instead, as his pre- and post-discussion scores on the looting scale suggest, he felt somewhat ambivalent toward the looting. Mike clearly understood event-related looting and fires as an opportunity for event participants to express complaints that had gone unheard by the system over the years. At the same time, however, his pre-discussion score on the arrests scale indicates that he viewed event-related arrests as "right." Mike ultimately resolved this apparent paradox by distinguishing between "right" and "wrong" for event participants. versus "right" and "wrong" in some more general sense. He seemed to priv-ilege the latter sense of "right" and "wrong" by defining event-related activ-ity as "crimes," thus explaining his support for event-related arrests. The other group members, in contrast, seemed to empathize with the "initial" anger of event participants toward the beating verdicts, but felt that this anger was quickly channeled into people taking advantage of the situation. As one informant put it, many event participants "cared more about steal-ing." The following exchange reflects the flavor of this debate:

MIKE: It was . . . I said it was right to arrest them during the looting because they were obviously committing crimes. You can't just let that happen, but, you know, why, why shouldn't they?

JILL: Well, it's one thing to be angry and express your opinion, but it's another thing just to make an excuse just to go out and loot –

MIKE: How long, how long have they been angry and expressing their opinions?

JILL: Well, it's like the straw that broke the camel's back.

MIKE: I mean, it's been years and years and years and years. How long do we expect them to be angry and express their opinions in –

JILL: But it's still not an excuse for them to go out and do illegal things.

MIKE: You can't . . . well, why not? They, I mean, they tried legal. They tried expressing their opinions legally. I mean, how long are they going to keep doing that without getting anywhere before they turn to illegal methods and ways to express themselves.

JILL: Well, in that case, why, why, why did you say it was right for them to arrest them?

MIKE: Because they were committing crimes.

JILL: But you said that that was right.

MIKE: Well, sure it's right for them, but you can't just let them commit crimes.

By far, this group made more overt references to "race" than any of the other white-raced groups. Informants clearly accepted the textual assump-tion that "race" was at the center of the events (assumption 6). Throughout the group's discussion, informants were preoccupied with coming to terms with raced tensions between "blacks" and "whites." Indeed, accepting the textual assumption that the black-raced community constituted the event insiders (assumption 7), informants expressed a general fear of "African Americans," a desire to live "far away" from South Central Los Angeles (an area they associated with "African Americans"):

LARRY: I'd, I'd have to say that, that, ah, I guess the whole racial issue about, is kind of all about it. Being that I'll probably live in an area or, or would live in an area, I guess, other than South Central Los Angeles, I guess, I don't think my kid would be in touch with that many African Americans. Just judging from the, you know, where I've come from, you know, I think there'd be a lot of confusion as to, you know, what African Americans are all about and seeing them on TV, you know, looting and beating up white people, especially white people. I don't think I would discuss it with him. I'd just kind of let him know that rioting's going on and that it's far away. And let him know, you know, that he's protected here.

JILL: It'd be so hard to like talk to him about it, though, and to try and change their opinions when they were like that young, I mean, if I was that young and I saw it, you know, a bunch of African Americans just beating up on white people and just like ruining, you know, just like starting fires and everything. And as much as I'd expect my parents to say something to me I don't know how much I would believe them. I'd just be so scared of black people after that, you know. At least when I was that age maybe, I mean, that's like a parent really actually talked it . . . over, you know, whatever. Friendly with black people, whatever . . . No, I meant like really good friends though, you know.

LARRY: Uh, huh.

While informants discussed their understandings of the events in terms of the KTTV text, they also voiced these understandings by referencing intertextual memories. Larry, for example, expressed his own angst over the events – the seemingly dismal prospects for US race relations – by recalling a movie he had seen titled *Little Man Tate*:[14]

LARRY: It's about a kid who feels so, a kid who's so burdened by the, ah, processes of society, burning down the rain forests, ah, all these different issues, that he almost feels like, almost like, ah, almost like suicidal.

In the final analysis, although this group accepted textual assumptions about the centrality of "race" (assumption 6) and the insider status of the black-raced community (assumption 7), informants attempted to distance themselves from what would likely be perceived as a racist position: that "blacks," as a category, are to blame for the events. As Joseph argued, all "blacks" are not "evil," even if they did initiate the events. Likewise, he concluded, all "whites" are not "evil," even if they "sort of drove the whole racial tensions to where it is now."

Conclusions

In this chapter, I sought to explore the process by which each white-raced study group made sense of the KTTV text. Several findings warrant summarizing:

First, the white-raced groups in this study tended to define the events as "crime." Accordingly, all of the groups accepted the textual assumption that the events were undesirable (assumption 1). Although many of the groups empathized with the anger they attributed to event participants, they felt that the "riots" were just too destructive and counter-productive. Indeed, the tendency among informants in these groups was to view the text as a narrative about the disintegration of order, the rise of lawlessness. Consistent with this general feeling, white-raced groups tended to support event-related arrests. Several of the groups also agreed with the textual assumption that event participants should have protested in more peaceful ways, preferably by voting (assumption 9).

Second, three of the groups (DORM1, DORM3, and JILL) decoded the text solely in a referential mode. That is, prior to specific prompting about news coverage, these groups tended to discuss the events strictly in terms of their own feelings or the text's narrative. The remaining two groups (MATES and DORM2) decoded the text in a combination of metalinguistic and referential modes. These latter groups were clearly familiar with discourses of media deconstruction, offering criticisms of the text as-construction prior to specific prompting about news coverage. Nonetheless, most of these criticisms tended to focus on KTTV personalities and styles, not on the validity, fairness or slant of the text. In short, the white-raced groups voiced little unprompted concern with KTTV's coverage of the events, treating it as a clear window onto events gone by.

Third, prolonged debate between informants occurred in three of the white-raced groups. In two of the groups (MATES and JILL), debate centered around the causes of the events and the motivations of event participants. Informants in these groups – regardless of the side they took in the debate – ultimately condemned the events as "wrong." In a third group (DORM2), the debate *was* about the morality of the events, and it was waged along raced lines: a Latina-raced informant versus two white-raced informants. The Latino-raced informant attributed the events to economic and raced oppression in the US. She, unlike her white-raced counterparts, refused to place a "good" or "bad" label on participants. Thus her pre- and post-discussion scores on the looting, fires and arrests scales fell in the ambivalent range.

Fourth, the white-raced groups' treatment of "race" followed two rather distinct patterns: "race" was either barely mentioned or it was a major item on the discussion agenda. Three of the five groups (DORM1, DORM2, and DORM3) exhibited the first pattern. That is, relative to other study groups, there was very little use of overtly raced labels and not much discussion (if any) of the raced meanings associated with the King beating verdicts or other issues identified in the text. In contrast, the two remaining groups (MATES and JILL) explicitly identified the black-raced community as the event insiders and were quite liberal – relative to the other study groups – in their use of raced labels. With few exceptions, however, the white-raced groups made no explicit references to "whites" in their discussion of the KTTV text.

Finally, in each group, intertextual memories seemed to shape how informants understood the events; these memories also affected informants' reception of the KTTV text, their reaction (or lack thereof) to its depiction of the events.

In part 3 – Analysis and conclusions – I embark on a more systematic consideration of the data collected from the Latino-raced, black-raced and white-raced study groups. Two concerns frame the remainder of the book: (1) establishing the role that "raced ways of seeing" played in informants' decoding of the KTTV text, and (2) exploring the relationship between meaning-making and resistance in the television experience.

PART III

Analysis and conclusions

7

Raced ways of seeing

> The way we see things is affected by what we know or believe. In the Middle Ages when men believed in the physical existence of Hell the sight of fire must have meant something different from what it means today. Nevertheless their ideas of Hell owed a lot to the sight of fire consuming and the ashes remaining – as well as to their experience of the pain of burns. (Berger, 1973, p. 8)

In chapters 4, 5 and 6, I explored in some detail how study groups found meaning in the KTTV text – their "ways of seeing." These groups, you will recall, were categorized by race-as-representation in order to facilitate an analysis of raced differences in this meaning-making process. But how valid were these a priori raced groupings? That is, with what degree of confidence can one attribute differences in decoding to differences in raced identification rather than some other variable or variables? After all, I did observe decoding differences *within* the raced groupings. Were these within-"race" differences sufficiently overshadowed by the between-"race" differences so that one might meaningfully speak of raced differences?

To proceed as if "race"-per-se explains differences in the television experience essentializes "race" and explains nothing. The real question, the one left unanswered by this type of approach, is as follows: *What is it* about race-as-representation in the US context that results in the decoding differences we encounter? To put it another way, how does raced subjectivity influence the television decoding process, and how does this process, in turn, influence the construction and reproduction of raced subjectivities?

In the present chapter, I attempt to tackle this question. By considering patterns in decoding between the various study groups, I aim to assess the importance of raced ways of seeing in the meaning-making process.

In the final chapter, chapter 8, I discuss the relationship of this meaning-making process to struggle and resistance in society.

Raced differences?

Between April 29, 1992 – the first day of the events – and July 29, 1992, Bobo *et al.* (1992) surveyed a representative sample of people in Los Angeles County and asked them about their understandings of the events. The results of this survey suggest that there existed rather striking differences at the time between raced groups in their views regarding the events. The majority of "black" respondents, the researchers found, viewed the events as "mainly protest" (67.5 percent), while the majority of "white" respondents (55.8 percent), "Hispanic" respondents (51.9 percent), and "Asian" respondents (50.5 percent) viewed the events primarily as "looting and street crime."[1] In other words, "white," "Hispanic" and "Asian" respondents were considerably less likely than their "black" counterparts to view the events as "mainly protest" (42.9 percent, 38.7 percent, and 37.4 percent, respectively).

These responses become more interesting when they are compared to the survey's finding that following the outbreak of the events there also existed important raced differences in respondents' perceived fairness of the system. That is, more than 75 percent of "black" respondents felt that "American society just hasn't dealt fairly with people from my background," while the figures for "Hispanic," "Asian" and "white" respondents were only about 45 percent, 36 percent and 15 percent, respectively. At first glance, these two survey items suggest that a connection may exist between perceptions of societal fairness and interpretations of the events.[2] That is, the tendency to interpret the events as "protest" seems consistent with the tendency to perceive US society as racially "unjust." Conversely, the tendency to make sense of the events as "crime" appears consistent with the tendency to feel less maligned by the system.

It seems reasonable to assume that these raced differences, if valid, should be echoed in viewers' decoding of televised representations of the events. This, of course, is exactly what we found in chapters 4, 5 and 6, when I presented audience ethnographies for each of the study groups. To black-raced informants, the KTTV text was about racial and economic injustice in the United States, a condition with which black-raced subjects, these informants argued, were quite familiar. These informants described the events as legitimate protest and spoke somewhat empathetically of event participants. A few black-raced informants even referred to the events as a "rebellion," feeling that "riot" misrepresented the nature of the events.

Latino-raced and white-raced[3] informants, in contrast, ultimately portrayed the events as crime in their discussions. Many informants sympathized with the frustration of event participants, but concluded that the events were an intolerable breach of order – too destructive and counter-productive. A few of these informants even criticized event participants for "taking advantage" of the situation to "loot" and pillage.

These ethnographic observations are underscored when we consider raced differences on three scales measuring informant attitudes toward event-related activity. These scales ranged from 1 to 10, with 1 indicating that informants felt the looting, fires or arrests were "right," and 10 indicating that informants felt each event-related activity was "wrong." Table 7.1 presents the average scores by raced grouping (i.e., "Latino-raced" versus "black-raced" versus "white-raced" informants) for each scale, administered after the screening of the KTTV text, prior to group discussions.

Three findings emerge from this table: first, black-raced informants were substantially more tolerant of event-related looting (mean = 5.7) than either Latino-raced (mean = 8.3) or white-raced informants (mean = 8.6); second, black-raced informants were somewhat more tolerant of event-related fires (mean = 7.8) than either Latino-raced (mean = 8.7) or white-raced informants (mean = 9.1); and third, black-raced informants were much less tolerant of event-related arrests (mean = 5.8) than either Latino-raced (mean = 3.7) or white-raced informants (mean = 2.9).

In fact, each scale finds the attitudes of black-raced informants to the left on a political stance continuum, toward support of the looting and fires and condemnation of the arrests; meanwhile, the attitudes of white-raced informants fall to the right, toward condemnation of the looting and fires and support of the arrests; the attitudes of Latino-raced informants fall in the middle, but closer to white-raced than to black-raced informants.

Do these findings constitute evidence of *raced* ways of seeing? How do we know that other variables do not explain the differences? Moreover, if raced ways of seeing are to blame for the differences, how exactly do raced subjectivities exert their influence in the meaning-making process? Finally, what are the implications for the construction and reproduction of raced subjectivities?

Below, I attempt to unpack the black box surrounding the meaning-making process so that we might trace and specify how race-as-representation exerted its influence on study informants. In particular, I explore the use of pronouns; effects of race-as-representation versus socio-economic status (SES) and gender; group viewing modes; group discussion modes; polarization outcomes by group; and the relationship between group characteristics, discussion dynamics, and polarization outcomes.

The use of pronouns

In chapter 2, I defined "race" as "the central axis of social relations" in the United States (Omi and Winant 1986, p. 61; 1994), a "collective representation" that serves to account for (and even legitimate) difference and stratification in society (Prager 1982, p. 102). Because race-as-representation is so pervasive in US culture, it acts as "a fundamental organizing principle of social relationships" (p. 66). At the micro-level, race-as-representation informs the construction and reproduction of identity. As Omi and Winant (1986) put it, "One of the first things we notice about people when we meet them (along with their sex) is their race . . . Without a racial identity, one is in danger of having no identity" (p. 62). But as Hall (1988) points out, identity is composed of multiple dimensions – including "race," gender, sexual orientation, class, and so on – the salience of each waxing and waning from situation to situation. How, then, are we to isolate an individual's raced identity as the source of his or her attitudes and actions? That is, how do we know whether what we have termed "raced ways of seeing" is really attributable to "race?"

One approach to answering this question involves identifying how social actors understand themselves, the immediate subject position from which they think and act. In respect to the question at hand, this *subjectivity* consists largely of what is often termed *racial consciousness* – "a set of political beliefs and action orientations" arising out of "the awareness of having ideas, feelings and interests similar to others who share the same [raced] characteristics" (Gurin *et al.* 1980, p. 30). Previous studies (e.g., Cramer and Schuman 1975) suggest that pronoun usage may serve as an insightful indicator of the solidarity social actors share with important ingroups and their distance from certain outgroups. When the referents of these pronouns are raced groups, raced solidarity and distance – raced subjectivity – may be established.

Table 7.2 reviews the rate of pronoun use for each group and raced category during the discussions following the screening of the KTTV text. I divided pronouns into two classes: pronouns of solidarity ("we," "us" and "our") and pronouns of distance ("they," "them" and "their"). The first finding that emerges from the table is that the black-raced groups had a higher average rate of solidarity pronoun use (2.54 per minute) than either Latino-raced (1.77 per minute) or white-raced groups (1.44 per minute). Black-raced groups also had a higher average rate of distance pronoun use (9.79 per minute) than either Latino-raced (5.42 per minute) or white-raced groups (4.01 per minute). The significance of these differences for the raced subjectivity question becomes clear when the referents of the pronouns used are explored.

Table 7.3 presents pronoun usage for each group and raced category by referent.[4] The first panel of the table presents the referents of solidarity pronouns ("we," "us" and "our"), while the second panel presents those of the distance pronouns ("they," "them" and "their"). Three important findings emerge from this table regarding the question of raced subjectivities. First, in their discussion of the events and KTTV text, informants in the Latino-raced groups seemed to understand themselves as members of their immediate study group (60 uses), while informants in the South Central groups also thought of themselves as people who live in South Central Los Angeles (48 uses) and as "Latinos" (11 uses):[5]

Not all of *us* were thugs. (mumbled something) That has nothing to do with it! But, you know, last year, I mean, they just, everybody in South Central, they're thugs. *We're* gangsters. *We're* . . .   (LATINA group)

It's about people trying to come up with money, with things, freeloading. Because that's what it's really all about. I mean, *our race*.   (YOUTH group)

At the same time, the Latino-raced groups generally talked about event participants (204 uses) and the media (163 uses) as if they were distant others:[6]

I understand *they* were very angry and I don't think that justifies anything that *they* did.   (MARIA group)

They [reporters] were scared because *they* thought *they* were going to get hurt too.
                                                              (FAMILY group)

Second, informants in the black-raced groups understood themselves first and foremost as "blacks" (101 uses):

We [blacks] cared about Rodney King, man, because that was one of *our* brothers.
                                                              (GANG group)

In two of the groups (CORNER and KEISHA) informants also expressed solidarity with event participants (11 uses):

I mean, but that was some stress that people needed to get off they chest, though. *We* really did.   (CORNER group)

This is a, umm, white-dominated society and black people have no, no, no – you know, they don't fit in anywhere. And so, I think that, that's why *we* rebel.
                                                              (KEISHA group)

In contrast, no such solidarity with event participants was expressed in any of the Latino-raced or white-raced groups. For the most part, however, black-raced groups also tended to discuss event participants as if they were distant others (133 uses):

I really don't know what *they* should have done, but that's just not . . . I don't have the answer really, but that, that did a lot of damage to the city and everything else.

(NORTH group)

Black-raced groups also tended to treat the media (173 uses), "whites" (35 uses) and the police (30 uses) as distant others:

During the Gulf War, okay. Wasn't *they* [the media] telling us to be strong, stick together, support your family? Okay, so why *they* wasn't doing that . . . even though it was a riot, but why *they* wasn't giving us moral support? From the media? You know, I mean *they* wasn't saying nothing.

(CORNER group)

We have to do it the white man's way. The only way we can beat, beat the game is to beat *them* [whites] at *their* own game.

(CHURCH group)

They [police] was out there by Fox Hills Mall, protecting it. As soon as you go out there, *they* all around you, waiting for somebody to do something.

(CORNER group)

Third, informants in the white-raced groups seemed to think of themselves primarily as members of their immediate study group (55 uses):

What's interesting about what *we* just watched [the KTTV text] is that it's so detached.

In three of these groups (MATES, DORM2 and DORM3) informants also talked about themselves as "Americans" (5 uses):

. . . You say, "That, that couldn't happen here." That total anarchy. You know, the country of Democracy that *we* have – just can't imagine that!   (DORM3 group)

But in none of the white-raced groups did informants use solidarity pronouns when speaking of "whites." At the same time, these informants talked about the media (162 uses), event participants (152 uses), and "blacks" (33 uses) as if they were distant others:

That's what happens when *they* [the media] get stories like this, when *they* don't have time for someone to write all of the lines for *them* . . .   (JILL group)

It [the events] was just an excuse for *them* to go wild – a bunch of, of animals.

(MATES group)

Well, I just never, I . . . growing up, I, I always felt that, ah, African Americans were more or less, ah, a whole separate culture. It was like a, ah, you really, you really, *they* wouldn't really interact with you. I think *they* felt, ah, more like a solidarity amongst *themselves*.   (JILL group).

In short, an analysis of pronoun usage suggests that when black-raced informants discussed the events and KTTV text they clearly understood themselves as "black" subjects. White-raced informants, in contrast, generally talked about themselves as members of their immediate study group, while Latino-raced informants seemed to approach the events and KTTV text from a variety of subject positions – "race" being just one.

Raced identification versus income and gender

Income and gender referents were not among those implicated by informant pronoun usage. Nonetheless, in order to distinguish the effect of raced subjectivity (or lack thereof) on informant understandings of the events from possible SES and gender effects, I tested a series of multiple regression models concerning the responses of individual informants on three of the attitudinal scales.[7] Table 7.4 presents the regression coefficients for three models assessing the effects of family income[8] and raced identification on informant feelings concerning the events. The dependent variable in Model 1 is informant support for event-related "looting;" the dependent variable in Model 2 is informant support for event-related fires; and the dependent variable in Model 3 is informant support for event-related arrests.[9]

In Model 1, I tested the null hypothesis that no differences existed between white-raced informants (the omitted group) and black-raced or Latino-raced informants in their support for event-related looting. The data do not support this hypothesis. Black-raced informants were less likely than their white-raced counterparts to agree that the looting was "wrong" (beta = −.55; p < .01). No significant difference, however, was detected between Latino-raced and white-raced informants concerning feelings about the looting. Furthermore, the proxy for SES, family income, did not appear to influence support for event-related looting. This model explained about 26 percent of the variance in the scale scores (adjusted r-square = .26).

In Model 2, I tested the null hypothesis that no differences existed between white-raced informants (the omitted group) and black-raced or Latino-raced informants in their support for event-related fires. The data appear to support this hypothesis. Although the beta for black-raced informants (−.32) is significant at the .05 level – which in and of itself suggests that black-raced informants may have been less likely than their white-raced counterparts to view event-related fires as "wrong" – the F statistic for the entire model is not significant. This model explained only about four percent of the variance in the scale scores (adjusted r-square = .04), suggesting that variables more important than raced identification or SES influenced informant feelings about the fires.

In Model 3, I tested the null hypothesis that no differences existed between white-raced informants (the omitted group) and black-raced or

Latino-raced informants in their support of event-related arrests. The data do not support this hypothesis. Black-raced informants were more likely than their white-raced counterparts to view event-related arrests as "wrong" (beta = .56; p < .01). No significant difference, however, was detected between Latino-raced and white-raced feelings about the arrests. Furthermore, family income did not appear to influence support for event-related arrests. This model explained about 18 percent of the variance in scale scores (adjusted r-square = .18).

Table 7.5 presents the regression coefficients for three models assessing the effects of gender and raced identification on informant feelings concerning the events. The dependent variable in Model 4 is informant support for event-related "looting;" the dependent variable in Model 5 is informant support for event-related fires; and the dependent variable in Model 6 is informant support for event-related arrests.[10]

In Model 4, I tested the null hypothesis that no differences existed between males (the omitted group) and females in their support for event-related looting. Dummy variables for black-raced and Latino-raced informants were left in the model to assess the effect of gender net of raced identification. On the basis of the data, I could not reject the null hypothesis. In other words, the beta for the female variable (.04) was not large enough to conclude that female informants were more or less likely to support event-related looting than were male informants. Despite the introduction of gender into the model, black-raced informants continued to be less likely than their white-raced counterparts to agree that the looting was "wrong" (beta = −.54; p < .01). As in Model 1, no significant difference was detected between Latino-raced and white-raced informants concerning feelings about the looting. This model explained about 24 percent of the variance in the scale scores (adjusted r-square = .24).

In Model 5, I tested the null hypothesis that no differences existed between males (the omitted group) and females in their support for event-related fires. Again, I could not reject this hypothesis on the basis of the data. That is, the beta for the female variable (.01) was not large enough to conclude that a difference existed between male and female informants regarding their support for event-related fires. This model explained only about two percent of the variance in the scale scores (adjusted r-square = .02), suggesting that variables more important than gender or raced identification influenced informant feelings about the fires.

In Model 6, I tested the null hypothesis that no differences existed between males (the omitted group) and females in their support of event-related arrests. Again, I could not reject this hypothesis on the basis of the data. In other words, the beta for the female variable (.19) was not large enough to conclude that female informants were any more or less likely than male informants to view event-related arrests as "right." As in Model 3, however, black-raced informants were found to be more likely than their white-raced counterparts to find event-related arrests "wrong" (beta = .48, p < .01), while there was no significant difference between Latino-raced and white-raced informants. This model explained about 23 percent of the variance in scale scores (adjusted r-square = .23).

In short, an individual-level analysis of racial effects supports the group-level findings: black-raced informants left the screening significantly more tolerant of event-related looting and significantly less supportive of event-related arrests than their white-raced and Latino-raced counterparts. Furthermore, socio-economic status and gender, net of raced identification, did *not* seem to be a major determinant of informants' attitudes toward event-related activities.[11] Other studies, of course, highlight the importance of both class and gender in shaping how people make sense of media (see Morley 1980, 1992; Press 1991), in channeling them to specific interpretive communities (Lindlof 1988). But the Los Angeles events were evidently so pregnant with racial meanings that raced subjectivity was the primary identity activated as informants made sense of the KTTV text.

Group viewing modes

If, as the findings above suggest, black-raced informants were more likely than white-raced or Latino-raced informants to perceive the events as protest, then one might expect to find that black-raced informants also received KTTV *representations* of the events differently than their white-raced and Latino-raced counterparts. That is, if – as I argued in chapter 3 – the assumptions embedded in the KTTV text condemn the events and event participants, then one might expect to find that most black-raced informants arrived at the screening predisposed to a more critical decoding of the text than either white-raced or Latino-raced informants.[12] Indeed, one might expect to find that black-raced informants were more likely to question the validity of reporter claims, react against any loaded terminology, talk back to the screen.

Alternatively, as media-powerful scholars might argue, the vividness of the text's representations may have submerged textual assumptions so deeply in a sea of image and sound that these assumptions, over time, became invisible to informants of all raced identifications, taken for granted. Given this scenario, one might expect to find that informants slipped further and further into the television experience during their respective screenings, that they lost both the will and the ability to adopt a critical stand outside the established frame, to challenge the face validity of media representations with alternative sources of knowledge. In other words, one might *not* expect to find major "race"-based differences in how informants received the KTTV text. The power of the representations might be expected to level any differences in group predispositions, to standardize informant reception modes.

For this case, at least, the validity of both perspectives may be tested by exploring what study informants actually *did* during their respective screenings of the KTTV text. In particular, I was interested in noting whether group members were animated during the screening, discussing and deconstructing textual representations with one another, or whether they were more passive, quietly processing the representations without consultation of the group. In particular, I sought to identify any visible reactions within each group at three points in the text: when one of the news anchors refers to event participants as "thugs;" when the same anchor describes the plight of an "Asian" victim who is "drenched in blood;" and during the anchors' "summary" at the end of the text – that is, when the anchors provide a unified interpretation of the day's events (see chapters 4, 5 and 6, for group-by-group descriptions). Group reactions that questioned the text, its use of labels and its narrative, I reasoned, would constitute evidence against the media-powerful argument as I have cast it.

Table 7.6 presents a summary of group viewing characteristics during the screening of the KTTV text. The most obvious finding in the table is that the white-raced groups tended to be visibly more passive in their reception of the text than either Latino-raced or black-raced groups. Viewers in the white-raced groups sat motionless and quietly throughout the 17-minute screening. I noted no visible reactions in these groups when the KTTV anchor referred to event participants as "thugs," or when the plight of the "Asian" man "drenched in blood" was described. In only one of the groups was there any talk when the KTTV anchors attempted to summarize the events, package them into a coherent, unified narrative. And this talk was *not* critical of KTTV efforts.

In contrast, table 7.6 indicates that black-raced groups were quite animated during the screening, with Latino-raced groups not far behind. Several of the black-raced groups and one of the Latino-raced groups promptly reacted with laughter or talk to the labeling of event participants as "thugs." At least two of the black-raced groups and three of the Latino-raced groups responded with talk or body gestures during the report of the "Asian" man "drenched in blood." All of the black-raced and Latino-raced groups engaged in continuous or intermittent episodes of talk during the anchors' summary of the events at the end of the KTTV text.[13]

My failure to note similar visible reactions within white-raced groups during key points in the screening, of course, does not preclude the possibility that invisible reactions were occurring within the heads of white-raced viewers. But when the dearth of *social* activity in white-raced groups is compared to the relative wealth of such activity in black-raced and Latino-raced groups, the case for "race"-based reception differences seems to gain strength.[14] Furthermore, no clear pattern emerged *within* black-raced and Latino-raced groups suggesting that socio-economic status made a difference in reception styles.[15]

Why did black-raced and Latino-raced groups feel it necessary *or* appropriate to be animated during the screenings? Did viewers in the white-raced groups find such activity during the screenings unnecessary or inappropriate? One possible interpretation of the differences in viewing styles between white-raced and non-white-raced informants (black-raced informants, in particular) is that white-raced informants arrived at the screening already in agreement with the textual assumption that "blacks" were the event insiders (assumption 7), feeling somewhat distant from the text and events.[16] Furthermore, the events had subsided more than eight months prior to the interviews. Perhaps white-raced informants simply were not aroused by the text; maybe they *valued* its meanings differently than black-raced and Latino-raced informants.[17] As one white-raced informant put it:

I mean, it's [the events] just, just kind of a memory that comes up occasionally. But it's not something that I take time, because I wasn't there and it didn't personally affect me.[18]

In contrast, Latino-raced informants who lived in the areas depicted in the text, and black-raced informants, who were depicted as event insiders, responded as if they had a stake both in the events and the KTTV text. Perhaps the zest with which these informants received the text was emblematic of their attempts to negotiate unresolved issues that were important to them.[19] Moreover, given the nature of the assumptions embedded in the text, maybe these informants were forced to "work harder" than their white-raced counterparts to resolve these issues in a satisfying way (see Condit 1994, p. 432).

Polarization by group

"Media-powerful" arguments aside, the finding that raced differences appear to exist in how study informants received the KTTV text should come as no surprise given the findings of Bobo *et al.* (1992): Race-as-representation clearly played an important role in how people understood the events. Nevertheless, the finding of raced reception differences is only the first step in the arduous task of tracing the influence of race-as-representation in informants' decoding of the KTTV text. An important subsequent step is attempting to understand how such differences are reproduced over time. This step would bring us much closer to understanding the meaning-making *process*.

In chapter 2, I proposed that small-group phenomena such as attitude polarization at the micro level feeds into the macro-level process by which raced group norms, expectations and boundaries are reproduced. Attitude polarization, you will recall, occurs when group interaction and discussion strengthens response predispositions generally favored by a subject popu-lation" (Myers and Lamm 1975, p. 299). It follows, then, that any pre-exist-ing attitude differences found *between* raced groupings in a given sample of informants should increase as informants participate in same-"race," group interaction.

Table 7.7 presents cases of attitude polarization (in italics) by group and attitude scale. The first finding that emerges is that attitude polarization occurred in only about 38 percent of the possible cases (17/45). This occur-rence rate, however, was not distributed equally across the raced groups. Polarization occurred most frequently in the Latino-raced groups, in about 53 percent of the cases (8/15); it occurred less frequently in the black-raced and white-raced groups, in about 33 percent (5/15) and 27 percent (4/15) of the cases, respectively.

The case for group influence, however, strengthens a bit when we con-sider simple attitude convergence. By "attitude convergence," I refer to a post-discussion decrease in the scale standard deviation, indicating, liter-ally, that group scores have converged about the scale mean. Table 7.8 again presents cases of attitude polarization (in italics), but this time cases of atti-tude convergence (double asterisks) are added as well. That is, an additional case is added for each raced category that supports the group-influence argument. Thus, in about 44 percent of the possible cases (20/45), support for the group influence argument – either attitude polarization or conver-gence – is evident. This number breaks down into 60 percent of the cases for Latino-raced groups (9/15), 40 percent for black-raced groups (6/15), and about 33 percent for white-raced groups (5/15). Unlike the Latino-raced groups, most black-raced groups felt somewhat ambivalent about the events (see chapter 5), perhaps explaining the relatively low rate of polar-ization or convergence in these groups. Furthermore, two of the white-raced groups (MATES and DORM2) were characterized by heated debates between one informant and the rest of the group members (see chapter 6). Perhaps these discussion environments account for the absence of polarization in the groups and the relatively low rate of polarization and convergence among the white-raced groups as a whole.

Table 7.9 presents scale outcomes correctly predicted by the polarization hypotheses.[20] These hypotheses correctly predicted scale outcomes in about 69 percent (31/45) of the cases. As with the *occurrence* of polarization, the *accuracy of predictions* was not evenly distributed across the raced groups. Among Latino-raced groups, outcomes were correctly predicted in about 80 percent of the cases (12/15); among black-raced and white-raced groups, outcomes were correctly predicted in about 60 percent (9/15) and 67 percent (10/15) of the cases, respectively. In short, the polarization hypotheses received a modest level of support from the data.

In the final analysis, although polarization only occurred in about half of the Latino-raced cases and a quarter of the white-raced ones, it generally led in these cases to increased condemnation of event-related fires and looting, and increased support for event-related arrests. In contrast, polarization only occurred in about a third of the cases among black-raced groups, but this polarization concerned event-related fires and arrests (i.e., not looting), decreasing black-raced support for *both* the former and the latter. The majority of black-raced group discussions, you will recall, were marked by a high degree of ambivalence toward event-related looting and arrests (see chapter 5). In short, attitude polarization – when observed – worked to sharpen the divide between black-raced informants on the one hand, and white-raced and Latino-raced informants on the other. Myers and Lamm (1975) speculated that this micro-level process might explain the reproduction over time of group differences in attitude. But in order to more clearly understand the *conditions* under which this process contributes to the negotiation of racial meanings, we must look beneath the numbers and explore any patterns between group characteristics, discussion dynamics and polarization outcomes.

Group characteristics, discussion dynamics and polarization

Table 7.10 presents summary information for each group concerning origin, racial make-up, discussion dynamics and polarization outcomes.[21] Among black-raced and Latino-raced groups, no clear pattern was found between group origin (i.e., South Central Los Angeles versus UCLA) and polarization outcomes.[22] That is, both South Central and UCLA groups were equally distributed across the high- and low-polarization categories.

Likewise, I found no clear pattern between group racial homogeneity and polarization outcomes.[23] That is, groups exhibiting high degrees of attitude polarization were equally distributed across the racially homogeneous and heterogenous categories, while those exhibiting low degrees of polarization were nearly equally distributed across the categories. At first glance, this finding might suggest that interpersonal comparison theory is "race" neutral. This theory, you will recall, argues that people desire to present themselves favorably relative to others. Thus, when a person finds in group discussion that others share his or her position on an issue, he or she may feel free to become an even stronger advocate of the position (Myers and Lamm 1975). If this theory were "race" neutral, then the raced identification of others to whom group members compare themselves would not matter.

An alternative interpretation, however, is that members of the racially heterogenous groups in which polarization did occur (i.e., in which interpersonal comparison processes may have been at work) may share commonalities or points of view that overshadowed raced differences, that facilitated interpersonal comparisons during discussion *despite* these differences. One might expect these groups – JULIO, NORTH, and DORM3 – to be less likely than the other groups to center "race" in their discussions of the text and the events. Detailed analysis of these groups' discussions (chapters 4 through 6) offers some support for this interpretation.[24]

While the data in table 7.10 suggest that a clear relationship between group racial homogeneity and polarization does *not* exist, they do reveal a clear pattern between these outcomes and discussion dynamics.[25] That is, study groups in which informants tended to support one another's statements and arguments (i.e., "unity") tended to exhibit a relatively high rate of polarization and/or convergence (5/7, or 71.4 percent). The remaining groups, groups in which informants frequently challenged one another's positions, tended to experience lower rates of polarization and/or convergence.

These findings, of course, are consistent with the logic of informational influence theory. This theory, you will recall, posits that group attitude polarization is the result of arguments generated during discussion that favor the initially dominant point of view. Some of these arguments may not have been considered before (or may have been forgotten) by certain members of the group, thereby leading to a strengthening of these members' original positions and to a hardening of the initially dominant point of view for the group as a whole (Myers and Lamm 1975). It follows that if arguments generated in discussion challenge each other (i.e., if there is no initially dominant point of view), these arguments are likely to cancel out the influence of one another across all group members, making polarization unlikely.

In sum, the low overall polarization rate noted above – 38 percent –

appears to be more a function of initial attitude differences among members in some groups and enduring ambivalence within black-raced groups than group racial heterogeneity. Consistent with both interpersonal comparison theory and informational influence theory, attitude polarization generally occurred in groups whose members were in initial agreement. And as I observed above, initial attitudes toward event-related looting differed significantly between black-raced and non-black-raced informants. In other words, when group discussion had any effect at all, it was generally to increase these initial differences between black-raced and non-black-raced groups.

Conclusions

When one surveys intergroup patterns in pronoun use, in attitudes toward event-related activities, in group viewing modes, and in polarization outcomes, evidence begins to mount for what I have referred to as "raced ways of seeing." Black-raced and Latino-raced study groups were quite animated during the screening of the KTTV text, while white-raced study groups watched quietly. For black-raced informants, in particular, raced subjectivity was clearly an important lens through which the events and text were viewed. The relatively low salience of raced subjectivity among Latino-raced and white-raced informants echoed the non-black-raced/black-raced divide observed in informant attitudes toward the events. That is, while white-raced and Latino-raced informants were *less* likely than their black-raced counterparts to talk about themselves in raced terms, they were *more* likely than black-raced informants to condemn the looting and fires and to support the arrests. Moreover, socio-economic status and gender seemed to have very little impact on these raced differences. There was clearly a link between racial subjectivity and how informants made sense of the events.

In many respects, the finding of attitude polarization and/or convergence (44 percent of the possible cases) is emblematic of the role that group pressures and expectations play in individual decoding behaviors. Each informant, of course, brought certain personal experiences and understandings concerning the events to his or her own screening and the discussion that followed. These experiences and understandings were in part the products of previous social interactions, previous discussions between the informant and important others. But as we saw in chapters 4 through 6, these experiences and understandings were also the product of *intertextual* relations, informants' continuous dialogue with other texts stored in memory. The group screenings and discussions analyzed in this study represent the intersection of both sets of relations at a given point in time. To put it another way, they represent yet another cycle in the process of meaning-making for the informants, a process that is ongoing.

This observation is important for the following reason: because "race" is not some fixed essence (Prager 1982; Omi and Winant 1986, 1994; Hall 1988, 1989), specific category attributes can be quite fluid and ambiguous from one moment to the next. And because category members often have an investment in their category membership (e.g., seeing it as integral part of identity), they must continually work to achieve and re-achieve membership status anew (Garfinkel 1967) – that is, in the eyes of important others (e.g., network members), and as measured by the texts that position them (Hall 1988; Gray 1995). In this sense, the study screenings and group discussions served as a forum for informants to "do-being Latino," "do-being black," or "do-being white" – to negotiate positions from which to make sense of the KTTV text *and* affirm their own raced subjectivities. In other words, informants activated memories of past experiences and other texts to negotiate group expectations about how Latino-raced, black-raced or white-raced subjects *should* discuss the KTTV text. Indeed, these expectations seemed to influence the subsequent performance and understandings of informants in the study.

For Latino-raced and black-raced informants, in particular, evidence of these expectations at work can be found in several of the arguments that emerged in the group discussions – for example, that people should "stick" to their own "race" (e.g., the FAMILY group) or that "blacks" must unify before they can effectively challenge the system or move ahead (e.g., the CHURCH and KEISHA groups). These prescriptions seem to echo other texts and discourses about key values in "Latino" and "black" culture.

For example, Marin and Marin (1991) argue that "Latino" culture tends to "emphasize the needs, objectives, and points of view of an ingroup," rather than the personal objectives, attitudes and values typically privileged in more individualistic cultures (p. 11). Among Chicanos, in particular, Blea (1988) notes that "[i]ndividualism is seen as Anglo, and profit is valued to the degree that it does not disrupt social relationships" (pp. 64–65). Most Latino-raced informants discussed the events as if they were *not* in the interest of the ingroup.[26] "Latinos" who participated in the events, they argued, were just taking advantage of the situation. Accordingly, Latino-raced informants found relatively little to criticize in the KTTV text's depiction of the events as "undesirable."

This was not the case for black-raced informants.

In his ethnographic study of everyday black-raced Americans, Gwaltney (1980) identifies ethnic solidarity as a key tenet of "black" culture. "White America," he notes, loomed large in his subjects' narratives concerning the history of "black" oppression and resistance. The black-raced informants in this study discussed the events in similar terms, returning again and again to issues of "white" racism and "black" solidarity. It was as if these informants – in accord with classic discourses on black-raced consciousness (see e.g., DuBois 1965; Fanon 1967) – were expected to trace their anxieties back to contact with the "white" world.[27] Indeed, consistent with recent texts highlighting a general "black" suspicion of official knowledge (Gabriel 1988; Turner 1993; Fiske 1994), black-raced informants (unlike their Latino-raced counterparts) seemed predisposed to questioning many of the assumptions embedded in the KTTV text, if not the text's construction itself. As Gray (1993, p. 191) put it,

Various reading strategies and practices produced by black audiences have been, indeed must be, critical, suspicious, and mindful of the dominant and dominating impulses of a racialized social and cultural order, an order that has historically stereotyped, excluded, objectified, and silenced black subjects.

Accordingly, black-raced informants received the KTTV text as a "white text" – one that might provide snippets of useful information,[28] but that ought not be taken at face value.

White-raced informants were much more at ease with the KTTV text, despite their familiarity with and enactment of discourses of media deconstruction. Three of the white-raced groups contained one or more Asian-raced members who agreed with white-raced members that the system was more or less fair, that the events were an undesirable, counterproductive breach of order. Accordingly, these groups sat quietly during the screening of the KTTV text, opting not to talk back to the screen. Furthermore, "race" – with a few exceptions – was not a salient topic in these group discussions. Informants in these groups were generally hesitant to talk about the events in raced terms, despite their frequent references to "blacks" and "African-Americans." Perhaps membership in the dominant "major race" (Hacker 1992) presented white-raced informants with the expectation and luxury to talk about themselves as "Americans" first – *not* as raced subjects (Waters 1990; Feagin and Vera 1995).

In short, while this study's exploration of group discussion and polarization effects treats "race" as a social construct whose reproduction is dependent upon an endless succession of micro-level interactions, the study also acknowledges that raced meanings are reified and reinforced at the macro-level of economics and politics (see Omi and Winant 1986, 1994). In other words, structures situate groups *vis-à-vis* one another in social space, while individuals continually decode the meanings of their unique situations in accordance with normative understandings and expectations (Fine and Kleinman 1983). Over time, this process leads to a patterning of individual-group relationships, thereby establishing an important micro-macro link (see chapter 2).

Nonetheless, the relationship at any given moment between raced identification and decoding – what I have termed "raced ways of seeing" – is always a probabilistic one, never a deterministic one (see Fiske 1987). For race-as-representation, as an *immediate* social force, is always experienced by actors through the conduit of concrete situations. In this case study, at least, raced ways of seeing appeared to be a critical factor in informants' decoding of the KTTV text. Moreover, as informants negotiated these ways of seeing, as they replayed intertextual memories and engaged themselves in discussion with network members, they also affirmed (directly or by default) their own raced subjectivities.

8

Meaning-making and resistance

If it is true that man cannot be conceived of except as historically determined man – i.e. man who has developed, and who lives, in certain conditions, in a particular social complex or totality of social relations – is it
then possible to take sociology as meaning simply the study of these conditions and the laws which regulate their development? Since the will and
initiative of men themselves cannot be left out of account, this notion
must be false. (Gramsci 1971, p. 244)

In chapter 2, you will recall, I proposed that the television experience is a
complex, iterative meaning-making process (see figure 2.3, appendix B).
That is, I proposed that race-as- representation (1) sets parameters for television texts (2) and organizes intertextual memory (3); at the same time, I
proposed that micro-level confrontations between television texts, intertextual memory, individual decodings (4), social network discussions (5), and
negotiated decodings (6) shape the meanings viewers take away from any
given encounter. Finally, I proposed that these macro- and micro-level
processes necessarily feed into one another, mutually (re)shaping meaning
with each iteration.

The findings that emerged from group discussions in this study seem to
support the proposed model. First, race-as-representation clearly shaped
the KTTV text's treatment of the events. KTTV newsworkers freely
employed racial labels to identify event participants and victims as if "race"
was somehow relevant to what was happening. Combined with the potent
symbols of the Rodney King beating verdicts (i.e., "white" officers beat
"black" man, acquitted by "white" jury), Watts (i.e., a militant "black
riot"), KTTV anchors and reporters (i.e., "non-black" interviewers), First
AME interviewees (i.e., "black" interviewees), and Reverend Washington
(i.e., "black" leader), this newsworker practice worked to structure a racial
dividing line into the KTTV text: "blacks" were syntagmatically marked as

event insiders, "non-blacks" as event observers and victims. That is, KTTV newsworkers relied upon race-as-representation – a primary explanatory framework in the US – to imbue event participants with ready-made motivations in the narrative. But from the vantage point of KTTV newsworkers, these motivations did not justify the means: the events were clearly undesirable. Voting and/or peaceful protest were presented as more desirable alternatives.

But study informants did not always decode the text as KTTV newsworkers intended. Intervening between the KTTV text and informant decoding practices were the intertextual memories of informants. Whether it was memories of *Roots* (used by one group to dramatize the legacy of slavery and black-raced oppression in America), Gulf War news coverage (used by one group to criticize the news reporters who covered the events), or *Malcolm X* (used by one group to criticize black-raced participation in the events, used by others to identify with this participation), the study groups' understandings of the events and reception of the KTTV text seemed to be profoundly affected. These negotiated decodings, of course, were forged through informants' interaction within their social networks, through discussion within the study groups (i.e., through attitude polarization and convergence). In short, the study interviews became one iteration in an ongoing meaning-making process for informants.   ·

Because meaning-making links private thoughts and action to social structure, the "end result" of this process has become *the* point of contention in many agency-versus-social- determination debates. In this book, I have defined audience-powerful and media-powerful perspectives as the rather idealized poles of this debate. Audience-powerful perspectives generally emphasize the tendency/ability of individuals to resist the ideologies inscribed in media texts – that is, to recognize them, challenge them, or otherwise subvert them (see Klapper 1960; Blumler and Katz 1974; Fiske 1987). In contrast, media-powerful perspectives tend to underscore the power of media texts to plant their intended meanings in the minds of individuals, to position them ideologically, to shape their views of the world and of themselves (e.g., Althusser 1971; Foster 1985). At best, this latter perspective treats resistance as a fleeting phenomenon whose cultural products are continually absorbed by the status quo, repackaged, and fed back to a consuming public (see chapter 2).

A central goal of this book, of course, was to employ empirical data in order to shed some light on this debate – to come to terms with the power of media to impose a particular view of reality on audiences versus the tendency of audience members to meaningfully resist. In this final chapter, I first take a closer look at the degree to which study groups tended to oppose or accept particular assumptions embedded in the KTTV text. Second, I reconsider the KTTV text in an attempt to uncover the origins of its assumptions, to name the ideological position(s) from which the text speaks. Finally, in light of this ideological analysis, I explore the social significance of informant opposition to textual assumptions, identifying any practices that might meaningfully constitute "resistance."

Informant opposition

If words speak the truth, people in the United States have little confidence in the media. Only 15.2 percent of those who responded to the 1990 General Social Survey claimed to have "a great deal" of confidence in the "people running" the press. An even smaller percentage, 13.9 percent, reported having faith in the television industry. In contrast, the overwhelming majority of respondents reported having "only some" to "hardly any" confidence in the "people running" the press and television (General Social Survey 1990).

But how do these *words* compare to *behavior*? Does a lack of professed confidence in media necessarily result in oppositional decodings? What about acts of viewer "resistance?" Or is media "bashing" merely a discourse – currently in vogue – that has little impact on the ability of media to influence and the tendency of viewers to "resist" in any meaningful way?

In chapter 7, I noted that black-raced informants were more tolerant of event-related "looting," somewhat more tolerant of the fires, and much less tolerant of the arrests than their white-raced and Latino-raced counterparts. That is, pre-discussion scale scores suggested that black-raced informants questioned the central textual assumption that the events were undesirable (assumption 1), while Latino-raced and white-raced informants embraced the assumption. Likewise, I found interesting raced differences in how study groups received the KTTV text during the screening. Black-raced and Latino-raced informants were quite animated during the screening, while white-raced informants generally watched quietly. These findings, of course, raise several questions: *How* did study groups talk about the KTTV text following the screening? *Referentially? Metalinguistically?* Was this decoding *mode* also patterned by raced identification? Moreover, which textual assumptions did study groups oppose in their discussions? Was the pattern of textual opposition consistent across raced groups? And what effect did instances of opposition have on how informants finally understood event-related activity – on post-discussion attitude scales?

Given the differences between how black-raced, white-raced and Latino-raced informants received the KTTV text during their respective screenings, one might expect to find corresponding raced differences in how informants talked about the events following the screening. "Metalinguistic" decodings of media texts, you will recall, were marked by discussions in which viewers display an unprompted awareness and appraisal of the techniques used in the text's construction. In contrast, "referential" decodings were defined by discussions in which viewers simply speak of a media text in terms of their own personal experiences or the text's narratives. Liebes and Katz (1988, 1993) found that viewers of television drama tend to either discuss these texts in a referential mode, directly connecting the narratives to their own lives, or shift back and forth between referential and metalinguistic modes in their discussions. In this study, I sought to explore the mode or modes of decoding employed by viewers of a television *news* text, how explicitly informants considered the techniques used in its construction. Was there a connection between informants' consideration (or lack thereof) of these techniques and their tendency to accept or reject the assumptions embedded in the KTTV text? Were raced differences in decoding mode evident?

Race, socioeconomic status, decoding mode and opposition

Table 8.1 presents summary data for each group regarding socio-economic status (SES), decoding mode and rate of opposition toward KTTV textual assumptions. The first finding that emerges from the table is that only one of the groups, CHURCH, began discussion of the KTTV text in a metalinguistic mode and maintained this mode of decoding throughout most of its discussion. Three other groups, KEISHA, MATES and DORM2, discussed the text using some combination of metalinguistic and referential decoding modes. The remaining eleven groups – accounting for over 73 percent of the sample – failed to explicitly consider the techniques used in the construction of the narrative until specifically prompted to do so.[1] One possible interpretation of this finding – that seems to fit with media-powerful conceptualizations of the media-audience relationship – is that the majority of study informants treated the KTTV text and its framing of the events as a clear window onto the world. In other words, one might argue that the vividness of the text's sound and images pulled the majority of informants so far into the television experience that these informants took the text's representations for granted, unable or unwilling to adopt a critical stand outside the established frame. That is, the case might be made that the text was successful in positioning informants as subjects who accept the veracity of news images.

However, support for the media-powerful interpretation seems mixed when one considers the relationship between decoding modes and the rate of group opposition toward assumptions embedded in the KTTV text. Despite decoding the text in a referential mode, four of the groups exhibited relatively high rates of opposition toward key textual assumptions during their discussion of what they had seen. That is, the LATINA, JULIO, GANG, and NORTH groups offered at least 0.81 arguments per minute that directly challenged a key textual assumption.[2] But rather than deconstruct the entire KTTV text as-construction, informants in these groups typically challenged particular textual issues on the basis of alternative sources of knowledge. The rate of opposition among these groups is noteworthy given the mean number of oppositional arguments per minute offered by each raced category: 1.01 for black-raced groups, and only 0.58 and 0.64 for Latino-raced and white-raced groups, respectively.[3] In short, referential discussion modes and high rates of opposition were *not* mutually exclusive options in these groups.

At the same time, however, there appears to have been a significant relationship between the rate of opposition and decoding mode.[4] That is, there were *no* groups that exhibited both a low rate of opposition *and* that decoded the text in a metalinguistic mode, suggesting that low rates of opposition and metalinguistic decodings were mutually exclusive options for informants.

Aside from the finding that the only predominantly metalinguistic decoding was offered by a black-raced group, and the finding that none of the Latino-raced groups offered a decoding that was even somewhat metalinguistic, there did not appear to be a clear pattern between raced identification and decoding modes.[5] That is, the remaining black-raced and white-raced groups offered both referential and partially metalinguistic decodings of the KTTV text.

Likewise, although all five of the lower SES groups made referential decodings of the text, six of the ten higher SES groups did as well, blurring any clear pattern between SES and decoding modes.[6] Yet the finding that none of the lower SES groups made metalinguistic decodings may be important in and of itself. David Morley (1974, 1980, 1992) has long argued that decoding strategies are a function of the institutions in which viewers are embedded and the discourses to which they are privy. Lower SES informants from South Central Los Angeles, unlike their more affluent counterparts from the Westside college groups and the CHURCH group, were clearly not exposed to discourses of media deconstruction. But informants in several of these lower SES groups still managed to challenge specific textual assumptions on the basis of members' experiences and intertextual memories.

Opposition by textual assumption

Table 8.2 presents opposition to KTTV textual assumptions by study group, raced identification, and assumption. Several important findings emerge from this table. First, nearly half of all oppositional arguments offered in group discussions (48 percent) concerned assumption 14 – that the role of news media is to serve their viewers by providing them with fair and factual coverage of the events. In short, congruent with previous findings concerning a general lack of confidence in the media in the US (see General Social Survey 1990), many study groups – LATINA, CHURCH, KEISHA, MATES, DORM2, and DORM3, in particular – were openly skeptical of news media in their discussions.

Second, challenges to the notion that the media are fair and factual (assumption 14) and that the events are undesirable (assumption 1) combined to account for more than three quarters (79 percent) of all oppositional arguments offered in group discussions.

Third, opposition toward textual assumptions seemed to be patterned by raced identification. Anti-media arguments (assumption 14) accounted for more than half of the oppositional arguments offered in Latino-raced and white-raced groups, 53 percent and 51 percent, respectively; they accounted for only about 40 percent of the oppositional arguments offered in black-raced groups. Meanwhile, arguments challenging the undesirability of the events (assumption 1) accounted for a larger portion of the oppositional arguments offered by the Latino-raced and black-raced groups (40 percent and 33 percent, respectively) than the white-raced groups (23 percent).

Furthermore, only two groups – YOUTH and FAMILY – failed to generate arguments that challenged the undesirability of the events (assumption 1). Both of these groups were Latino-raced groups from South Central Los Angeles. Meanwhile, both black-raced and white-raced groups – GANG,[7] DORM1 and DORM3, in particular – offered challenges to the assumption that the events were caused by the King beating verdicts (assumption 4). Latino-raced groups did not question this assumption.

In the final analysis, table 8.2 suggests, Latino-raced opposition focused on two textual assumptions: that the events were undesirable (assumption 1) and that the media are fair and factual (assumption 14). Arguments challenging these assumptions accounted for about 93 percent of all oppositional arguments offered in Latino-raced group discussions. In contrast, black-raced and white-raced groups were more diversified in their opposition toward textual assumptions. About 88 percent of the oppositional arguments offered in black-raced group discussions concerned four assumptions: that the events are undesirable (assumption 1), that the media are fair and factual (assumption 14), that the King beating verdicts caused the events (assumption 4), and that ministers have a special role in efforts to restore calm (assumption 8). Likewise, about 92 percent of the oppositional arguments offered in white-raced group discussions was distributed across four assumptions: the first three challenged by black-raced groups, as well as the assumption that "race" was a central factor in the events (assumption 6). The other nine textual assumptions – that the events were centered in South Central Los Angeles (assumption 2), that elected officials should become more involved (assumption 3), that the events were "riots" (assumption 5), that "blacks" were events insiders (assumption 7), that voting is the appropriate outlet for change (assumption 9), that police should have had more of a presence (assumption 10), that the events were similar to the Watts riots (assumption 11), that the First AME rally was a reasonable response (assumption 12), and that prayer was a reasonable strategy (assumption 13) – were left largely unchallenged by study groups.

Terminology and opposition

Opposition toward key textual assumptions might also be assessed by considering the terminology informants used to discuss the events and KTTV's depiction of them. Table 8.3 presents the usage of key terms by group and raced identification. Several interesting findings emerge from this table. First, congruent with the paucity of opposition toward assumption 5 (that the events constituted a "riot"), "riot" was clearly the preferred term for the events among informants. This term was used 57 times in the white-raced groups, 38 times in the Latino-raced groups and 28 times in the black-raced groups. With one exception, only black-raced groups – CHURCH and KEISHA – used terms other than "riot" to refer to the events. That is, the term "rebellion" was used five times by these groups, and "uprising" was used once.[8] This observation, of course, is consistent with the finding that black-raced informants tended to be less condemning of the events than either white-raced or Latino-raced informants (see chapter 7).

Second, while explicit references to Rodney "King" or the "verdict(s)" occurred 35 times in the white-raced groups and 34 times in the black-raced groups, these references only occurred 16 times in the Latino-raced groups. Perhaps the greater number of references to the verdicts in black-raced and white-raced groups was a reflection of these groups' opposition to the assumption that the verdicts *caused* the events (assumption 4). In contrast, Latino-raced groups seemed to take this assumption for granted, finding little reason to debate the significance of the verdicts in their discussions.

Third, while the term "thugs" was used by one of the Latino-raced groups (LATINA) and two of the black-raced groups (KEISHA and NORTH), it was not used by any of the white-raced groups. Not surprisingly, perhaps, the use of this term in the discussions mirrored group responses to its emergence in the KTTV text. That is, the term only appeared in the discussions of the groups that visibly reacted during the screening to the anchor's characterization of event participants as "thugs." And these groups were highly critical of *both* the KTTV anchor who used the term and the notion that the media are fair and factual (assumption 14).

Fourth, echoing the text's definition of the events as crime and its portrayal of event-related activity as "looting," the term "loot(er)(ing)" was clearly the preferred term among informants to describe such activity.[9] The term was used more frequently in white-raced groups (37 times), than in Latino-raced and black-raced groups (19 times and 25 times, respectively). No other term or interpretation was offered for this event-related activity in group discussions. Nonetheless, prior to discussion, black-raced informants were considerably less condemning of this activity than white-raced and Latino-raced informants (see chapter 7). When this observation is combined with black-raced informants' lack of support for event-related arrests, it becomes clear that black-raced informants opposed the text's depiction of the events as crime, despite their use of the crime signifying term "loot(er)(ing)."

In short, the few instances in which informants challenged textual terminology occurred in black-raced or Latino-raced groups. Moreover, their rather animated screening behaviors, their often raucous discussions, and their expression of opposition through humor, wit and irony suggests that these groups worked harder than the white-raced groups to derive pleasure from the KTTV text (see Condit 1994). Indeed, it appears that the assumptions embedded in the text were not nearly as bothersome to white-raced informants, informants who sat passively throughout most of the screenings and spoke in measured tones during the discussions (see chapter 6).

Oppositional arguments and attitude change

Table 8.4 presents pre- and post-discussion scale averages regarding event-related looting, fires and arrests by raced identification.[10] Despite the finding that 40 percent of the oppositional arguments offered by Latino-raced groups and 23 percent of those offered by white-raced groups challenged assumption 1 – that the events were undesirable – post-discussion scale averages suggest that Latino-raced and white-raced informants continued to find the events undesirable. That is, Latino-raced and white-raced informants ultimately found event-related looting "wrong" (means = 8.9

and 8.7, respectively), event-related fires "wrong" (means = 8.7 and 8.9, respectively), and event-related arrests "right" (means = 3.8 and 3.3, respectively).[11] In Latino-raced and white-raced group discussions, perhaps, arguments more supportive of assumption 1 worked to offset those that challenged it. Chapters 4 and 6, which detail Latino-raced and white-raced discussions by group, suggest that this was indeed the case. Latino-raced and white-raced groups tended to perceive the action of event participants as inappropriate, too destructive, even counter-productive. In most of these groups, a lone "devil's advocate" was the source of most oppositional arguments regarding the assumption. Apparently these arguments did not persuade other group members.

In contrast, the post-discussion scale averages for black-raced informants were quite consistent with the high rate of opposition toward assumption 1 exhibited in the group discussions (33 percent of all oppositional arguments). That is, following these discussions, black-raced informants remained quite ambivalent regarding whether event-related looting was "right" or "wrong" (mean = 6.2). These informants continued to find the fires "wrong," but they were less vehement in this feeling than Latino-raced or white-raced informants (mean = 7.8). Finally, black-raced informants actually moved from having ambivalent feelings about event-related arrests to concluding that these arrests were "wrong" (mean = 7.2). As I noted in chapter 5, all of the black-raced groups were somewhat sympathetic to the events and/or event participants. From the perspective of these groups, the events were symptomatic of racial and economic injustice in the US.

In the final analysis, study informants opposed the KTTV text in a variety of ways – through metalinguistic decoding, by challenging embedded assumptions, and through the use of alternative terminology. At the same time, however, many informants seemed to accept key assumptions embedded in the text. In other words, study groups generally made *negotiated* decodings of the KTTV text: they decoded this text according to various mixtures of dominant *and* oppositional codes (see figure 2.2, appendix B). Moreover, the distribution of informant opposition/acceptance seemed to be patterned to some extent by the raced groupings. Before we might understand these patterns in terms of "resistance," however, we must first revisit the KTTV text and establish *how* it worked as a hegemonic text.

The KTTV text revisited

In chapter 2, you will recall, I argued that news construction is inherently an ideological enterprise, one that works to buttress societal hegemony. Indeed, "news" is the result of a complex social process, not simply the product of professional newsworkers who objectively report on some reality out there (see Lippmann 1922; Epstein 1973; Tuchman 1978; Altheide and Snow 1979; Gans 1979; Fishman 1980; Parenti 1986; Herman and Chomsky 1988). This process, you will recall, consists of several factors, including (but not limited to) *journalistic values*, *newswork routines*, *entertainment value*, and *the socio-political climate*. The ideological nature of the assumptions embedded in the KTTV text becomes more clear when considered in light of these factors.

Journalistic values The preeminent US journalistic value, of course, is objectivity. This value came into prominence early in the twentieth century in order to legitimate the journalistic enterprise in a time when the line between "news" and propaganda became increasingly blurred (Schudson 1978). Indeed, objectivity has become more a practice for newsworkers than an actual belief or achievement (Tuchman 1978). Accordingly, throughout the KTTV text, newsworkers fluctuated between paying homage to the objectivity ideal and slipping into emotional pronouncements about the events and participants. On the one hand, newsworkers advertised their attempts to "confirm" reports and avoid being "unfair" in their characterization of the events and participants; on the other hand, they referred to participants as "thugs" and continually lamented the "unfortunate" nature of the events.[12] Nonetheless, "live" (read "self-evident") footage dominated KTTV's coverage of the events, buttressing efforts to validate an indispensable presupposition: the role of KTTV news is to serve its viewers by providing them with fair and factual coverage (assumption 14). Indeed, terms like "objectivity," "fairness," and "balance" permeated the discourse of KTTV newsworkers long after the events had subsided. KTTV's managing editor during the events, for example, described KTTV coverage of the events as "fair" and "balanced" because it played down "rhetoric." For an important mission of television news, as he put it, is to provide an "accurate" reflection of today's events.[13] Likewise, another KTTV newsworker – the reporter who conducted the First AME interviews featured in the text – spoke passionately about journalists' responsibility to "balance" newscasts.[14] In short, for journalists to eschew the labels "objective," "fair" or "balanced" in reference to their news production is tantamount to professional suicide. KTTV newsworkers were no exception. While the KTTV text clearly fell far short of achieving the ideal of "objective," "fair" or "balanced," journalistic legitimacy demanded that KTTV newsworkers feign as if the text was precisely that.

Journalistic routines These routines, you will recall, facilitate newsworkers' selection of "newsworthy" events from the proliferation of other events/occurrences on the societal horizon (Tuchman 1978). More germane to this case, routines provided KTTV newsworkers with *pre- developed* strategies for collecting and reporting "news." And these routines, of course, made the KTTV text what it is. First, from the newsworker's perspective, the most important characteristic of the events was probably the speed at which they were unfolding. Because the events spontaneously erupted and spread, newsworkers were pressured to react quickly. As the events grew and metamorphosed, newsworkers struggled to keep up, to compare favorably with their competitors at other news media. In a zero-sum world of time and resources, analysis of causes and long-term significance necessarily took a back seat as newsworkers shifted into a familiar journalistic routine, the *breaking news mode.* The luxury of scripted reports disappeared. This reporting environment, of course, produced a multitude of off-the-cuff newsworker comments, appraisals, and comparisons in the KTTV news text. An anchor's labeling of event participants as "thugs" and the helicopter reporter's comparison of the events to the Watts riots (assumption 11) stand out as prime examples.

Second, the saturation of the text with fire footage *sans* analysis of causes – "helicopter journalism" (Tice 1992) – represented what must have been seen by Los Angeles news media as state-of-the-art crisis coverage. In this media environment, the *"live" mode* became both a journalistic routine and a selling point. Finally, the jump-on-the-bandwagon routine is evident in the locations KTTV newsworkers selected for news coverage. In lock-step with its competitors, for example, KTTV singled out the First AME gathering from a multitude of other event-related activities for special attention. Thus KTTV repeatedly returned to First AME throughout the first evening of the events, effectively affirming the gathering's centrality to efforts to restore order (assumptions 12 and 13). This "rally," of course, was attended by important city and community officials – important "newsmakers." For in the KTTV text, interviewees enjoyed one of two statuses: either they were witnesses to "significant" event-related activity (e.g., the First AME "rally," which other news media also treated as newsworthy) or they were officials of some sort (e.g., Reverend Washington). Officials – unlike other interviewees – were granted the distinction of being able to engage in ongoing dialogue with newsworkers, of being allowed to clarify their emerging analysis of event-related activities. In the end, KTTV's adherence to journalistic routines (e.g., favoring official sources and focusing on "significant" activity) necessarily resulted in a rendering of the events that alternative routines might not produce.

Entertainment value Because television news is a business dependent upon the attraction of audiences and advertisers, it must be entertaining. Indeed, information has become a necessary but not sufficient component of television "news." "Newsworthy" information must be packaged; it must be decontextualized and then recontextualized, presented in some action-packed, coherent format that piques audience needs, curiosity and/or fear. Although commercials were suspended throughout much of KTTV's coverage during the first night of the events (e.g., none appear in the text),[15] the KTTV text was clearly designed to entertain. First, graphics were used throughout the text to anchor KTTV's packaging of the events: "Cops on Trial: The Rodney King Case." The drama of the events was thus provided with an inciting incident. The tension appeared to escalate as newsworkers emphasized immediacy, action, fires. "I'm Carol Lin reporting *live* [emphasis added] at First A.M.E" (20).[16] "What you're looking at right now – and I don't have a monitor here, but I believe what you're looking at right now are two fires burning simultaneously on the corner of Western and Slauson" (20). As a consequence of routine concerns for entertainment value, of the breaking news format, newsworkers talked about the King beating verdicts (assumption 5) as if they emerged in a vacuum, unrelated to larger issues of societal fairness and equity.[17] That is, they were, by default, treated by newsworkers as the consequences of isolated, individual actions – *not* systemic forces. The social history of the verdicts was not germane to the immediate drama.[18]

Socio-political climate The socio-political climate shapes the tenor of news texts by defining who the "legitimate" sources are, the sources (typically elite "officials") newsworkers tend to rely upon when ferreting out "news" and/or interpreting its social significance. Indeed, when elite consensus on policy and tactics dissolves from time to time, this discord is routinely reflected in the media's coverage (Hallin 1984). However, this was not the case with the events. The *official* definition of the situation as "lawlessness" was established soon after the outbreak of the events, when word of possible National Guard deployment and other efforts to restore order were reported. The next seventy-two hours saw key "officials" reinforce this definition by presenting a united front in their condemnation of the events and participants:

We simply cannot condone violence as a way of changing the system . . . I will keep telling the country that we must stand up against *lawlessness* and *crime*, wherever it takes place [emphasis added].[19]

We are determined that this city is not going to suffer the kind of *terrorizing* that some people seem bent on inflicting upon it [emphasis added].[20]

I'm not going to relax and assume it's over . . . I don't believe it's over. I want us to show by the massive . . . force we are putting on the streets here that we are determined to maintain control.[21]

Echoing this official understanding of the situation, KTTV newsworkers depicted the events as undesirable (assumption 1) – as "riots" (assumption 6) centered in South Central Los Angeles (assumption 2). Newsworkers toed the official line and assumed that a police presence was desirable to protect whatever order remained in event-torn areas of the city (assumption 10). Indeed, consistent with the 1968 Kerner Commission report recommendations,[22] newsworkers even cooperated with police in the exchange of information about event locations and participants. Because newsworkers assumed that the Rodney King beating verdicts (i.e., "white"officers acquitted on charges of beating a "black" man) were the root cause of the events (assumption 5), "blacks" were labeled the event "insiders" (assumptions 3 and 7), thereby downplaying the multi-racial nature of the events.[23] Meanwhile, common sense concerns for safety and property led to depictions of the events as a "senseless" breach of order. Accordingly, newsworkers assumed that ministers (assumption 8) and other community leaders (assumption 4) might be in a position to convince people to "do the right thing," to "remain calm," that it "makes more sense" to vent their "frustrations" at the polling place (assumption 9). Finally, the discourse of criminality was invoked by newsworkers to explain the behavior of event participants. That is, the burning of buildings became "arson" and the action of removing goods from stores was defined as "looting" – or as one informant in the MATES group put it, "hoodlum behavior." But as Fiske (1994b) points out:

... "[L]ooting" cannot be understood as simple theft; indeed, it cannot be understood simply at all. It is an engagement in a multifrontal struggle where antagonistic social relations are contested in the domains of law and economics and in the material and psychic conditions of everyday life. (p. 169)

In short, the KTTV text works to bury the political meanings of event-related activity with the vocabulary of crime; as a result, "America" itself, the *system* that gave birth to the events, is shrouded by a routine diversion of newsworker scrutiny. Indeed, in an updated version of "blaming the victim,"[24] the text locates responsibility for the events with deficiencies in event participants themselves.

In contrast, KTTV newsworkers might have portrayed the events as an unfortunate, but necessary wake-up call for the government, an important societal agent that had neglected innercity needs for years (see Johnson *et al.* 1992). Or they might have depicted the events in more systemic terms, as emblematic of struggles between haves and have-nots in a classist and racist society (see Robinson 1993). By any measure, the implications of the events easily dwarf the "venting of frustration" and "crime" frames circulated by news media. Indeed, the events clearly qualify as political activity, as "rebellion," as "dissent." The events were *triggered* by a perceived failure of social justice (i.e., the King beating verdicts); they continued for several days in defiance of civil authority (i.e., the US president, the mayor of Los Angeles, the Los Angeles Police Department, National Guard Troops, and so on); a substantial amount of the activity seems to have been patterned, rather than randomly distributed (Davis 1992; Dentler 1992; Johnson *et al.* 1992; Noel 1992); many event participants forcefully articulated the various political, racial and economic factors that motivated them (Johnson *et al.* 1992; Noel 1992; Winant 1994);[25] and an alliance between formerly warring gangs produced a proposal for rejuvenating the socio-economic infrastructure of South Los Angeles (Madhabuti 1993). In an historical analysis of the "Watts riots" that occurred in Los Angeles twenty-seven years earlier, Horne (1995) found similar circumstances and patterns. He also found that those "senseless" events contributed over the years to progressive (if not revolutionary) changes in consciousness and imbalances in the hegemonic order.[26]

In other words, consistent with the *conflict* perspective[27] of social relations I proposed in chapter 2, KTTV's construction of the events worked to reinforce societal hegemony – "the 'spontaneous' consent given by the great masses of the population to the general direction imposed on social life by the dominant fundamental group" (Gramsci 1971, p. 12). The ideologies inscribed in the KTTV text first worked to interpellate viewers as those who accept the veracity of news images; the text then worked to establish the "senselessness" of the events, to downplay their legitimacy as political activity. Gitlin (1980, p. 253) nicely summarizes how hegemony is facilitated by the transmission of commonsense ideas and assumptions:

hegemony is a ruling class's (or alliance's) domination of subordinate classes and groups through the elaboration and penetration of ideology (ideas and assumptions) into their common sense and everyday practice; it is the systematic (*but not necessarily or even usually deliberate*) engineering of mass consent to the established order. (emphasis added)

In short, simply by doing their jobs, KTTV newsworkers fashioned a text that works to reproduce common sense, status quo versions of reality. That is, journalistic values and routines – as filtered through the sieve of KTTV-TV's commercial concerns (i.e., entertainment value and the socio-political climate) – designated certain questions concerning the *nature* of the US system either off-limits for KTTV newsworkers, *or* not germane to the immediate "riot" story. Indeed, because the resulting news text does not challenge status quo perspectives of the events, the text, by default, affirms these perspectives. In all fairness, however, it should be noted that the "blame" for this text should not be placed on KTTV or its employees. By many accounts, KTTV's coverage of the events was among the "best" offered by local news operations.[28] Instead, the "blame" must be laid squarely at the feet of journalism as an institution, its conflicting array of allegiances, its concurrent proclivity to produce hegemonic texts.

Given the enduring media-powerful versus audience-powerful debate that motivates this study, an obvious question remains: To what degree can we conclude that informants' *opposition* to the assumptions embedded in this hegemonic text constitute acts of *resistance*?

From opposition to resistance

In chapter 2, you will recall, I employed Gramsci's notion of "war of position" and argued for the theoretical and practical possibility of *real* audience resistance. This perspective views societal struggle as one waged on many fronts – economic, political and ideological. Indeed, because there is no definite correspondence between these fronts, social formations at any given moment appear exceedingly complex and often contradictory. Hegemony is thus inherently unstable, facilitating an ongoing struggle, one that produces no decisive victories. In such an environment, practical everyday consciousness becomes a societal linchpin. As this "organic ideology" informs individual action, it necessarily shapes the trajectory of the ongoing war of position. Opposition thus becomes resistance when it is informed by an organic ideology that challenges hegemonic views of reality; it becomes resistance when it supports subordinate forces in the war of position. While the assumptions embedded in the KTTV text supported hegemonic views of reality in a number of important ways, informant opposition, from time to time, produced counter-hegemonic ammunition:

By proclaiming the events "undesirable" (assumption 1), the KTTV text works to affirm the desirability of order (read the current *order*) at all costs. But a sizable percentage of all oppositional arguments, particularly among Latino-raced and black-raced groups, seemed to challenge this rather unproblematic judgment of the events. In the end, though, it was generally black-raced informants who seemed to resist this assumption by declaring their ambivalence toward event-related looting and fires, and opposition to event-related arrests. For these informants, the hegemonic ideology of "property rights" was balanced by the organic ideology of "survival in an oppressive order."

By centering the events in South Central Los Angeles (assumption 2), the text works to apply political triage, to isolate the events, to reduce the risk that blame might bleed into the broader community. Informants, for the most part, did not challenge this assumption. Nonetheless, many of the black-raced and Latino-raced groups still managed to indict the system as a cause of the events. White-raced informants generally accepted the text's relegation of the events to South Central Los Angeles *and* the corresponding notion that the broader system was not to blame.

By identifying the King beating verdicts as the cause of the events (assumption 4), the text again works to isolate the significance of the events, to divert attention away from broader, systemic causes. Many black-raced groups resisted this assumption, talking explicitly of societal racism and classism as causes. In contrast, Latino-raced and white-raced groups generally accepted the text's framing in this regard.

By defining the events as "riots" (assumption 5), the text works to discount their political significance. "Riot" is the only term of the *riot/uprising/revolt/rebellion/insurrection/revolution* continuum that does *not* explicitly denote an act against the government or established authority.[29] Consistent with this framing, most informants understood the events as "riots." Only two of the black-raced groups used alternative terms, terms that more explicitly linked the events to the hegemonic order. Nonetheless, many of the black-raced informants, in particular, demonstrated their awareness of this link through their discussion of the events and perceived causes. These informants' failure to adopt alternative terminology seems to be more a function of the vocabulary available to them at the time than the ultimate meaning they attached to the term "riot."[30]

By identifying race as a central factor in the events (assumption 6) and blacks as event insiders (assumption 7), the text works to activate (albeit rather covertly) the discourse of race and its well-stocked warehouse of assumptions and representations. Indeed, by designating one group as the event insiders, and highlighting conflict between various raced groups, the text works to reduce the likelihood of cross-raced alliances in the war of position. While several white-raced informants resisted (or failed to acknowledge?) this assumption, black-raced and Latino-raced informants generally seemed to accept it. Perhaps this observation is a classic example of the doublebind that subordinate-raced groups face in the US racial order: in order to fight racism (and its reification of "race") you have to notice (and risk reifying) "race" (Omi and Winant 1986, 1994). In other words, because "colorblind" stances deny the enduring significance of racism, these stances become, by default (or design), hegemonic stances.[31]

By identifying voting as the appropriate outlet for change (assumption 9), the text works to inoculate the status quo (which escapes newsworker analysis) against counter-hegemonic accusations – i.e., "Nothing is wrong with the system, but it provides reasonable outlets for dissent anyway." Few informants openly resisted this assumption in group discussions. However, as noted above, black-raced informants still managed to resist the textual assumption that the events were undesirable. This observation suggests that these informants did not dismiss, as the text does, the notion of "working outside of the system" for change.

By declaring that police should have been present at the site of the events (assumption 10), the text works to legitimate an agency of state coercion against the subordinate forces of dissent. Again, few informants openly resisted this assumption in group discussions. Nonetheless, black-raced informants – unlike Latino-raced and white-raced informants – were quite clear in their opposition to the event-related arrests. This resistance, of course, echoes a long history of black-raced suffering and repression facilitated by the dominant group's use of police force and the justice system (Berry 1994). The King beating seems to have been little more than an immediate symbol for black-raced informants of a system that has always been stacked against "just-us."[32]

By proclaiming that KTTV's role is to serve its viewers by providing them with fair and factual coverage of the events (assumption 14), the text works to both reinforce the image of journalists as professionals and legitimate the mission of journalism as an institution. In a rather twisted turn of events, the text borrows from journalism's store of goodwill as Fourth Estate to *bolster* rather than *check* the power of the other three. As I noted above, however, nearly 48 percent of all informant opposition toward textual assumptions concerned this particular assumption. That is, many informants – even some who accepted other textual assumptions – resisted the hegemonic assumption of fair and factual news media.

Conclusions

Study groups generally made negotiated decodings of the KTTV text. That is, they decoded the text according to various mixtures of dominant and oppositional codes. In the crudest terms, what I have described in this book as informant opposition to the text's assumptions might be seen in one of two ways: either as acts of resistance, or acts of pseudo-resistance. I argue for the former interpretation. My finding that KTTV framed the events largely in accord with status quo, hegemonic conceptions of society, and that many study groups (black-raced groups, in particular) challenged this framing, is my rationale. Indeed, consistent with audience-powerful and in-between perspectives that acknowledge the ability and/or tendency of individuals to resist the ideologies inscribed in media texts (see Inglis 1990;

Berger 1973; Fiske 1987, 1989a, 1990; Dates and Barlow 1990; Lipsitz 1990), several study groups managed to subvert the hegemonic meanings encoded in the KTTV text, to turn the text to uses other than those intended. In this sense, I cautiously celebrate instances of viewer opposition to the assumptions embedded in the KTTV text; we might see these as either constituting meaningful acts of resistance in their own right, or contributing to a consciousness necessary for meaningful social action at some later moment in time.

But the same findings suggest a different interpretation when viewed from the vantage point of those who discount the possibility of resistance. Here, media-powerful perspectives tend to underscore the power of media texts to inject their intended meanings (directly or indirectly) into the minds of individuals, to influence them, to shape their views of the world and of themselves over the long run (see Althusser 1971). At best, this latter perspective treats resistance as momentary pauses along an endless path toward ideological conformity (Adorno 1991a, 1991b). The cultural products emerging from these moments of resistance, the argument goes, are eventually absorbed by the status quo, repackaged, and sold back to a consuming public (Foster 1985). From this vantage point, informant opposition to assumptions embedded in the KTTV text would signal little cause for celebration; it would constitute little more than pseudo-resistance, a vicarious venting of frustration that has become fashionable in the private sphere (e.g., media bashing), but that ultimately leaves the status quo unscathed. Where is the meaningful political action? What are the prospects for change?

As I argued in chapter 2, however, it seems unreasonable to dismiss, *a priori*, acts of audience opposition as mere pseudo-resistance. At the level of micro-politics, audience opposition to hegemonic media assumptions is an end in and of itself (Fiske 1989a). Regardless of whether these decodings are directly translated into social action they nonetheless leave an imprint on the consciousness of social actors. Even Althusser (1990) acknowledges the importance of this consciousness: "every struggle implies the intervention of people's 'consciousness'; every struggle involves a conflict between convictions, beliefs, and representations of the world" (p. 36). In other words, the struggle (or lack thereof) for meaning between the KTTV text and study informants was necessarily dependent upon the consciousness of the latter. But this consciousness – filed in and retrieved from intertextual memories – was much more than just a guide for informant decoding practices: it also provide(d)(s) informants with the meaning and motivation essential for any future social action.

As I noted in this chapter and the previous one, black-raced informants exhibited a consciousness qualitatively different from that exhibited by Latino-raced and white-raced informants. Although several Latino-raced and white-raced informants questioned the textual assumption that the events were undesirable, when the dust settled, Latino-raced and white-raced informants generally understood the events as they were depicted in the KTTV text – as crime. But for black-raced informants, the KTTV text was about struggle, about another engagement in a protracted, raced war in the US that engulfed them, their mothers and fathers, and the "black" mothers and fathers before them. Consequently, black-raced informants tended to sympathize with event participants, if not their tactics. They were generally hostile toward KTTV assumptions that localized the significance of the events, that blurred the events' connection to issues of systemic racial and economic injustice in the US. Here, of course, we are presented with a case where textual interpellations and audience resistance are intimately connected to raced ways of seeing.

In the end, however, it is significant that certain Latino-raced and white-raced (as well as black-raced) study groups challenged the textual assumption that the news media are fair and factual. That is, this finding at least holds open the possibility that news representations of the world – if not the events in question – might be received by viewers with some measure of skepticism. Some observers, of course, might interpret this informant opposition as little more than "media bashing," at worst a Right-wing tactic, at best a fashionable discourse (e.g., see General Social Survey 1990). In any event, we must ask ourselves why this activity is so popular at this moment in history. Perhaps the popularity of this skepticism signals that a potentially progressive consciousness permeates US culture. As Fiske (1989a, 1989b) has argued, popular culture is *popular* because its texts are polysemic, because these texts provide space for social actors to create – within limits (Hall 1973) – their own meanings. And the pleasures that result from this meaning-making process are "the reward[s] of grasping the opportunities offered by [the] unstable forces of empowering and enhancing one's social agency" against the forces of subordination (Fiske 1989a, p. 181). In other words, meaning-making and resistance are inexorably linked, always different sides of the same coin. The widespread lack of confidence in social institutions in the US (e.g., the media), and the pleasure people derive from countering their official meanings, may be emblematic of the powerlessness people feel relative to these institutions.

Which brings us to the "what might be?" so central to critical approaches. Whether one laments or celebrates the skepticism and cynicism so widespread in US culture today probably depends on the image of society held. Those who view society as essentially just (although they often recognize minor faults) might criticize widespread skepticism as a barrier to solidarity, a drain on progress. On the other hand, those who recognize major inequities in the very structure of society are from time to time encouraged that widespread skepticism – precisely because it involves consciousness – may hold promise for social action and future change. The image of US society offered by this book, of course, is more consistent with the latter view. The obvious question, then, becomes: How might we harness widespread skepticism so that it at least offers progressive potential in the ongoing war of position?

Because hegemony depends heavily upon commonsense, taken-for-granted definitions, beliefs, and justifications, anything we can do to challenge these ways of seeing necessarily threatens to destabilize the status quo. This order, of course, is quite elastic and can expand to accommodate challenges. But that is not to say, as some have argued (e.g., Newcomb 1984), that the notion of hegemony precludes the possibility of change. Today's hegemonic order, despite its continuing problems, is qualitatively different from the one that existed, for example, when the events erupted in Watts in 1965. For one thing, important changes in race-as-representation officially prohibit the overt use of racist sentiments and feelings to justify racist actions (Omi and Winant 1986, 1994). Today, such actions must be cloaked in non-racialized garb, which arguably changes the tenor of race relations and creates new spaces for counter-hegemonic incursions. Indeed, at critical moments in history, the hegemonic order may expand to the point where, in terms of the experiences and life chances of social actors, it is no longer the same order.

With this said, there are a few things I believe we can do to facilitate these critical moments. First and foremost, we should work at every opportunity to expose the constructed nature of basic ideologies (e.g., "equal opportunity," "meritocracy," "individualism," "free enterprise," and "property rights") and representations (e.g., "race," "class," "gender," and "sexual orientation"). Meanwhile, official (i.e., hegemonic) language should be subjected to constant scrutiny. As a beginning, we should work to defuse the vocabulary of crime associated with urban unrest: "riot" might be relabeled "rebellion," "looting" relabeled "seizing," "gang" relabeled "network," and so on. Indeed, we should engage in these consciousness-raising practices on a number of different fronts: in our political affiliations, in our work, in our home. But a united and uni-vocal assault is not required, and might even be counter-productive. Aside from offering a larger and more defined target for backlash, canonized means only work to alienate marginalized voices and lessen the chances for short-term, cross-interest alliances.

In short, I propose that those of us interested in change engage in *more* of what we are already doing, that we encourage *more* of what is already taking place. Indeed, it is only when we think in terms of "war of maneuver" – in terms of decisive victories – that we fail to recognize the oppositional decodings of study informants as acts of resistance. It is only when we think in terms of "war of position" – in terms of ongoing struggle – that we appreciate the promise these decodings hold for progressive change.

Postscript

Whatever the 1992 Los Angeles rebellion may ultimately mean in the annals of United States history, for a moment at least, it seemed to find an important niche in US popular culture. Five months after the fires, the *Los Angeles Times*[1] reported that the "riots" had become television's "new theme" in the 1992–93 season. Shows as diverse as *Fresh Prince of Bel Air, Knots Landing, A Different World* and *Doogie Howser* featured episodes devoted to the rebellion.

From a "war of maneuver" perspective it looked as though the rebellion was headed the way of the Malcolm X moniker – toward cultural appropriation (cf. Foster 1985; Featherstone 1991). The rebellion, it seemed, had been reduced to a cultural product for sale to a consuming public, an icon of resistance that was being commodified and defused by the system. From around-the-clock news coverage to situation comedies, the societal differences laid bare by the rebellion were being appropriated for "fresh" television narratives. In short, it appeared as though the hegemonic order had expanded to the point where any oppositional meanings expressed through the rebellion would be safely contained.

But when conditions are right, people do take stands against cultural appropriation and containment. The group interviews conducted for this study coincided with this period of containment. Nonetheless, the personal experience, intertextual memories and raced subjectivity of many informants seemed to counterbalance the forces of incorporation. As sources of resistance, informant ways of seeing safeguarded certain heartfelt meanings associated with the rebellion, while challenging other more hegemonic ones. For example, it is no accident that black-raced informants exhibited the highest rate of opposition toward the assumptions embedded in the KTTV text – that they were more tolerant of rebellion-related "seizing," somewhat more tolerant of the fires, and much less tolerant of the arrests than their Latino-raced and white-raced counterparts. Black-raced informants, the data suggest, understood themselves first and foremost as *"black"* subjects *vis-à-vis* the events and KTTV text. In the face of images that worked to circumscribe the meaning of the rebellion, to leave the status quo unscathed, black-raced informants – more so than their Latino-raced or white-raced counterparts – viewed the rebellion as a commentary on society's fatal flaws. As countless scholars have pointed out (e.g., DuBois 1965; Franklin 1965; Farley and Allen 1989; Hacker 1992, and so on), black-raced subjects in the US have endured a long history of suffering because of these flaws. Accordingly, black-raced informants in this study used the interviews as an opportunity to take oppositional stands and, in the process, (re)affirm their own raced subjectivities.

At the same time, however, I found less significant, but nonetheless interesting *intra-racial* differences in how informants understood the rebellion and KTTV text. These findings suggest – as other media scholars have argued (e.g, see Morley 1992; Ang 1989) – that the outcome of the struggle between a text's dominant meanings, and those that historically situated viewers are likely to prefer, is always an open, empirical question. In light of the raced patterns I observed, raced ways of seeing should never be discounted in these investigations, particularly in the US context. Indeed, future studies of this variety would benefit from an increase in the number and kind of study groups – to ferret out additional details of the meaning-making process. For example, the effects of group racial heterogeneity and homogeneity on polarization outcomes might be studied more carefully by increasing the number of both types of groups and comparing them to one another. Similar design recommendations seem warranted for gender heterogeneity and homogeneity as well.

In the final analysis, then, what are we to make of this study's findings of informant opposition? Did (or will) the kinds of consciousness that shaped informant decoding practices in any way facilitate future change? As I write this note, more than four years have elapsed since the rebellion erupted in Los Angeles. It would be difficult to trace, of course, the effect that specific acts of resistance like oppositional decoding might have on the probability of other types of social action. We can, however, explore from a "war of position" perspective the effect that oppositional consciousness – which necessarily informs these decoding practices – has had on the broader ongoing struggle.

For example, the Los Angeles rebellion cast a heavy shadow on the national elections of 1992. Incumbent George Bush stood firm in his early denouncement of the rebellion as "the brutality of a mob, pure and simple."[2] Touring through the fire-damaged areas, he parroted the Republican line and essentially blamed the rebellion on a lack of personal responsibility that grew out of overly generous liberal welfare programs (Omi and Winant 1994). But protests of solidarity with the Los Angeles rebellion had occurred in several US cities – New York, San Francisco, Atlanta, Seattle and Las Vegas, just to name a few (Hazen 1992). Many of these remote participants and sympathizers undoubtedly rejected Bush's assessment. Mobilized by the rebellion, and solidified against the president's stand, many voters registered who may not have otherwise done so.[3] Indeed, a Census Bureau survey reported that a higher percentage of respondents voted in the election (61.3 percent) than in the previous presidential election (57.4 percent).[4] Meanwhile, fear of the rebellion among traditional Republican voters may have bred dissatisfaction with the standard Republican policy of urban neglect (Omi and Winant 1993; Winant 1994). The 1965 Watts rebellion, in fact, had led to massive white flight out of innercity Los Angeles to the safety of gated communities and surrounding suburbs (Davis 1990).

When the electoral dust settled, Democrat Bill Clinton was elected 42nd president on November 3, 1992. Black-raced and Latino-raced voters in California had overwhelmingly cast their ballots for the new president, while Clinton's margin of victory among white-raced and Asian-raced voters was more narrow.[5] Women and minorities also gained seats in Congress as twenty incumbents fell to the "voters' wrath."[6] While the new administration's "neoliberal" policies were no panacea for the structural problems plaguing the nation (e.g., see Omi and Winant 1994), they were clearly more progressive than those of the previous administration. In other words, an important advance had been made by progressive forces in the war of position, one that opened new space for challenging and (re)shaping the hegemonic order. And this advance, of course, was predicated on the kinds of oppositional consciousness exhibited by study informants.

But as was the case in the aftermath of the 1965 rebellion (Horne 1995), forward progress is often met with backlash. Hegemonic forces soon mobilized on national, state and local fronts to contain the progressive incursions fueled by the 1992 Los Angeles rebellion.

For example, while early coverage of the 1992 rebellion labeled "blacks" as the event insiders, the faces captured in subsequent coverage suggested that many "Latinos" participated in rebellion-related "seizing" and other activity. Indeed, the area identified by the media as the center of the rebellion was roughly half "Latino" at the time (Johnson *et al.* 1992). Many of these residents were recent immigrants, some undocumented. Arrest figures also suggest that Latino- raced involvement in the rebellion was at least as great as black-raced involvement.[7] Many of these participants, as Latino-raced study informants put it, undoubtedly saw the rebellion as an opportunity to "come up" – a momentary chance to "seize" a piece of the economic pie that had been systematically denied them. At least one Los Angeles-based news reporters was heard to point to Latino-raced participants during live coverage and speculate as to their legal status.[8] Perhaps it is no mere coincidence that in November of 1994 California voters overwhelmingly approved Proposition 187. This so-called "Save Our State" legislation was designed to curb the flow of "illegal aliens" into the state. According to the voter pamphlet, Proposition 187:

> * Makes illegal aliens ineligible for public social services, public health care services (unless emergency under federal law), and public school education at elementary, secondary, and post-secondary levels.
> * Requires various state and local agencies to report persons who are suspected illegal aliens to the California Attorney General and the United States Immigration and Naturalization Service. Mandates California Attorney General to transmit reports to Immigration and Naturalization Service and maintain records of such reports.
> * Makes it a felony to manufacture, distribute, sell or use false citizenship or residence documents.[9]

The "illegal aliens" targeted by this legislation, of course, were "Latinos." In recent years, Latino-raced immigrants had been flowing into the state in record numbers,[10] particularly into Southern California. Indeed, the 1990 US census revealed that the city of Los Angeles had no "racial" majority, and that "Hispanics" had surpassed white-raced residents as the plurality.[11] In the context of resentment and fear left by the 1992 rebellion, it had undoubtedly become easier for hegemonic forces to successfully scapegoat "illegal aliens," as they had done in the past,[12] for the economic ills facing the state. Although the incumbent president, Bill Clinton, was an outspoken opponent of the legislation, the Republican governor of California, Pete Wilson, was quite influential as a supporter.

But the hegemonic order is inherently unstable. Organic consciousness is a constant threat to this order, always the potential ally of progressive forces. One bright note surrounding the passage of Proposition 187 is that Latino-raced, black-raced and Asian-raced voters largely rejected it.[13] Moreover, about 40 percent of those opposing the legislation said they did so because it was patently racist or "anti-Latino."[14] This oppositional consciousness, if nourished and properly applied, has progressive potential for the ongoing war of position.

Note: Upon passage of Propostion 187, oppositional forces quickly moved to challenge the legislation's legality in court. On November 20, 1995, a US District judge ruled that the voters of California had overstepped their bounds by attempting to regulate immigration policy.[15] This activity, according to the judge, is reserved by the Constitution for the federal government. As Pro-Proposition 187 forces plan their appeal, the struggle continues on many fronts.

Appendix A

Data and methods

The research design for this study consisted of two interrelated components: an ethnographic component and an experimental one. The first component *qualitatively* searched for any patterns that might link informant
decoding behaviors, group discussions and "race." The second component
sought to *quantitatively* evaluate these patterns and determine to what
degree, if any, group discussion influenced individual decoding of the
selected news text.

More specifically, I sought to answer the following research questions:

1. What key assumptions were encoded in the news text screened for the
    study groups?
2. Immediately following the screening, did individual group members tend
    to perceive the events negatively, positively, or somewhere in between?
3. How did group members discuss – negotiate – the meanings of the news
    text amongst themselves?
4. To what degree did groups accept or oppose textual assumptions?
5. Did group discussion affect individual perceptions of the events or
    news text?
6. Did group discussion topics, styles, or opposition vary by raced groupings?
7. What role, if any, did intertextual memories play in group decodings of
    the text and events?
8. What role, if any, did "raced ways of seeing" play in the meaning-
    making process?

Sampling procedure

Informants were selected in the first stage of a two-stage snowball sample
in order to target three group "types:"

1. College-aged, black-raced informants from South Central Los Angeles and black-raced students living on Los Angeles' affluent Westside $(n = 5)$[1]
2. College-aged, Latino-raced informants from South Central Los Angeles and Latino-raced students living on Los Angeles' affluent Westside $(n = 5)$
3. White-raced college students living on Los Angeles' affluent Westside $(n = 5)$

Each of the informants identified in the first stage was asked to nominate four (4) other informants with whom he or she *regularly* watches television *or* discusses issues of mutual interest.[2] Each of these nominees was also required to know one another. Fifteen groups were thus identified, resulting in an overall sample size of sixty-five informants.

My goal in targeting different "types" of viewers was to explore any raced-grouping, class (i.e., socioeconomic status as proxy), and/or gender differences in the meaning-making process among informants. That is, I was interested in analyzing *how* the social locations of informants may have influenced this process. My goal was *not* to make generalizations about how *all* black-raced viewers, *all* white-raced viewers, *all* Latino-raced viewers, *all* viewers from South Central Los Angeles, or *all* viewers from the Westside would likely decode the selected news text. Groups from South Central Los Angeles were identified with the assistance of staff at community-based organizations; these organizations included high schools, youth development centers and churches. The Westside college groups were identified by paid interviewers, several of whom were solicited through an advertisement placed in the campus newspaper.

I targeted college-aged informants because this age cohort had not yet been born when the bulk of the 1960s "riots" occurred. I was particularly interested in examining the sources of knowledge this group referred to when decoding the selected news text.

Table A.1 presents key demographic data for informants by group.[3] Note that several of the groups were racially heterogenous. This occurred as a result of the sampling procedure, which asked the first-stage informant to nominate the other group members, members of his or her social network. Note also that only one of the groups from South Central – GANG – was racially heterogenous, while nearly all of the college groups from the Westside were. These findings belie very different patterns of raced interaction in the two environments.[4]

Table A.1 also indicates that group socio-economic status (SES) was very nearly synonymous with group origin. That is, with one exception –

Table A1. *Key demographic characteristics of discussion groups.*

	Latino-raced groups				
	YOUTH	FAMILY	LATINA	MARIA	JULIO
N	3	5	4	4	4
Mean family income (1)	$17,138	$16,903	$17,495	$49,567	$40,232
Racial mean			$28,267		
HS degree	66.7%	40.0%	50.0%	100.0%	100.0%
College participation	66.7%	20.0%	25.0%	100.0%	100.0%
Father some college	0.0%	0.0%*	0.0%*	75.0%	100.0%
Mother some college	0.0%	0.0%*	0.0%*	75.0%	100.0%
Percent female	33.3%	60.0%	100.0%	100.0%	25.0%
Mean age	20.7	23.0	17.5	18.8	21.0
Racial composition (2)	3 Lat	5 Lat	4 Lat	3 Lat 1 Wht	1 Lat 3 Wht
Origin	South Central	South Central	South Central	UCLA	UCLA

	Black-raced groups				
	GANG	CHURCH	CORNER	KEISHA	NORTH
N	4	5	6	5	5
Mean family income (1)	$21,736	$30,969	$18,074	$38,585	$32,139
Racial mean			$28,300		
HS degree	50.0%	80.0%	16.7%	100.0%	100.0%
College participation	0.0%	60.0%	16.7%	100.0%	100.0%
Father some college	25.0%	100.0%	33.4%	80.0%	40.0%
Mother some college	25.0%	60.0%	16.7%	80.0%	80.0%

Table A1. *(cont.)*

	Black-raced groups				
	GANG	CHURCH	CORNER	KELSHA	NORTH
Percent female	0.0%	40.0%	66.7%	100.0%	100.0%
Mean age	16.8	18.6	25.5	21.0	17.8
Racial composition (2)	2 Blk 2 Lat	5 Blk	6 Blk	5 Blk	4 Blk 1 Mly
Origin	South Central	South Central	South Central	UCLA	UCLA

	White-raced groups				
	MATES	DORM 1	DORM 2	DORM 3	JILL
N	4	4	4	4	4
Mean family income (1)	$56,857	$32,697	$37,243	$50,118	$54,171
Racial mean			$46,217		
HS degree	100.0%	100.0%	100.0%	100.0%	100.0%
College participation	100.0%	100.0%	100.0%	100.0%	100.0%
Father some college	100.0%	75.0%	100.0%	75.0%	100.0%
Mother some college	100.0%	75.0%	75.0%	75.0%	100.0%
Percent female	100.0%	0.0%	25.0%	50.0%	25.0%
Mean age	19.0	18.7	19.0	19.3	20.8
Racial composition (2)	3 Wht 1 Chn 1 Fil	1 Wht 2 Kor	3 Wht 1 Lat	2 Wht 2 Chn	4 Wht
Origin	UCLA	UCLA	UCLA	UCLA	UCLA

Notes:
(1) Based on an average of the median family incomes for the zip codes in which informants' parents reside. (2) Lat = Latino; Blk = Black; Wht = White; Kor = Korean; Fil =Filipino; Mly = Malaysian * Also high school completion rate.
Sources: Survey of informants; "Summary of Key 1990 Census Data," Western Economic Research, Co. Panorama City, CA.

Table A.2. *Media consumption and previous event-related discussion, entire sample (N = 65).*

	Total %
TV news	
none	3.1
< 1 hour	4.6
1 to 3 hour	20.0
> 3 hours	26.2
all evening	44.6
missing	1.5
	100.0
LA Times	
never	43.1
sometimes	36.9
every day	20.0
	100.0
Discussion	
never	26.2
< once/month	32.3
once/month	27.7
once/week	4.6
several/week	3.1
every day	1.5
several/day	3.1
missing	1.5
	100.0

Source: Post-discussion questionnaires.

CHURCH – mean family incomes and college participation rates were considerably lower for the groups from South Central Los Angeles than those from the Westside. And as one might expect (cf. Farley and Allen 1989), the white-raced groups were considerably more affluent than the Latino-raced or black-raced groups. For example, the mean family income figure for the white-raced groups was $46,217, compared to $28,267 and $28,300 for the Latino-raced and black-raced groups, respectively.

Table A.2 presents data on media consumption and previous event-related discussion for the entire sample. First, this table reveals that most informants heavily consumed television news coverage during the first night of the events. About 45 percent of the sample reported that they watched news coverage of the events "all evening," while about 26 percent said they watched three hours or more, 20 percent said they watched between one and three hours, and 5 percent said they watched less than one hour of this coverage. Only about 3 percent of the respondents reported watching no news coverage of the events the first evening.

Second, while informants were quite dependent upon television news for their information about the events (at least that first evening), they had considerably less use for the major local newspaper. Only about 20 percent of the sample reported reading the *Los Angeles Times* "every day" during the events, while about 37 percent said they read it "sometimes," and 43 percent said they "never" read it during the period.

Finally, informants, in general, had not discussed the events very frequently with their fellow group members in the months following the outbreak. Less than 14 percent of the informants reported discussing the events "once per week" or more with other members of their group. The largest portion of the sample, about 32 percent, reported discussing the events "less than once per month" with other group members. About 26 percent said they "never" discussed the events with other group members. (Chapters 4 through 6 present the breakdown of these characteristics by study group.)

Ethnographic[5] component

The fifteen study groups were shown a 17-minute extract from news coverage of the first day of the Los Angeles events (see appendix C for transcript).[6] At the conclusion of each screening, groups were instructed as follows:

Imagine that you are the parent of a 12-year-old son or daughter. You both just watched this news together. What would you say to him or her about what you just saw? Why? You have up to 30 minutes to discuss this amongst yourselves.

This scenario was designed to minimize cross-group differences in the possible response effect due to respondent expectations regarding the study (Bradburn 1983). That is, each group was instructed to interpret the task before them in a uniform, concrete manner that seemed consistent with the stated purpose of the study.[7] Facilitator-respondent interactions were minimized in order to allow the groups to set the discussion agenda through members' interaction with one another. A few standard questions were posed when group discussion stalled prematurely (i.e., before 30 minutes).[8]

Same-raced facilitators were used for each group to minimize any possible response effects due to interviewer "role characteristics" (Bradburn 1983).[9]

The group discussions *and* the screenings that preceded them were video-taped and transcribed for analysis. From this data, I sought to understand how viewers in each group made sense of, "decoded," the selected news text. My indicators of this meaning-making process included: (1) group viewing modes; (2) group discussion modes; (3) opposition toward textual assumptions; and (4) the use of pronouns.[10]

1. *Group viewing modes* Here, I was interested in what viewers did or said at key points during the screening. These points included the following: the reference to an Asian man "drenched in blood"; the labelling of event participants as "thugs"; and the event summary at the end of the text (see appendix C for complete transcript). I was interested in whether informants viewed the text in passive modes (i.e., sitting quiet, still) or more active modes (i.e., communicating amongst themselves, "talking back to the screen") at these points in the screening. Active viewing modes, I hypothesized, are more indicative of viewer opposition or resistance than are passive ones.

2. *Group discussion modes* Liebes and Katz (1988, 1993) found that viewers of television drama tend to either discuss these texts in a "referential" mode or shift back and forth between "referential" and "metalinguistic" modes in their discussions. Metalinguistic decodings of texts are characterized by discussions (i.e., the proxy for the social processes behind decoding) in which viewers display an unprompted awareness and appraisal of the techniques used in the text's construction. In contrast, referential decodings are characterized by discussions in which viewers simply discuss media texts in terms of their own personal experiences or the text's narratives. In this study, I sought to explore the mode or modes of decoding employed by viewers of a television *news* text. I was concerned with identifying how explicitly viewers considered the techniques used in the construction of the selected news text. After viewing the videotapes, I coded each group's discussion mode as either referential, metalinguistic, or some combination of the two. "Metalinguistic" group discussions were defined as those that included episodes of talk which explicitly considered the techniques used to construct the selected news text – *prior* to specific prompts about media coverage. "Referential" group discussions were defined as those that either included no episodes of talk which explicitly considered these techniques, or that did so only *after* informants were specifically prompted about media coverage.

Although the literature is not explicit concerning the relationship between decoding mode and opposition, I expected to find that groups who discuss texts in a metalinguistic mode are more likely to oppose textual assumptions than are those who discuss the text in a referential mode.

3. *Opposition toward textual assumptions* In order to facilitate an analysis of viewer opposition, I first analyzed the verbatim transcript of the selected news text, identifying what I felt were fourteen key assumptions underlying its framing of the events (see chapter 3). Next, I derived a list of propositions/arguments from the verbatim transcript of each group's discussion. These propositions/arguments were coded (1) to identify the relevant textual assumption(s) and (2) whether they were "oppositional" to the assumption(s) or "other."[11] I then tabulated, by group and raced category, the rate of opposition for each of the fourteen textual assumptions. My goal was to identify the issues (1) for which media depictions of the events were *not* met with viewer opposition, and (2) for which these depictions *were* met with such opposition.

4. *The use of pronouns* Previous studies (e.g., Cramer and Schuman 1975) suggest that pronoun usage may serve as an insightful indicator of informants' feelings of solidarity with important ingroups and distance from outgroups. In this study, I sought to analyze informant pronoun use as it refers to solidarity or distance from event participants and raced group status. Accordingly, I computer searched the verbatim transcript of each group discussion in order to identify occurrences of key "we" (us, our) and "they" (them, their) pronoun use. The primary referent(s) of these pronouns were tabulated for each group. I treated groups that referred to event participants or a raced group primarily with "we" pronouns as exhibiting a measure of solidarity with the referent. Conversely, I treated groups that used primarily "they" pronouns as exhibiting less solidarity with the referents.

Experimental component

In addition to the ethnographic analysis, I conducted a quasi-experiment in order to *quantitatively* describe group differences and similarities, and to determine if group discussion influenced the decoding behaviors of individual group members (i.e., attitude polarization). In particular, I sought to measure any (1) raced group and (2) SES or gender differences in perceptions of the events; (3) the prevalence of attitude polarization; and (4) the significance of patterns between group characteristics, viewing modes, discussion dynamics and polarization prevalence.

1. *Raced Differences*: Printed questionnaires – Survey 1 – were administered immediately after each group screening (i.e., before discussion) to measure individual attitudes regarding three key issues alluded to in the selected text (see appendix D for questionnaires):

1. the degree to which event-related "looting" was "right" or "wrong"
2. the degree to which the starting of event-related fires was "right" or "wrong"
3. the degree to which event-related arrests were "right" or "wrong"

Each of these survey items consisted of a ten-point scale, where 1 = "right" and 10 = "wrong." Mean values were computed for each of the fifteen viewing groups and for each of the raced categories – "Latinos," "blacks" and "whites." On the basis of this latter set of means, raced differences were assessed.

2. *SES and gender differences* In order to simultaneously assess the effect of raced identification, socio-economic status (SES) and gender on the three scale items, I tested six multiple regression models which included both raced identification and SES or raced identification and gender as predictor variables. As an indicator of SES, I used the median family income for the zip code in which each respondent's parents currently lived.[12] Model 1, tested the null hypothesis that no differences existed, net of SES, between white-raced informants (the omitted group) and black-raced or Latino-raced informants in their support for event-related looting; it also tested the null hypothesis that median family income had no effect, net of raced grouping, on attitudes toward looting. Models 2 and 3 substituted attitudes toward event-related fires and arrests, respectively, as the outcome variables. In Models 4 through 6, I replaced SES with gender as a predictor variable for each of the scale scores.[13]

3. *Attitude polarization* Immediately following each group discussion, another printed questionnaire – Survey 2 – was administered. This questionnaire repeated the "looting," fires and arrests scales found in the first questionnaire, but interspersed these items among dozens of other attitudinal and demographic items. Here, the goal was to isolate and *quantitatively* describe any effects of group discussion – net of viewing the news text – on post-treatment decodings. In other words, the change in *mean* values (Survey 1 minus Survey 2) for each of the three scales was computed by group. A diagram of the experimental design is as follows:

N-groups	Treatment
15	Video/Q1/discussion/Q2

Consistent with Myers and Lamm's (1975) overview of the polarizing effects of group discussion, the following hypotheses were proposed:

1. Decoding polarization will only occur in groups where the pre-treatment decodings among viewers fall on the same side of a 10-point scale (i.e., either between 1.0 and 5.0 *or* between 6.0 and 10.0).

2. Group averages for a decoding scale that are relatively low before discussion (i.e., between 5.0 and 3.0 on a 10-point scale) will *decrease* in magnitude after discussion.
3. Group averages for a decoding scale that are relatively high before discussion (i.e., between 6.0 and 8.0 on a 10-point scale) will *increase* in magnitude after discussion.
4. Extreme pre-discussion decodings (i.e., average group scores above 8.0 *or* below 3.0) will result in little if any polarization after discussion.

Given the time lapse between the actual outbreak of the events and study screenings,[14] I treated any resulting attitude polarization as an indicator of the continuing influence of group norming processes. Throughout these processes, I assumed, group members would invoke race-as-representation in their arguments and explanations.

I also treated attitude polarization as an indicator of group *insulation* against media influence when resulting attitudes conflicted with the assumptions embedded in the selected news text; I treated it as a *facilitator* of media influence when the resulting attitudes were congruent with textual assumptions.

4. *Group characteristics, viewing modes, discussion dynamics and polarization* Finally, I sought to test the significance of any possible patterns between group characteristics, viewing modes, discussion dynamics and polarization. The sample of 15 groups was dichotomized along a number of different dimensions: (1) black-raced versus non-black-raced; (2) Westside (UCLA) versus South Central; (3) high versus low SES; (4) racially homogeneous versus racially heterogeneous; (5) passive versus active viewing modes; (6) referential versus metalinguistic decoding modes; (7) unified discussions versus conflict-laden discussions; (8) high rates of opposition versus low rates of opposition; (9) high degrees of polarization versus low degrees of polarization. Fishers Exact Probability Test (Siegel 1956) was used to test the significance of any apparent associations between the various dimensions.[15]

Appendix B

Figures

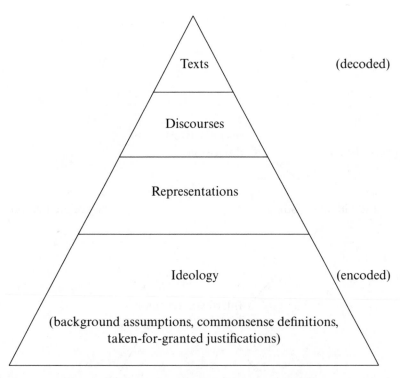

Figure 2.1 The proposed relationship between texts, discourses, representations and ideology

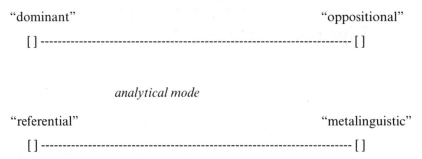

Figure 2.2 The proposed decoding dimension continua

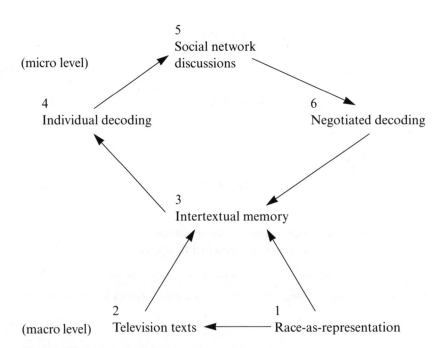

Figure 2.3 The proposed television experience model

Appendix C

KTTV transcript

AUDIO

VIDEO

Tony Valdez (1):

. . . The scene here again . . . I hate
to draw the comparison, but it is
the same thing that we saw twenty-
seven years ago in Watts . . . this,
this part of the city just destroying
itself, burning itself up. The streets
themselves are, ah, are extremely
dangerous. There are cars running,
ah, we clocked one at about sixty
miles per hour, ah, running down
the street, no lights on, ah, we see
that constantly. We took a break,
to, to brush some of the glass off of
us and, ah, get something to drink,
ah. We were next to a shopping
center. A car drove into that area
and just started firing shots
randomly into cars parked in the
parking lot. We have seen at least
three gas stations being held up,
ah, by people, and they are taking
cans, whatever kind of containers
they have so that they can fill up
their containers and presumably
start fires. It is just a situation
absolutely out of control, ah, from

Night. Aerial shots of burning
buildings.

AUDIO	VIDEO

roughly the, ah, well I would say Washington Boulevard south.

Patti Suarez (2):
Tony, expound on, on brushing the glass off if you would. What happened . . .

Tony Valdez (3):
We, we, we were here at the intersection of Normandie and Florence, ah, there was a man we found sitting in the middle of the street, ah, he appeared to be an Asian man. He was sitting drenched in blood. There was a, an African-American man who appeared to be a minister. He was standing over him, trying to use his body to shield him from all the rocks and bottles and everything else that was being fired here. We pulled over, we were trying to find a way that we could rescue this man, pull him out. But it got to the point where it was either him or the rest of us. We were at that point taking rocks and bottles and there was occasionally some gunfire. We had to pull out and in the process of doing that, our front window on our news van was smashed. We took rocks and bottles, both sides of it, ah, and you know, I hate to tell you this Patti, but we feel guilty for this man, for having left him here. I, I, I presume, however, that, ah, that someone did get to him. I see him gone now. We can only hope he is in good condition now, but there is no love lost out here for the media and as

FADE TO: Anchor desk with Suarez and Harris.

CUT TO: Aerial shot of burning buildings

AUDIO   VIDEO

soon as they can identify any of our
vehicles, we are under a barrage.

Chris Harris (4):
Tony, rest easy as far as that
gentleman is concerned, ah, by all
accounts now the injured people
from that immediate area, the ones
that were beaten up by the thugs in
the intersections have all been
gotten out and ah, have been taken
to hospitals. So rest easy on that
score. We have been talking to you
over some video shot some time
ago from the helicopter of the fires
you've been talking about and they
seem to be everywhere.

Tony Valdez (5):
They are indeed everywhere. Ah,
and we see a band of cars. We see
gutted cars, fire gutted cars, just
about everywhere we go. Ah, ah, the
fire department, unfortunately, in
too many instances, can do nothing.
They don't have police backup to
protect them to go in and fight these
fires and so they are left just to
watch them burn. I should also tell
you that as we monitor the police
activity, ah, hardly a five-minute
span of time goes by without us
hearing a call of an officer needing
assistance, an officer being fired
upon, it's lawlessness, Chris.

Chris Harris (6):
Tony, you were, you were talking
about the parameters roughly of
what you have traversed tonight.
What are the East-West

AUDIO

VIDEO

boundaries, ah, and North-South
ones again.

Tony Valdez (7):
As far as we have been able to
determine, Chris, the western
boundary is Crenshaw Avenue,
more or less. We are hearing activity,
we have seen some activity as far
East as, ah, Avalon, ah, well, even
going beyond that, ah, to Central
and beyond that. Probably going all
the way out to, ah, I would guess,
Alameda, ah, eastern boundaries.
Curiously, these are basically the
same boundaries, ah, we saw during
the Watts Riots in August of 1965.

Patti Suarez (8):
Okay, Tony, thanks very much.
And, and, that's good information
about the police officers being in
presence. Perhaps, perhaps we've
been a little bit unfair through the
evening, by, by continuing,
continually saying, "No police
presence. No police presence."
Now Tony Valdez tells us they are
in the area and, ah, especially right
on that intersection where it first
began. And, Tony, you be careful.

Chris Harris (9):
Using his parameters, again, of the
geography. That explains why the
Harbor Freeway, we've had the
report that the Harbor Freeway,
both ways, has been closed between
Century Boulevard on the South
and the Santa Monica Freeway on
the North because that would

FADE TO: Anchor desk with Suarez
and Harris.

AUDIO	VIDEO
traverse right directly through the area that Tony was telling us about where all problems are.	
Patti Suarez (10): We want to go back now to the AME church where people are raising their voices in protest, in song, and in prayer. And Christine Devine.	CUT TO GRAPHIC: "Cops On Trial: The Rodney King Case." Split-screen between anchor desk and FAME location.
Christine Devine (11): Hi Patti. The rally wrapped up about 30 minutes ago. This place, if you recall, was packed. There were three thousand people inside this building. I'm told just as many outside. The main message here was, "Stay calm, remain calm. Let's take out our frustrations at the, the polling place." Right now, we're gonna talk with some people who are here attending this rally, attending this meeting. Angela, you are not a member of the First AME church, but I wanted to get your thoughts on the rally.	CUT TO: Devine stand up at FAME. Interviewees in background.
Angela (12): Ah, my boyfriend and I came down because this was a primary point of reference for people, that they were saying if you wanted to come and vent your frustrations or just to find out what was going on in the community to come down. But I have to admit I'm very disappointed in the rally. I thought that the black leaders had all congregated here – and it was a safe haven for people to come and talk – but they didn't	PAN TO: Closeup of Angela.

AUDIO

VIDEO

say anything. When they should
have been out there in the streets
with the people who were really
angry and venting their frustrations
like the fires we're seeing across the
street. There are people shooting –
they should be out there in the
streets with the people, and telling
them what we should be doing,
what is our next step. And, and, I
felt like it turned into a musical,
into a concert; it ends with a rap, a
rapper, it was, it, it was nonsense.

ZOOM OUT AND PAN TO: Devine
with microphone

Christine Devine (13):
Okay, Angela had mentioned there
was a fire across the street. We
understand it possibly may be a gas
station or perhaps an apartment
building. Ah, somebody ran in here
a few minutes ago asking for
people to come out and help. We
cannot confirm that at this point
because we are inside talking with
people here. We will check that out.
But let's talk with some more
people. Denver, what were your
thoughts on the rally?

PAN AND ZOOM IN TO: Denver

Denver (14):
Ah, I feel that, ah, the rally, you
know, should have, you know,
addressed, you know, more, more
about the Rodney King beating,
you know, and, you know. We talk
so much about, you know, trying to
get Gates out. But, you see, putting
another person in is not going to
change anything. You see, if the
people are gonna, if the people are
gonna change it, the people are

AUDIO   VIDEO

gonna change it. All the leaders can
do is just give us guidance.

Christine Devine (15):
Okay, let's move over here. Kevin,
you're not a member of the church
either, but you showed up tonight.

Kevin (16):   PAN TO: Kevin.
Ah, yes. I have kinda the same
feelings as Angela. I was very
disappointed, ah, about this, ah,
rally here tonight. They really didn't
let the people voice their opinion.
Ah, basically I want to speak out to
my brothers and sisters for you to
quit all this destruction in the city
and throughout the city. We're
actually stuck in this church here –
Crenshaw and Adams, Florence,
Manchester, Century is blocked off,
the Harbor Freeway. We have to
come together as one, quit
patronating, patronizing these
Orientals and all these other
nationalities, businesses and come
together as one and get our
ministers in the church to quite
playing church and acting the
church and give us a proposal like
this one young black lady spoke,
they were trying to knock her off
the podium . . . but she was saying
more real stuff than, ah, the elected
officials. She spoke better than
Mayor Bradley.

Christine Devine (17):   PAN TO: Devine.
Kevin, of course, is referring to the
lady that we showed you a little,
little while ago. She, ah, had sat

AUDIO

VIDEO

outside listening to the rally, was
upset, did not like what she was
hearing from city officials so she
came inside and challenged them.
She spoke up and, and, they tried to
usher her out. The crowd said, "No,
let her speak, let her speak." So they
brought her up on stage and let her
talk and she, she said she didn't like
what the politicians were doing, she
said it really was not enough. Let's
get one more opinion, shall we?

PAN AND ZOOM TO: Shelly.

Shelly Henderson (18):
My name is Shelly Henderson and
I'm a, representing the Black
Student Association of Occidental
College. And we're here . . . I just
want everyone to know that we're
outraged and that we are planning
on mobilizing and getting ourselves
together, organizing and doing
some things in the community. One
thing I did want to say was that I
think that the police . . . for
instance, we're stuck here and the
police are nowhere to be found. The
police are gonna let us tear up this
because we're in the hood. We're on
Adams and Western. The police
aren't gonna come and help us here.
But if we go to Beverly Hills they'll
probably drop tear gas on us. So I
just want to admonish everyone to
stop all the violence. It's not helping
any. All they're gonna do is call out
the National Guard and then we're
all gonna be destroyed. Let's come
together as one, and let's take care
of this problem. Thank you.

AUDIO

VIDEO

Christine Devine (19):
Okay that's the reaction from some
of the people who are attending
this rally here that started at seven
o'clock and ended about nine
fifteen. A few minutes ago there
was a prayer over here. I know
downstairs some of the male
leaders of the church are meeting,
trying to again call for calm. And
we're hearing about some unrest
outside, so we're gonna go and
check that out and check back with
you a little later. But let me now
put Carol, Reporter Carol Lin . . .
she was here to file another report.
So Carol, I'm gonna hand over the
mic to you . . . if you can step right
in front of the camera here and
take over.

PAN AND ZOOM OUT TO: Devine.

Lin steps in front of the camera
and takes the microphone

Carol Lin (20):
Thanks Christine. Thanks a lot.
Chris and Patti, we just got back
from witnessing some of the events
that are happening out in South
Central. Ah, right now we're gonna
roll some videotape which we shot,
we shot within the last hour or so.
What you're looking at right now –
and I don't have a monitor here,
but I believe what you're looking at
right now are two fires burning
simultaneously on the corner of
Western and Slauson. This,
unfortunately, despite the calls for
peace, ah, despite the calls for, ah,
ah, lack of action, and, ah, taking
action at the polls instead of out
on the streets . . . these fires

CUT TO: Night. Various buildings
burning, shot through the window
of a moving vehicle. Streets are
busy with traffic.

AUDIO   VIDEO

erupted shortly after sundown, ah, I
think we counted about, I would
say, anywhere between six and ten
fires as we drove done the Harbor
Freeway southbound. There were
fires burning off of, ah, Manchester
Avenue. The power was completely
out. And as we drove down the
street, as cautiously as we could, we
saw people looting in the stores,
carrying whatever they could – large
tv sets, clothing shoes, anything that
they could carry away – there was,
ah, people running, they were
people running out in the streets, ah,
fires were burning on the other side,
both sides of the Harbor Freeway.
Ah, they're weren't any fire engines,
they're weren't any police officers in
the area to control the crowds. I
believe primarily, and this is the
sense we got from the command
post at Van Ness and fifty-fourth,
that ah, the police feel at this point
that by going into these areas they
simply will incite more, ah, just
more rioting, ah, more trouble,
more anxiety on the community's
part. Ah, I can understand people's
feelings here at First AME that
they, they need the police into these
areas. We were hearing from some
people here at the church that
there's an apartment building across
the street that's burning and that
adults were called across the street
to, ah, rescue some of the children
which may be trapped, ah, inside
the building. And, ah, we have a

AUDIO

VIDEO

crew over there right now getting
those, ah, pictures. But out
there, right now, Chris and
Patti, there is just a sense of, truly
of anger. Ah, nobody is laughing
out there. This, this wasn't a joke.
These, these weren't just kids out
there playing. They were throwing
rocks. They were throwing bottles.
They were shooting, ah, at people
on the street – including the news
crews including ourselves, in fact.
Ah, we were driving northbound
on Western, just west of Adams
and, ah, we heard five gunshots
and, ah, our car is now pock-
marked and beer was thrown inside
and glass and rocks. Ah, these
people mean business. Ah, I
happen to be shooting with a
photographer named Chad
Molinex. He happens to be white.
He got a lot of abuse. He was
sitting in the passenger seat, ah,
rolling on whatever videotape he
could and, ah, we had to quickly
escape some of these areas. Ah, it,
it is a serious situation out there
we're very sorry to report. I'm
Carol Lin reporting live at First
AME. Back to you Chris and Patti.

CUT TO: Lin standup at FAME

CUT TO GRAPHIC: "Cops on Trial:
The Rodney King Case." Split
screen with anchor desk and Lin
at FAME.

Chris Harris (21):
This First AME church has been
the site tonight of a, ah, of a huge
rally in terms of numbers of people
– several thousand. Ah, city
officials, religious leaders, all
praying and pushing and working

CUT TO: Anchor desk with Harris
and Suarez.

AUDIO

VIDEO

as best they can for everyone to remain calm, and unfortunately not all of us are listening to that. The Reverend Carl Washington joins us now with, ah, his own view of what has been happening . . . Not of the verdict anymore – we're past that. But Reverend Washington, I think your view of what we've seen in terms of the video, of parts of South Central Los Angeles burning to the ground.

Reverend Washington (22): Absolutely. Ah, one of the most remarkable things about this is that, ah, is the cry we made, ah, some three or four days ago, ah, for the people not to participate in riots, ah, fell on deaf ears. Ah, but we are still . . . we'll be leaving, going back to the streets again, ah, Chris, with the same message . . . ah, to convince those not rioting not to go out into the streets. And we're sending a message to every home, to family, parents, to get they kids, take them in the house, make their family safe . . . and then I think we can, ah, avoid a lot of people running the streets. But right now it's chaos. Ah, we as ministers, ah, will continue our jobs as we done for the last three days – to go back to the streets.

CUT TO: Rev. Washington at anchor desk with Harris and Suarez.
CUT TO: Close-up of Washington.

CUT TO: Rev. Washington at anchor desk with Harris and Suarez.

Patti Suarez (23): You've been particularly, ah, articulate the last, ah, few days in this message. I, I keep getting the image of, of a fighter pilot who

CUT TO: Three-shot of anchor desk.

AUDIO

VIDEO

says, "I've tried 'A,' I've tried 'B,'
I've tried 'C." They go through the
list and they can't figure out what's
wrong. But, you, that must be what
you're feeling. You've tried
everything you know how to try. Is
there anything left –

CUT TO: Close-up of Rev.
Washington.

Reverend Washington (24):
Ah –

Patti Suarez (25):
– for you to say?

Reverend Washington (26):
Again, ah, to say there's really
nothing left to say, but, ah, now it's
our job as ministers to go down on
our knees in prayer and ask for a
higher resource to intervene in this
matter. Ah, it's totally disgusting,
ah, I had never thought that I would
see another time like this in history.
Ah, but history was made today
when the verdicts came in. Ah –

Chris Harris (27):
Tomorrow morning we're going to
see ashes in a great many parts –
just ashes and perhaps a few
smoldering embers and California
National Guard troops patrolling
parts of South Central Los Angeles.
What will be the message then?

CUT TO: Close-up of Harris.

CUT TO: Three-shot of anchor
desk.

Reverend Washington (28):
Ah, ah, to continue, ah, again we
will be saying the same thing to the
people. It's ah, stay calm, stay in
your houses. Ah, this is far from
being over with. Ah, this is, ah, a
episode of life that, ah, has

CUT TO: Close-up of Rev.
Washington.

AUDIO   VIDEO

disgraced many of us. Ah, it's not
only in the, the African-American
communities. But there are a
number of people participating after
watching down at the Parker Center.
There's . . . everybody's involved
with this thing. Ah, those who were
opposed to the, ah, decisions that
came down, that the verdict came
to. Ah, we started out saying that
whatever the verdict will be we
would remain calm and peaceful.
That's still our message. Ah, we're
going back to the communities –
even though it sounds impossible.
We're not Superman. But there are
some people we can reach. And
that's the message we want to say
Chris, ah, Chris and Patti, that we
will continue to look for the higher
resources – even in the dilemma of
this matter that's at hand right now.

Chris Harris (29):
Reverend Washington, thank you.
Please stay with us. We need your
voice, ah, tonight.

Reverend Washington (30):
Okay.

Chris Harris (31):
Stay with us.

Patti Suarez (32):   CUT TO: Two-shot of Suarez and
If you have a few minutes we'd   Harris.
appreciate it .

Reverend Washington (33):
Sure.

Chris Harris (34):
It is, ah, now ten o'clock and, ah,

AUDIO

VIDEO

tonight a community is venting its
fury over the verdicts in the
Rodney King beating trial. Fires
are raging in South Central Los
Angeles at this hour – a testament
to the anger and frustration felt by
many residents tonight. They're
angry over the not-guilty verdicts
delivered earlier today by the jury
in the Rodney King beating trial in
Simi Valley. Now this is where
some of the worst violence is
taking place, near the corner of
Florence and Normandie . . . this
videotape shot late this afternoon
. . . began just a few hours after the
verdicts were announced. People
began looting stores and setting
them on fire, beating people up.
Four drivers, at least, pulled from
their vehicles and severely beaten,
including the man there by that
truck.

FADE TO: Aerial shot of fires.

FADE TO: Black youth attacking
cars in intersection.

CUT TO: Shot of debris from
looting on sidewalks

CUT TO: Aerial shot of truck
driver laying in street beside his rig.
Black males watch middle of street.

Patti Suarez (35):
Chaos also erupted, ah, at the
downtown Parker Center, L.A.'s
police headquarters. Scuffles broke
out throughout the evening. A
parking lot kiosk, as you see there,
was toppled and then set afire. At
this hour, police in riot gear can
only stand by hoping, by their
presence, to somehow keep a grasp
on order. Tonight, Los Angeles is
under a state of emergency.

FADE TO: Police rushing crowds
at police headquarters.

CUT TO: Shot of kiosk being
turned over by a large, multi-racial
group.

(Music)

Announcer (36):
From KTTV Los Angeles, this is
Fox News.

Fox News logo flips in,
superimposed over footage of
the kiosk's destruction.

Appendix D

Questionnaires

Survey 1: Pre-discussion Questionnaire

Your initials _____   G| _____

Today's date _____   (leave blank)

1. How would you describe what you just saw to a friend or family member?

2. On a scale from 1 to 10, do you feel the looting that occurred during the Los Angeles riots was "right," "wrong," or somewhere in between?

   right ___ ___ ___ ___ ___ ___ ___ ___ ___ ___ wrong
   　　　　1　2　3　4　5　6　7　8　9　10

3. On a scale from 1 to 10, do you feel the starting of fires during the riots was "right," "wrong" or somewhere in between?

   right ___ ___ ___ ___ ___ ___ ___ ___ ___ ___ wrong
   　　　　1　2　3　4　5　6　7　8　9　10

4. On a scale from 1 to 10, do you feel the arrests made during the riots were "right," "wrong" or somewhere in between?

   right ___ ___ ___ ___ ___ ___ ___ ___ ___ ___ wrong
   　　　　1　2　3　4　5　6　7　8　9　10

5. On a scale from 1 to 10, does what you just saw about the riots make you feel "very hopeful," "not at all hopeful," or somewhere in between?

   very　 ___ ___ ___ ___ ___ ___ ___ ___ ___ ___ not at all
   hopeful 1　2　3　4　5　6　7　8　9　10　hopeful

Survey 2: Post-discussion Questionnaire

Your initials _____   G| _____

Today's date _____   (leave blank)

1. What were you doing during the first day of the riots?

2. Why do you think the riots started?

3. On a scale from 1 to 10, how important a role do you think race played in the riots?

    very ___ ___ ___ ___ ___ ___ ___ ___ ___ ___ not at all
    important 1   2   3   4   5   6   7   8   9   10 important

4. On a scale from 1 to 10, does what you just saw about the riots make you feel "not at all hopeful," "very hopeful" or somewhere in between?

    not at all ___ ___ ___ ___ ___ ___ ___ ___ ___ ___ very
    hopeful 1   2   3   4   5   6   7   8   9   10 hopeful

4a. Why do you feel this way about what you just saw?

5. On a scale from 1 to 10, do you feel the looting that occurred during the Los Angeles riots was "wrong," "right" or somewhere in between?

    wrong ___ ___ ___ ___ ___ ___ ___ ___ ___ ___ right
           1   2   3   4   5   6   7   8   9   10

6. On a scale from 1 to 10, do you feel the starting of fires during the riots was "wrong," "right" or somewhere in between?

    wrong ___ ___ ___ ___ ___ ___ ___ ___ ___ ___ right
           1   2   3   4   5   6   7   8   9   10

6a. Why do you feel this way?

7. On a scale from 1 to 10, do you feel the arrests made during the riots were "wrong," "right" or somewhere in between?

    wrong ___ ___ ___ ___ ___ ___ ___ ___ ___ ___ right
           1   2   3   4   5   6   7   8   9   10

8. How much television news coverage did you watch during the first day of the riots (after the police beating verdicts came in)?

    none ___
    less than an hour ___
    between 1 and 3 hours ___

more than three hours ___
all evening ___

9. How often did you read the *Los Angeles Times* during the riots?

never ___
sometimes ___
every day ___

10. Are you currently a student?

yes ___
no ___

10a. If yes, where do you go to school?

_____

10b. If yes, what is your major?

_____

11. What do your *parents* do for a living?

a. Your mother?

b. Your father?

12. What is your parents' home zip code(s)?

_____

13. What is your *mother's* level of education?

less than high school degree ___
high school degree ___
some college ___
bachelor's degree ___
some graduate work ___
graduate degree ___

14. What is your *father's* level of education?

less than high school degree ___
high school degree ___
some college ___
bachelor's degree ___
some graduate work ___
graduate degree ___

15. What is *your* level of education?

less than high school degree ___

high school degree ___
some college ___
bachelor's degree ___
some graduate work ___
graduate degree ___

16. What sex are you?

male ___
female ___

17. What race are you?

White or Caucasian ___
African American ___
Latino ___
Korean American ___
Japanese American ___
Chinese American ___
Other _____ (please specify)

18. How old are you? _____

19. How religious are you?
very religious ___
somewhat religious ___
not at all religious ___

20. How often since the riots occurred have you discussed them with the people who are here now participating in this study with you?

never ___
less than once a month ___
about once a month ___
about once a week ___
several times a week ___
about every day ___
several times a day or more ___

21. How do you know each of the people who are here now participating in this study with you? Please use their initials to write briefly about each person.

22. If you could, how would you change this questionnaire?

Appendix E

Tables

Table 3.1. *Key assumptions embedded in the KTTV text.*

assumption
1. The events are undesirable.
2. The events are centered in South Central Los Angeles.
3. Elected officials/community leaders could/should say something to event participants that would influence them one way or another.
4. The events were caused by the Rodney King beating verdicts.
5. The events are "riots."
6. Race is a central factor in the events.
7. Blacks are "event insiders."
8. Ministers have a special responsibility to help restore calm.
9. Voting is the appropriate outlet for change.
10. Police ought to have a significant presence at the site(s) of the events.
11. The events are similar to the Watts riots.
12. The First AME "rally" was a reasonable response to the events.
13. Prayer is a reasonable strategy for addressing the events.
14. The role of news media is to serve their viewers by providing them with fair and factual coverage of the events.

Source: Analysis of the verbatim transcript of the text (see appendix C).

Table 4.1. *Media consumption and previous event-related discussion,*
Latino-raced groups (in percentages).

	Latino-raced groups				
	YOUTH (N = 3)	FAMILY (N = 5)	LATINA (N = 4)	MARIA (N = 4)	JULIO (N = 4)
TV News					
none	0.0	0.0	0.0	0.0	0.0
< 1 hour	0.0	0.0	0.0	0.0	0.0
1 to 3 hours	33.3	20.0	0.0	0.0	75.0
> 3 hours	66.7	20.0	25.0	25.0	25.0
all evening	0.0	60.0	75.0	75.0	0.0
Total	100.0	100.0	100.0	100.0	100.0
LA Times					
never	33.3	40.0	25.0	50.0	75.0
sometimes	66.7	40.0	75.0	25.0	25.0
every day	0.0	20.0	0.0	25.0	0.0
Total	100.0	100.0	100.0	100.0	100.0
Discussion					
never	0.0	60.0	0.0	25.0	0.0
< once/month	33.3	0.0	50.0	75.0	75.0
once/month	66.7	20.0	50.0	0.0	25.0
once/week	0.0	0.0	0.0	0.0	0.0
several/week	0.0	20.0	0.0	0.0	0.0
every day	0.0	0.0	0.0	0.0	0.0
several/day	0.0	0.0	0.0	0.0	0.0
Total	100.0	100.0	100.0	100.0	100.0

Source: Post-discussion questionnaire.

Table 4.2. *Key arguments emerging from YOUTH discussion, in order of emergence.**

Relevant assumptions	Argument
	Prompt 1
(1)	People should have found less destructive ways of protesting.
(6)	There exists too much racial tension in Los Angeles.
(6)	*The events were not caused by race or the Rodney King incident; they were the result of socio-economic frustration.*
(1)	People should have found less destructive ways of protesting.
(1)	Two wrongs do not make a right.
(1)	The events have sparked little if any change.
(1)	People should look beyond their own interests and think about the needs of others.
(6)	There exists too much racial tension in Los Angeles.
(1)	The short-term gains from looting are not worth the long-term costs.
(10)	The police should have had a significant presence at the site(s) of the events.
(1)	Later on in life we will look back on the events and regret them.
(3)	Community leaders failed to provide leadership.
	Prompt 2
	(19:22)
(8)	Reverend Washington was right in his plea for calm.
(14)	*Media coverage was "sensationalistic."*
	People should come together as one.
(14)	Media coverage alerted people to what was happening.
(14)	*Media coverage incited violence.*
(10)	Problems with Los Angeles police (LAPD) can be traced to a few "bad apples."
(4)	If police had put themselves in King's position, the events would not have started.
(10)	*Police are indiscriminately brutal today.*
	End
	(29:10)

Note:
* Italicized arguments denote cases of informant opposition.
Source: Analysis of verbatim transcript, YOUTH Group.

Table 4.3. *Average scores on looting, fires and arrests scales, by Latino-raced group, before and after discussion.*

Latino-raced groups	Scale averages*		
	Loot1/loot2	Fires1/fires2	Arrest1/arrest2
YOUTH	9.3/10.0	10.0/10.0	2.7/2.7
FAMILY	9.8/10.0	10.0/10.0	1.0/1.0
LATINA	8.8/8.8	8.5/8.0	6.3/5.5
MARIA	7.3/7.8	8.8/8.8	5.3/5.5
JULIO	6.3/8.0	6.0/6.5	3.0/4.1

Note:
* Possible scale scores ranged from 1 to 10, with 1 indicating that informants felt the looting, fires or arrests were "right," and 10 indicating that informants felt each event-related activity was "wrong."

Source: Pre- and post-discussion surveys.

Table 4.4. *Key arguments emerging from FAMILY discussion, in order of emergence.*

Relevant assumptions	Argument
	Prompt 1
(1)	Event participants reacted in the "wrong way."
(1)	Event participants just took advantage of the situation.
(1)	Stealing is "wrong."
(1)	Event participants just took advantage of the situation.
	Residents of the area were not safe during the events.
	The events were like a war.
	Prompt 2
	(7:33)
	The most important news in the text concerned the burning.
(4)	The most important news in the text concerned the verdicts.
(4)	The events started when people took out their frustrations over the verdicts.
	The most important news in the text concerned the burning.
(1)	Event participants were "out of their minds."
(14)	*Media coverage incited the events.*

Table 4.4. (*cont.*)

Relevant assumptions	Argument
	Prompt 3
	(11:17)
	The most important news in the text concerned the burning.
	The events were like a war.
(1)	Event participants were acting "stupid."
(1)	Event participants just took advantage of the situation.
(14)	The news reporters let the world know what was going on.
(14)	*The news reporters were motivated by money.*
(14)	The news reporters risked their lives.
(8)(12)	*Church officials cannot make people stop participating in the events.*
(7)	Church officials could not possibly be afraid for their safety because they are black.
	Television pleas to restore calm were doomed to fail because South Central residents had no electricity and could not watch television.
	Prompt 4
	(14:54)
	Interviewee calls for calm could not be heard by area residents because of the power outages.
	Prompt 5
	(16:55)
	Police will be prepared for the outbreak of similar events in future.
(6)	The Ku Klux Klan was pleased by the events.
(1)	The events were acts of self-destruction.
(6)	Latino event participants were primarily from El Salvador.
(6)	Salvadorans should be sent back to El Salvador.
(6)	Blacks should be sent back to Africa.
(6)	Mexicans should be sent back to Mexico.
(6)	Southern California *is* Mexico today.
(6)	The Ku Klux Klan was pleased by the events.

Table 4.4. (*cont.*)

Relevant assumptions	Argument
(6)	Koreans suffered most from the events.
(6)	Asians participated in the events.
(6)	The events embarrassed the Latino community.
(1)	Event participants just took advantage of the situation.
(1)	Event participants just took advantage of the situation.
(4)	The Rodney King incident "was none of their [Latinos'] business."
(6)	Everyone should "stick to their own race."
(6)	Latinos are not as unified as blacks.
(6)	There are prejudiced individuals within every racial group.
(6)	A large percentage of blacks is ignorant.
(6)	Most Latinos living in the area are scared of blacks.
(6)	Latinos are the primary victims of black muggers in the area.
(6)	Latinos are small in stature relative to blacks.
(6)	Blacks commit most of the muggings in the area.
(6)	Blacks take advantage of Latinos.

End
(30:08)

Source: Analysis of verbatim transcript, FAMILY Group.

Table 4.5. *Key arguments emerging from LATINA discussion, in order of emergence.*

Relevant assumptions	Argument
	Prompt 1
(1)	Event participants were ignorant.
(1)	The events were not the "right" way to vent anger.
(1)	Nothing was gained from burning down buildings.
(1)	Because stores were burned down, we have to travel farther to shop. You must instill in your children a sense of right and wrong when they are young.
	Prompt 2
	(4:48)
(14)	*The media did not report the events the way we saw them.*
(14)	*The media did not adequately cover the events.*
(14)	*News reports incorrectly labelled all event participants "thugs."*
(14)	*The media present the residents of South Central as "thugs" and "low-lifes."*
(14)	*Not every resident of South Central is a low-life.*
(14)	*Reporters who covered the events made racist comments.*
(14)	*The media only showed people being destructive during the events; they did not show people helping others.*
(14)	*The media only showed people helping others on the third day of the events, after the events and interest in the news had waned.*
(14)	*The media repeatedly reported that "thugs" were doing the looting.*
(12)	The only positive images in the video were of FAME interviewees.
	People will always follow the bad rather than good.
(14)	*The news media always exaggerate the situation.*
(14)	*The entire news report was "dumb." Nothing was good about it.*
(12)	The only good thing about the video was that it showed people at FAME talking, trying to help the situation.
	The "stay calm" message sent out by leaders was ridiculous because people who lived near the events were threatened by the fires. Many also had no food or electricity.
(1)	It was "sad" to see mothers looting with their kids.

Table 4.5. (*cont.*)

Relevant assumptions	Argument
(1)	*Some people had to loot in order to get food.*
(1)	Some people looted items they did not need.
(1)	It was "dumb" to break into buildings.
(1)	It was "ridiculous" to burn buildings.
(6)	A lot of black people are innocent.
(14)(6)	*The white reporters were beat up because they were trying to be "nosey."*
(14)	The white reporters were just trying to inform us.
(14)	*We did not need to be informed because we were where the events were occurring.*
(14)	The media were needed to inform the rest of the world about what was happening.
(14)	*The media blew the events out of proportion.*

Prompt 3

(10:33)

The people interviewed in the video made fools of themselves.

Interviewees were just trying to get publicity.

(14)	*The reporters did not have anything informative to say; they repeated the same information over and over again.*
(14)	*The reporters did not know what to say.*
(14)	The reporters were scared.
(14)	*It was "dumb" for the media to repeat the same news over and over again.*
(3)	Elected officials did not intervene soon enough. When they did, they offered no specific solutions.
(14)	The reporters were just doing their job.
(14)	The reporters were risking their lives.
(14)	*The reporters did not do a good job covering the events.*

Prompt 4

(14:08)

(7)	The majority of event participants were black.
(7)	Hispanics had nothing to do with the events. They should not have participated.

Table 4.5. (*cont.*)

Relevant assumptions	Argument
(1)	*Some Hispanics who looted, looted out of necessity.*
(1)	Looting for food and necessities is reasonable. Looting for televisions, stereos and other merchandise was unnecessary.
(1)	Looters took too much merchandise.
(2)	South Central is not a ghetto; residents are just poor people.
(14)	*South Central is portrayed as a "low-life" area in the media.*
(2)	Everyone thinks that South Central is a "low-life" area.
(2)	It is not right for you to refer to your own community as "low-life."
(2)	South Central is not in a good part of town, but it is not a ghetto.
(1)	Words cannot do much now because everything is destroyed.
(9)	The system is "messed up."
(9)	The people who do not vote are the ones most likely to complain about the situation.
	You can rebuild buildings.
(1)	It will take years to rebuild South Central.
(1)	Those who died in the events were at fault for being out in the streets.
	Many of the victims were innocent, just in the wrong place at the wrong time. They did not know what was happening.
	Some people were beat up for being "nosey."
	Some people were beat up as they tried to get home from work.
	Most victims were probably out participating in the events.
(1)	The looting scenes were "sad."
	The curfew was "dumb."
	The curfew was good in that it decreased "trouble" in the area.
	It was "wrong" that many people were arrested because of the curfew.
	The curfew was "dumb" because people had things to do; it should have been set for a later hour.
	People should have been able to present an excuse for being out past curfew.

Table 4.5. (*cont.*)

Relevant assumptions	Argument
	People could not prove that they had a valid excuse.
(2)	South Central has the image of being a "low-life" area.
(2)	The idea that South Central is an area of "low-lifes" is "wrong."
(14)	*The media have convinced some of us that we are "low-lifes."*
(1)	Event participants were acting like "thugs."
(14)	*The media stereotyped everyone in South Central as "thugs."*
(2)	Some of the participants were "thugs," but that is not the same as saying that everyone in South Central is.
(14)	*The media say they are not racist, but they continually stereotype people.*
(14)	*The media always specify in news reports the race of suspected criminals when they are black or Hispanic.*
(14)(6)	*People should be treated as people, not colors.*
(14)	*The media may not be intentionally racist, but they always portray minorities negatively or not at all.*
(14)	*The news is racist because the majority of people in America are white.*
(6)	Everyone is raised to refer to people by race.
(6)	We owe it to ourselves to admit our own racism.
(6)	We all stereotype people.
(6)	We should refer to white people as Caucasians.
(6)	We are raised to refer to people in terms of color.
(6)	We were raised to refer to people in terms of color.
(6)	You have to start from the beginning to teach your children not to refer to people in terms of color.
(6)	It's not right to label people in terms of color.
(6)	Race was the main issue in the events.
(14)	*The media incited the events by playing the beating video over and over again.*
(4)	It was wrong for the officers to beat Rodney King.
(4)	It seems ridiculous for people to make such a big deal over the Rodney King beating when similar beatings "happen every day."

Table 4.5. (*cont.*)

Relevant assumptions	Argument
(1)	The events were just people taking advantage of the situation.
(1)	*The events were not just people taking advantage of the situation.*
(4)(1)	The events started with anger and ended with people taking advantage of the situation.
	Event participants were angry because they are not educated.
	We are educated.
(2)	If the people in the area were educated the events would not have occurred.
	We are educated, but not properly because the school system is "messed up."
(1)	*Event participants were fighting about justice because everything is "messed up."*

End
(29:30)

Source: Analysis of verbatim transcript, LATINA Group.

Table 4.6. *Key arguments emerging from MARIA discussion, in order of emergence.*

Relevant assumptions	Argument
	Prompt 1
(1)	The events were a "stupid" way for participants to take out their frustrations.
(1)	*It made sense for people from certain backgrounds to participate in the events.*
(1)	Event participants displayed a total lack of respect for personal property.
(6)	Racism motivated some people to participate in the events.
(1)	Immediately after seeing the video you would not think about racism or other issues. You would just come to the conclusion that people were destroying each other's property.

Table 4.6. (*cont.*)

Relevant assumptions	Argument
	You react to the events now on video differently than you did as they were occurring.
(1)	When the events were occurring the participants seemed like "idiots."
(1)	*The event participants were not "idiots."*
(1)	*The event participants were just fighting for what they believed in.*
(1)	Event participants "went about it the wrong way" because they did not have a leader.
(1)	Event participants were laughing and taking advantage of the situation.
(1)	Event participants did not care about the effects of what they were doing.
(1)	*The events meant survival to participants.*
(1)	You cannot justify the actions of event participants because many of them were drinking.
(1)	The events were "wrong."
(1)	The majority of participants were not involved for political reasons.
(4)	The verdicts were upsetting.
(1)	*The events were a way for participants to speak out.*
(1)	*The events were not "wrong."*
(1)	The events should have been organized so that participants would not destroy their own community.
(10)	A police presence in South Central could have prevented some of the damage.
(10)	Police did not try to control the events because they do not care about South Central.
(10)	Police did not control the events because they were overwhelmed.
(10)	Police did not think that the events would spread the way they did.
(10)	Police did not try to control the events because they do not care about South Central.

Table 4.6. (*cont.*)

Relevant assumptions	Argument
(10)	Police did not try to control the events earlier because they did not want to incite more activity.
(10)	Police could have controlled the events if they had acted when the events first started.
(1)	*Event participants were not "idiots."*
(1)	Event participants showed a complete lack of respect for personal property.
(1)	*Event participants were not destroying their own neighborhood because they do not own property.*
(1)	Event participants showed a complete lack of regard for personal property.
(1)	The events were not the proper way to address the situation.
(1)	*Event participants were not "just destroying themselves."*
(1)	The events were "stupid" and unjustified. Anger does not justify the actions of event participants.
(1)	Nothing positive has come out of the events.
(1)	The events just created more problems.
(1)	The events were not the most effective way of expressing anger.
(1)	Event participants were selfish, laughing as they beat people.
(1)	Event participants did not view their actions as protest.
(12)	The people at FAME were venting their anger in a more positive way.
(4)(1)	The events were prompted by anger, but then people joined "just to be part of the crowd."
(1)	Event participants were destroying their own neighborhoods.
(1)	*The events were positive because participants got a lot of media attention.*
(1)	A gigantic protest in which the whole city gathered together would be a more positive alternative to the events.
(1)	The protest at Parker Center suggests that a city-wide, non-violent protest could have been organized.
(1)	Many event participants were selfish and just took advantage of the situation.
(1)	*The events were initiated to get attention.*

Table 4.6. (*cont.*)

Relevant assumptions	Argument
(10)	If the events had spread into other areas they would have been stopped by the police.
(1)	The events could have been handled in a better, less destructive way.
(1)	Event participants were destructive because they suddenly felt they "could get away with doing something."
(1)	Event participants suddenly felt like they had power because they "could get away with doing something."
(1)	*It is not bad that event participants had power.*
(1)	The fire and destruction that resulted from the events was unnecessary.
(1)	Event participants took advantage of the situation when they started to have fun with it.

Prompt 2
(14:29)

	The interviewee from Occidental College was good.
	The speech of the interviewee from Occidental College sounded too "prepared."
	The interviewee from Occidental College "just told the truth."
	The interviewee from Occidental College was being more realistic than people are accustomed to.
	The interviewee from Occidental College did not speak "from the heart."
	The speech of the interviewee from Occidental College sounded too "prepared."
	The interviewee from Occidental College had to be "prepared" in order to make her points.
(12)	Interviews at FAME were different from most of the other media interviews that focused on looters and event participants.
(12)	Interviews at FAME seemed "real" because the interviewees appeared to be genuinely concerned about the cause.
	Interviewees who showed the most concern about the events were probably better educated than less-concerned people.

Table 4.6. (*cont.*)

Relevant assumptions	Argument
(2)	Many people from South Central are poorly educated because of the poor quality of the school system.
	The system is designed to prevent minorities from getting a good education.
(14)	The newscasters in the video "looked good" and seemed "real."
(14)	*The newscasters in the video were "good," but others who covered the events were not.*
(14)	*Most reporters repeated themselves throughout the course of their coverage.*
(14)	The events lasted so long that reporters ran out of things to say.
(14)	The media's identification of where the events were occurring had the mixed effect of helping people avoid the areas and directing would-be participants to the area.
(14)	*Media coverage probably encouraged people to join the events.*
(14)	*Many people probably would not have participated in the events had the media not informed them of what was happening.*
	End
	(22:00)

Source: Analysis of verbatim transcript, MARIA Group.

Table 4.7. *Key arguments emerging from JULIO discussion, in order of emergence.**

Relevant assumptions	Argument
	Prompt 1
	It's a "mad" world.
(1)	*Event participants were oppressed people who expressed their anger and frustration through the events.*
	You should let your children reach their own conclusions regarding important social issues.
(1)	Nothing good is likely to come out of the events.
(1)	*The events are the type of occurrence that happens in the world from time to time. The events are nothing to be mad or depressed about.*
	You should warn your children that the events are dangerous and that they should not be out after dark.
(7)	*White people also participated in the looting.*
(7)	White people did not participate in the looting.
	You should explain to your child how dangerous the events are, while at the same time instilling hope in them for the future.
(4)	*The events are connected to other events occurring around world.*
	You should ask your children what they think about the events rather than lecture at them.
	Children may just see the events as an opportunity to avoid going to school.
(1)	The events are detrimental to the economy.
(1)	*The events are not detrimental to the economy because people have to be hired to rebuild the city.*
(1)	*The "violence" connected with the events is creating more jobs.*
(1)	*The "violence" connected with the events is creating more jobs just like during war time.*
(1)	*During war the economy improves because the nation increases its production.*
(1)	*The economy improved after the Gulf War because the nation had to produce more ammunition.*
(6)	Children will recognize the racial overtones of the events when they see the white man being beaten on television.

Table 4.7. (*cont.*)

Relevant assumptions	Argument
(6)	Children see people of all races being beaten all the time. You may have to explain to them beatings that took place during the events, however, because they were inflicted due to skin color.
	You cannot "get into the technical stuff" when explaining the events to twelve year olds.
(6)	Children know the difference between black and white.
(1)	The events were "rudimentary ways of expressing our" anger.
(1)(6)	*Event participants were reacting to institutionalized racism in America.*
(1)	*The actions of event participants were "okay."*
(1)	The actions of event participants were not "okay."
(1)(5)	"Rioting" is not the answer to disagreements in society.
(1)	*Because the events occurred, they must have served some function in society.*
(1)	Violence is not the solution to problems in society.
(1)	*Event participants were "rebelling" because they are not typically "heard" in society.*
(1)	The events made an impact in that event participants were heard around the world, but they could have spoken with less violence and injury.
(1)	*Injury is the price we pay for confronting injustice.*
(1)	The events were an "awful" occurrence.
(1)	*Things happen in the real world that we cannot control.*
	The situation in America will worsen if nothing good comes out of the events.
(1)	*It is good that the events occurred.*
	We need to "make something good out of" the events.

Prompt 2
(13:07)

(12)	One positive aspect of the video was that it showed people who were doing things other than participating in the events.

Table 4.7. (*cont.*)

Relevant assumptions	Argument

Prompt 3
(13:37)

(14)	*The telephone reporter in the video was monotonous.*
(12)	The FAME interviews showed that people were doing things other than responding violently. It presented viewers with options other than looting.
(8)	*The media should not have interviewed the minister as an authority on the events because most people do not agree with organized religion on socio-political issues.*
(14)	*I have been desensitized by the news because I have seen it before.*
(14)	*The newscast was boring because it was the second time I have seen it.*
(14)	*Fox News is "tacky."*
(14)	*The newscast was boring because it was the second time I have seen it.*
	The events are likely to happen again.
(4)	The police who beat Rodney King probably will not be found guilty in the second trial.
(4)	People will probably be mad even if a guilty verdict does come out because it will remind them of how unjust the system is.
(4)	The police who beat King should not spend the rest of their lives in jail.
	Oppression is not what society does to you; it is what you do to yourself.

End
(21:20)

Source: Analysis of verbatim transcript, JULIO Group.

Table 5.1. *Media consumption and previous event-related discussion, black-raced groups (in percentages).*

	Black-raced groups				
	GANG (N = 4)	CHURCH (N = 5)	CORNER (N = 6)	KEISHA (N = 5)	NORTH (N = 5)
TV News					
none	0.0	0.0	0.0	0.0	0.0
< 1 hour	0.0	20.0	16.7	0.0	0.0
1 to 3 hours	0.0	0.0	66.7	0.0	40.0
> 3 hours	50.0	40.0	0.0	0.0	20.0
all evening	25.0	40.0	16.7	100.0	40.0
missing	25.0	0.0	0.0	0.0	0.0
Total	100.0	100.0	100.0	100.0	100.0
LA Times					
never	25.0	80.0	33.3	60.0	100.0
sometimes	75.0	20.0	33.3	40.0	0.0
every day	0.0	0.0	33.3	0.0	0.0
Total	100.0	100.0	100.0	100.0	100.0
Discussion					
never	25.0	20.0	16.7	0.0	0.0
< once/month	25.0	40.0	0.0	60.0	20.0
once/month	50.0	0.0	16.7	0.0	60.0
once/week	0.0	40.0	16.7	20.0	20.0
several/week	0.0	0.0	16.7	0.0	0.0
every day	0.0	0.0	0.0	20.0	0.0
several/day	0.0	0.0	16.7	0.0	0.0
missing	0.0	0.0	16.7	0.0	0.0
Total	100.0	100.0	100.0	100.0	100.0

Source: Post-discussion questionnaire.

Table 5.2. *Key arguments emerging from* GANG *discussion, in order of emergence.*

Relevant assumptions	Argument
	Prompt 1
(5)	*The events were "not just a riot."*
	Many event participants were looting because they normally could not afford the merchandise.
(1)	*Many event participants were "fighting for what they believed in."*
(1)	*Blacks beat Denny to make the point that blacks and whites are treated differently by the judicial system.*
(1)	It was "wrong" for event participants to "burn up the neighborhood."
(1)	*Event participants did not "burn up the neighborhood."*
	Event participants did "burn up the neighborhood."
(1)	I participated in looting even though I did not feel that it was "right."
(14)	*News coverage of the events "hyped" me, motivated me to participate.*
(1)	It was "wrong" to loot the Asian people's stores.
(1)	*The Asian stores were going to be burned anyway so why not loot them?*
(2)	Event participants only burned buildings in South Central.
(4)	*The events had nothing to do with Rodney King.*
(4)	We [blacks] did care about Rodney King.
(4)	*We [Latinos] did not care about Rodney King.*
(4)	*For many participants, the events were "just about coming up."*
(4)	Latinos did not care about Rodney King because all they wanted was "some new furniture."
(4)	Blacks cared about Rodney King because "that was one of our brothers."
(4)	*Participants only cared about King at the very beginning of the events and at the very end.*
(6)(4)	If King was Latino, Latinos would have "cared about it."
(6)(4)	It hurts blacks to see one of their own being exploited by whites.

Table 5.2. (*cont.*)

Relevant assumptions	Argument
(4)	*The events were initiated by the King beating verdicts, but people eventually participated in order to "come up."*
(4)	*The events were "all about coming up."*
(7)	*Very few looters were black.*
(6)	Blacks looted Korean businesses in retaliation for the Latasha Harlins incident.
(6)	"Different things were going on between the Koreans and the blacks and the whites and the blacks" during the events.
	Prompt 2 (7:17)
(12)	The most important news in the video "showed a positive thing," people coming together at FAME
(14)	*Media coverage inflamed the situation at Florence and Normandie.*
	Prompt 3 (8:12)
(12)	What I liked about the video was how people were "coming to church to help put the fires out rather than start the fires."
	Prompt 4 (8:24)
(1)	The burning of neighborhood stores and markets makes it hard to get what we need today.
	Prompt 5 (8:41)
(14)	I do not have any feelings toward the reporters; they were just making money.
	Prompt 6 (9:05)
(12)	I was "on like the same level" with what the people interviewed in the church were saying.
	End (9:45)

Source: Analysis of verbatim transcript, GANG Group.

Table 5.3. *Average scores on looting, fires and arrests scales, by black-raced group.*

Black-raced groups	Scale averages*		
	Loot1/loot2	Fires1/fires2	Arrest1/arrest2
GANG	5.8/6.0	8.3/6.5	4.3/6.0
CHURCH	8.8/9.4	8.6/9.1	5.0/8.6
CORNER	4.0/5.2	9.0/9.7	5.7/6.0
KEISHA	4.6/5.0	5.2/6.0	7.4/8.6
NORTH	5.2/5.4	7.8/7.8	6.4/7.0

Note:
* Possible scale scores ranged from 1 to 10, with 1 indicating that informants felt the looting, fires or arrests were "right," and 10 indicating that informants felt each event-related activity was "wrong."
Source: Pre- and post-discussion surveys.

Table 5.4. *Key arguments emerging from C H U R C H discussion, in order of emergence.*

Relevant assumptions	Argument
	Prompt 1
(14)	*News coverage was not factual.*
(14)	*News coverage was exaggerated.*
(14)	*Television always negatively portrays the black person.*
(2)(14)	*News coverage only focused on South Central.*
(7)	*Mexicans and Asians did most of the looting.*
(14)	*News coverage focused on black areas of the city.*
(10)	The police abandoned South Central in order to protect Beverly Hills.
(6)	The whole system is racist.
(14)	*News coverage ignored blacks who were either victims of the event or heroes.*
(4)	The Rodney King and Reginald Denny events are comparable.
(4)	Rodney King's attackers were acquitted because they are policemen.
(9)(1)	You must work within the system to change it.

Table 5.4. (*cont.*)

Relevant assumptions	Argument
(1)	Event participants were ignorant of how to best bring about change.
(14)	*News reports of no police presence incited more violence.*
(1)	Many event participants just took advantage of the situation.
(6)	Reginald Denny's attackers were quickly jailed because they are black.
(4)	The Rodney King and Reginald Denny incidents are comparable.
	The new police chief will make a positive difference.
(6)	The whole system is racist.
(9)	The system effectively neutralizes those who challenge it.
(6)	The white power structure allows drugs to enter the innercity so that blacks will be destroyed.

Prompt 2
(7:38)

(14)	*Nothing in the KTTV text was important news.*
(14)	*The aim of the news coverage was simply to negatively portray blacks.*

Prompt 3
(8:18)

(14)	*The news reporters were doing what they were paid to do, exploit the situation.*

Prompt 4
(8:45)

	Many of the interviewees were "ignorant."
(1)	*It takes episodes like the events to bring about change.*
(6)	Blacks need to unify before they can effectively challenge the system.
(6)	It is hard to love yourself as a black person when you see footage like the KTTV text.

Prompt 5
(10:06)

	Event participants attacked news workers in order to get attention.

Table 5.4. (*cont.*)

Relevant assumptions	Argument
(14)	*Event participants attacked news workers because they knew that they would be negatively portrayed in news coverage.*
(14)	*The media rarely cover negative stories in the white community with comparable energy.*
(11)	*The events are not comparable to the Watts riots.*
(11)	*The Watts riots erupted out of community frustration.*
(14)	*The events were incited by media reports of no police presence.*

End
(12:02)

Source: Analysis of verbatim transcript, CHURCH Group.

Table 5.5. *Key arguments emerging from* CORNER *discussion, in order of emergence.*

Relevant assumptions	Argument
	Prompt 1
(1)	*Looting was "okay," but the wrong items were looted.*
(1)	The violence against people was "wrong."
(1)	*The events were needed to provide resources for the community.*
(1)	*Event participants should have targeted other areas of the city.*
(1)	*Looting was "okay," but the fires and violence against people were "wrong."*
(4)	If the police chief had been fired, the events would not have started.
(1)	*The events were needed to relieve stress in the community.*
(1)	*The looting was "okay," but the fires were "wrong."*
(4)	*People participated in the events because they were "tired of everything."*
(6)	The police who attacked Rodney King were acquitted because they are white and King is black.
(1)	*The looting was "okay," but the fires were "wrong."*

Table 5.5. (*cont.*)

Relevant assumptions	Argument
(4)	The Rodney King and Reginald Denny beatings are comparable.
(1)	*The events unified the community.*
(1)	*The events brought the gangs together.*
	Police later broke up the gang unity.
(6)	Neither blacks nor Mexicans had the same rights as whites or Koreans.
(1)	*Event participants had "nothing to lose."*
(1)	*The events led to opportunities for blacks in the community.*
	Police will be prepared if similar events erupt in the future.
(1)	The first day of the events was sufficient.
(1)	Event participants "pushed it to the limit."
(1)	The events resulted in the destruction of popular stores and shops in the community.

Prompt 2
(15:05)

(1)	The fires were "wrong."
(1)	The violence against people was "wrong."
(3)	Black officials should have been in the streets trying to calm event participants.
(3)	*Event participants would not have listened to black officials.*
(1)	Event participants were primarily pursuing their own personal interests.

Prompt 3
(17:40)

(6)	Media workers were targeted by event participants because they were white.

Prompt 4
(18:10)

(14)	*News reporters did not talk "about the total situation."*
(14)	News reporters simply report the news as it occurs.
(14)	*News reporters decide what they want to cover.*
(14)	News reporters were doing their job.

Table 5.5. (*cont.*)

Relevant assumptions	Argument
(14)	*News reporters are often biased.*
(10)	The police abandoned the area.
(14)	News reports of no police presence in the area prompted people to participate in the events.
(1)	Residents of the area destroyed their own community.
(1)	Residents of the community will regret the destruction.

End
(23:27)

Source: Analysis of verbatim transcript, CORNER Group.

Table 5.6. *Key arguments emerging from KEISHA discussion, in order of emergence.*

Relevant assumptions	Argument
	Prompt 1
(5)	*The events were not a "riot;" they were a "rebellion" against the not-guilty verdicts and the way blacks are treated in America.*
(6)	America is a white-dominated society and blacks do not fit in anywhere.
(1)	*Blacks did not rebel because they were ignorant. When you "don't have anything" and see an opportunity to "get something" you are going to "go after it."*
(6)	Event participants were just fed up with white-dominated society.
	Some of the looters were not poor.
(4)	The events had more to do with injustice than poverty.
(4)	*The Latasha Harlins case was one of the underlying causes of the events.*
(6)	Blacks are not as "strong" today as they were during the height of the civil rights struggles in the 1960s.
(6)	If it were not for the sit-ins and other activities during the civil rights era, blacks would not be where they are today.

Table 5.6. (*cont.*)

Relevant assumptions	Argument
(6)	This is a white-ruled world.
(6)	Black efforts to make more progress in America do not seem to be working.
(6)	Blacks have "come a long way" over the years. For example, schools are integrated now.
(6)	There is more interaction between blacks and whites today than in the past, so white racism tends to be covert.
(6)	Whites still see blacks as "Niggers" today.
(1)(13)	You should think before you act and call on a "higher source" for guidance.
	The world is falling apart and it is getting increasingly difficult to instill hope in people.
(6)	We must preach "unification" of blacks in order to make more progress in society. This does not necessitate preaching hate.
(6)	In the dictionary, "black" is defined as the opposite of pure and innocent. It is defined as "everything negative."
(7)	*Blacks were not the only people looting.*
(14)	*The media always focus on blacks as "scapegoats."*
(6)	Blacks were more unified in the 1960s than they are today.
(6)	Education in American schools is "Eurocentric" and cannot facilitate black unity.
(6)	College provides opportunities to learn about black history.
(6)	One must search intently for information about black history in the typical college curriculum.
(6)	Math and science classes often fail to acknowledge black contributions to the disciplines.
(6)	America is a white, Anglo-Saxon, male-dominated society.
(6)	Whites are not going to teach minorities that they have any positive role in society. Instead, they will emphasize that America is a white-dominated culture that subordinates all others.
(6)	Blacks must "stick together."
(6)	Blacks have lost too much of their heritage over the years and cannot afford to "mix" with other groups today, especially whites.

Table 5.6. (*cont.*)

Relevant assumptions	Argument
(6)	When you "mix" with other groups, someone has to give up their culture.
(6)	Whites will not give up their culture when they "mix" with other groups because their culture is dominant in America.
(6)	The "African American race" has been "diluted" by mixing with other groups. In the past this mixing was forced, now it is by choice.
(4)	When the King beating verdicts were announced, the notion of non-violence "went out the window."
(1)	*Event participants should have moved the events to Beverly Hills.*
(1)	"We should not have torn up our own neighborhood."
(1)	*Event participants destroyed what they had access to at the time.*
(1)	Blacks need to think more before they act.
(6)	When the King beating trial was moved to Simi Valley and an all-white jury was selected, not-guilty verdicts became inevitable.
(4)	Jurors were simply following the instructions of the judge when they found the officers not guilty.
(4)	The jurors should have recognized – irrespective of the judge's instructions – that what they saw on the videotape was an illegal beating.
(4)	The verdicts were caused by the judge's instructions.
(4)	The people in Simi Valley did not really care about the King beating.
(6)	We need to go beyond the individual level and attack racism at the system level.
(6)	"Adverse" racism is worse than overt racism because people do not realize that they are being racist.
(6)	In the past, racism was overt; now it is more covert.
(14)	*Black children need to be shielded from the media and told that "black is beautiful."*
(6)	Blacks need to start teaching their children that whites are not superior to blacks.
(6)	It is hard to instill high self-esteem in black children today because they increasingly belong to single-parent families in

Table 5.6. (*cont.*)

Relevant assumptions	Argument
	which the mother spends much time working outside of the home.
(14)	*Television has become a guide for young black males who have no male role models when growing up. This is a problem because whites control television.*
(6)	Blacks need to unify in order to make progress in society.
(6)	I believe in the "preservation of the race," but I cannot help it that I am "mixed."
(6)	If I looked less black I might feel differently about my racial identity.
(6)	"Mixed" children should learn about both of their cultures.
(6)	You have no control over your racial makeup.
(6)	The race you identify with is more important than your actual racial makeup.
(6)	If you are black and identify with whites then you "got a problem."
(6)	If you have one "drop of [black] blood" you are considered black.
(6)	The only reason a black person would chose to identify with whites is that it is more profitable in America to be white.
(6)	Our parents tried to shield us from the racial tensions they endured when they were growing up.
(6)	Blacks in America still suffer today from "mind slavery."
(6)	Blacks learn about their slavery heritage at an early age because blacks are continually degraded in America, never treated as the equals of whites.
(6)	Children know that whites are advantaged, that "white is better."
(6)	White dolls – Barbies, and so on – teach children that whites are superior to other groups.

Prompt 2
(19:47)

(14)	*Newscasters do not do any research. They are not prepared for impromptu occurrences like the events.*

Table 5.6. (*cont.*)

Relevant assumptions	Argument
(14)	When newscasters are unprepared to cover a story they may slip and use labels like "thugs" that they may not regularly use.
(14)	The label "thugs" would never have been used had the coverage been scripted.
(14)	*Newscasters are not in touch with society.*
(14)(4)	*Newscaster remarks that they could only "assume" that the events had something to do with the King beating verdicts illustrates how estranged newscasters are from society.*
(6)	If white reporters were "in touch" with society they would have had "better sense" than to travel to South Central to cover the events.
(14)(6)	*The true feelings of white reporters were revealed when they used labels like "thugs" to describe event participants.*
(14)	*News coverage of the events did little to educate whites about the social issues that face black America.*
(14)(6)	*It is surprising that the media did not find "ignorant" blacks to interview.*
(14)(6)	*If we had watched more of the media's coverage of the events we would have seen interviews with "ignorant" blacks.*
(14)	*Media coverage of fires and looting did not provide viewers with an understanding of "what was going on."*
(5)(14)	*Media coverage made the events look like a "riot."*
(14)	The KTTV coverage was "better" than some we have seen.
(14)(2)	*The only reason KTTV did not interview a black person who "looked ignorant" is that reporters could not go down to South Central to find one. If reporters had had an opportunity to look for one, they would have.*
(4)	The King beating was "just as bad" as the Denny beating.
(1)	*People who were appalled by the Denny beating failed to consider what Denny may have been saying when driving through the intersection. He may have been saying, "Nigger."*
(6)	If whites could, they would refer to black event participants as "Niggers."
(8)(14)	*It was "stereotypical" of the media to select a minister as the spokesperson for blacks.*

Table 5.6. (*cont.*)

Relevant assumptions	Argument
(8)	*Blacks have other people who can speak for the community other than ministers.*
(8)(14)	*The media could have interviewed a black professor of sociology rather than a minister.*
(14)	*The media did not want to interview blacks who might encourage event participants to continue their activities.*
(8)(14)	*When the media want experts on abortion, they do not interview ministers. Why interview ministers in this case?*
(8)	*The use of ministers as spokespersons for the black community is "stereotypical."*

End

(26:34)

Source: Analysis of verbatim transcript, KEISHA Group.

Table 5.7. *Key arguments emerging from NORTH discussion, in order of emergence.*

Relevant assumptions	Argument
Prompt 1	
(4)	Event participants were upset about the King verdicts.
(1)	*Maybe the events were "wrong to a certain extent," but people had to let out their anger and emotions.*
(1)	*We tried legal ways of protesting in the past to no avail.*
(1)	It is "wrong" to destroy your own community.
(1)	Maybe event participants "chose the wrong way to go about it," but their anger was justified.
(1)	The looting was unnecessary.
(1)	The looting was not the "right" way to protest.
(1)	*Event participants had no other options for protesting other than their actions during the events.*
(1)	The events caused a lot of damage to the city and people will be out of jobs.

Table 5.7. (*cont.*)

Relevant assumptions	Argument
(1)	The events were not "helping anything."
(1)	*The events were necessary to make a point.*
(1)	*Event participants felt like they had nothing to lose.*
(1)	*Event participants owned nothing in their neighborhood. Why not burn it down?*
(1)	It's "wrong" to destroy other people's property. But I understand why people did it.
(4)	Blacks get beaten up by the police all the time. The King incident was just captured on videotape.
(1)	*Event participants should have moved the events to Simi Valley or Beverly Hills.*
(6)	The people in Beverly Hills are the ones who "control all the stuff in Los Angeles" and who are oppressing blacks.
(1)	*Event participants should move the events to the seat of power in Washington, D.C.*
(1)	*Event participants need to attack the power structure, not just individual businesses.*
(6)	No matter how much money blacks have, they are still "Niggers" to most whites.
(6)	Every white male in America with money has the power to oppress us. Looting a store in Beverly Hills will not change anything.
(6)	No white man can oppress me right now.
(6)	If you are looking for a job, a white male employer can decide not to hire you because of your race.
(6)	If I am just a student I am not vulnerable to the oppression of white males.
(6)	A white male professor can be "racist against you" and give you a lower grade than you deserve.
(6)	"There's tons of rich black people." They are still targets of white racism.
	We need to attack the power structure at the highest levels. The LA Four will probably be found guilty.
(2)	If the LA Four are found guilty, events will break out in Beverly Hills because there is nothing left in South Central to destroy.

Table 5.7. (*cont.*)

Relevant assumptions	Argument
	We should be organizing for the LA Four decision now.
(4)	It is "the saddest thing" that anyone can look at the videotape of the King beating and conclude that he deserved it.
(4)	King's civil rights were violated when the officers hit him in the head.
(4)	The officers could have subdued King without resorting to the beating they inflicted upon him.

Prompt 2
(11:10)

	The most important news in the video was the location of the events because you could use the information to stay calm and in your house.
(14)	*The newscaster who called event participants "thugs" may as well have called them "Niggers."*
(12)	The FAME interviews were important because they talked to intelligent black people who were not out in the streets.

Prompt 3
(11:54)

(6)	*The worst thing about the video was that there were no black reporters.*
(14)(6)	*The video failed to show white people who were "making an ass of themselves."*
(14)(6)	*The media did not show any racial tensions.*
(14)(6)	*If a viewer had just arrived in America and turned on the television, he or she would have no idea why blacks were acting the way they were.*

Prompt 4
(12:57)

(6)	KTTV was "bold" to send the Asian reporter to FAME.
(14)	Television reporters get paid handsomely.

Prompt 5
(14:51)

(14)	The news reporters were "okay."

Table 5.7. (*cont.*)

Relevant assumptions	Argument
(14)	*The newscaster who labelled event participants "thugs" should be fired.*
(14)	*The newscaster probably used the term "thugs" because he did not understand the "whole situation."*
(14)	It may have been instinctual for the newscaster to use the term "thugs," but you are not supposed to use "biased" terms like that in journalism.

End
(16:00)

Source: Analysis of verbatim transcript, NORTH Group.

Table 6.1. *Media consumption and previous event-related discussion, white-raced groups (in percentages).*

	White-raced groups				
	MATES (N = 4)	DORM1 (N = 4)	DORM2 (N = 4)	DORM3 (N = 4)	JILL (N = 4)
TV News					
none	25.0	0.0	0.0	25.0	0.0
< 1 hour	0.0	25.0	0.0	0.0	0.0
1 to 3 hours	0.0	0.0	25.0	25.0	0.0
> 3 hours	75.0	25.0	50.0	0.0	50.0
all evening	0.0	50.0	25.0	50.0	50.0
Total	100.0	100.0	100.0	100.0	100.0
LA Times					
never	25.0	0.0	50.0	25.0	0.0
sometimes	50.0	50.0	0.0	50.0	50.0
every day	25.0	50.0	50.0	25.0	50.0
Total	100.0	100.0	100.0	100.0	100.0
Discussion					
never	50.0	75.0	75.0	25.0	25.0
< once/month	25.0	25.0	0.0	25.0	50.0
once/month	25.0	0.0	0.0	50.0	25.0

Table 6.1. (*cont.*)

	White-raced groups				
	MATES (N = 4)	DORM1 (N = 4)	DORM2 (N = 4)	DORM3 (N = 4)	JILL (N = 4)
once/week	0.0	0.0	0.0	0.0	0.0
several/week	0.0	0.0	0.0	0.0	0.0
every day	0.0	0.0	0.0	0.0	0.0
several/day	0.0	0.0	0.0	0.0	0.0
missing	0.0	0.0	25.0	0.0	0.0
Total	100.0	100.0	100.0	100.0	100.0

Source: Post-discussion questionnaire.

Table 6.2. *Key arguments emerging from* MATES *discussion, in order of emergence.*

Relevant assumptions	Argument
	Prompt 1
	The events were an explosion of "pent-up" emotions and frustrations.
(1)	Event participants immediately reacted without thinking.
(1)	The events were "wrong." Violence is not the appropriate response to the verdicts.
(1)	Event participants' actions were a reflection of their "mentality."
(1)(4)	Even though "I didn't agree with the verdict," the way event participants handled the situation was "wrong."
(1)	It is "scary" that people in our society would participate in the events.
(1)	Activity like the events should not happen in the twentieth century.
(1)	Event participants were not thinking.
(1)	Many event participants were taking advantage of the situation.
(1)	A bad economy led participants to take advantage of the situation.

Table 6.2. (*cont.*)

Relevant assumptions	Argument
(1)	Event participants were taking advantage of the situation.
(1)	Violence is never the answer.
(1)	Two wrongs do not make a right.
(1)	Event participants were breaking the law and acting like "idiots."
(1)	The events were neither legal nor "right."
(1)	*Event participants may not have had any other options for addressing the situation.*
(1)	Destruction is never the answer.
	Everyone was confused at the time of the events.
(1)	Event participants did not think.
(1)	You cannot just react to things that anger you.
(14)	The images in the video seemed "detached" and far away.
(14)	The media are always "detached."
(14)	The media are "right there" in some instances, such as in the beating of Denny.
(14)	*The media always select certain images over others.*
(14)	Seeing the events on television is very different from experiencing them up close.
(1)	The rest of the nation thinks that Los Angeles was "behaving like a bunch of pigs" during the events.
	People who lived in Los Angeles during the events were a little bit more "in touch" with what was happening than people living in other places.
(1)	Event participants were destroying the economy.
(6)	The East Coast is racist.
(14)	*The media portrayed the events as a "black thing."*
(6)	*The causes of the events were much more "deep-rooted" than just race.*

Prompt 2
(5:44)

(1)	People should practice restraint.

Table 6.2. (*cont.*)

Relevant assumptions	Argument
	Prompt 3 (5:53)
	Prompt 4 (6:47)
(14)	The video was "pretty accurate" in its portrayal of the events.
(14)	*Media coverage is always negative because it never shows any of the "good things," never concentrates enough on the people who are not "rioting," who want peace.*
(14)	*The people who do the "wrong things" get all of the media attention.*
(14)	*The media only show what they want to be seen.*
(14)	*Aside from the beating of the truck driver, the media failed to report that people were being "hurt by this whole thing."*
(14)	*There was a quick shot here and there of the events effect on average people, but the media tended just to focus on fires.*
(7)	*Many different races were involved in looting, not just blacks.*
(14)	*Media coverage is often full of mistakes. It does not exactly mirror reality.*
(14)	Everyone is biased.
	Prompt 5 (9:43)
(14)	*The media do not always present all of the facts.*
(14)	*It would be hard to "really understand what's going on" during the events unless you were there.*
(14)	The media may not be perfect, but they are our main source of information regarding the events.
(14)	*The media are our main source of information about "what's happening" across the country. But we must realize that media workers select certain images over others.*
(14)	*The media are biased; you cannot believe everything you read and see.*
(14)	*The media may present only one part of the story. There are many other sides.*

Table 6.2. (*cont.*)

Relevant assumptions	Argument
	If we were explaining the events to our children in the "heat of the moment" we probably would not discuss media coverage.
	You would have to discuss media coverage with your children regardless because most of us experienced the events through the media.
(1)	The events were "not the way to solve the problem."
(14)	*The media showed the same images over and over again.*
(14)	The media did not have anything else to show.

Prompt 6
(13:14)

Prompt 7
(13:28)

(1)	The most important news in the video was that the law was being broken.
(1)	The most important news in the video was that people reacted to the situation by stealing and committing acts of violence.
(14)	The media are supposed to be impartial.

Prompt 8
(14:23)

(14)	The reporters did a "good job" describing what was happening during the fire scenes.
(2)(7)	The events did not really affect me.
	People interviewed in the video were "on the margins," they were not event participants.
(2)(7)	The neighbors of the people interviewed in the video did participate in the events.
	The people who went to FAME "needed someone to talk to about it."
(2)(7)	The people at FAME were "in touch" with the events because their neighbors were involved and it was their neighborhoods that were on fire.
(14)	The media could not reach event participants for interviews.
(14)	The interviewers did a "good" job.

Table 6.2. (*cont.*)

Relevant assumptions	Argument
(14)	It was "cool" that the media interviewed a student who was not "militant."
(14)	*The media did not interview event participants.*
(14)	*The media did not report the fact that "everyone's getting hurt." They only focused on "people that are in between," not those at "one extreme or the other extreme."*
(2)	Only a small group of people were involved in the events.
(2)	The events only affected a small geographical area.
(2)(7)	The events did not affect me; once they were over they were "out of my mind."
(2)	The events were not as "monumental" as people think they were.
(2)	The events did not personally affect me and I have a hard time relating to them. Most of society probably feels the same way.
(2)(6)	Most of white society may feel unaffected by the events, but not other segments of society.
(7)(2)	Most of my black friends at UCLA would probably say that the events do not affect them today. So I do not think that only white society felt distant from the events.
(6)	*When people talk about white and black involvement in the events they imply that race was a root cause. The events had more to do with "your social standing."*

Prompt 9
(19:13)

(14)	The events were so "visual" that if there was no television coverage of the events people's perceptions of the events would be different.
(14)	Sometimes your mind is more creative when it is not provided with images.
	The events were "history in the making."
(1)	It is sad that mankind is capable of initiating the events.

Prompt 10
(21:31)

(4)	The events were caused by racial tensions that built up over the Rodney King case.

Table 6.2. (*cont.*)

Relevant assumptions	Argument
	Prompt 11 (22:34)
(6)(1)	The events started as a racial thing before quickly transforming into people taking advantage of the situation.
(6)(1)	The events started as a racial thing before quickly transforming into people taking advantage of the situation. After the first few hours the events were about "crappy economics."
(6)	*Many event participants did not have any "racial problems, they just wanted merchandise. For example, looting took place in Hollywood and there are not many racial tensions there.*
(6)	There may be many people who took advantage of the situation, but it was not totally economic.
(6)	It is hard for me to appreciate the built-up racial tensions felt by event participants because we do not see "the day-to-day situation."
(6)	We do not see racial tensions because we do not discriminate.
(6)	Racial discrimination exists at UCLA.
(6)	I have not seen any racial discrimination at UCLA.
(6)	The events were racially motivated.
(6)	The events were racially motivated, but they eventually became in part an "economic thing."
(6)(2)	The events were a "racial issue" in South Central.
(6)	As a minority I can understand prejudice, but I do not understand "the extent of like what a lot of those people [event participants] feel."
(6)	*Many racists and "hyper-PC" people built the events into more of a "racial thing" than they were.*
(6)	*Race played a role in the events, but not to the extent that some people say.*
(4)	*The King beating verdict was just used as an excuse to participate in the events, to take advantage of the situation.*
(6)	*The events should not be viewed in racial terms because they were initially portrayed as a black-white conflict despite the fact that most of the stores destroyed were Asian owned.*

Table 6.2. (*cont.*)

Relevant assumptions	Argument
(14)	*I only take what I see on television as true when I read it in the newspaper first.*
(6)	*Racial tension was just used as an excuse for participants to loot.*
(2)(7)	An isolated group of "uneducated" people participated in the events.
	You do not know "who's out there" because you were not.
(2)	Due to the low education level in South Central you can make a case that low education contributed to participation in the events.
(2)	Better-educated UCLA students were protesting peacefully, not damaging property.
(2)	Very little event activity occurred in Westwood.
(1)	The events were just an excuse for participants to "go wild."
(1)	*If you were not there you cannot possibly know what motivated participants.*
(1)	There must be underlying factors that make people act like "hoodlums."
(1)	*All of the event participants were not "hoodlums."*
	You must separate the behavior from the person when discussing the actions of event participants.
(1)	Looting is a "hoodlum behavior."
	The protesting at Parker Center was "great" and deserved media coverage.
(1)	I understand why people looted, but that does not make it "right."
(7)	Martin Luther King was blacks' "biggest leader." He protested peacefully. Why don't blacks protest peacefully anymore?
(1)	*Many participants felt that peaceful protesting had failed to work in the past, so they tried violence.*
(1)	Event participants did not really think through their actions logically. They just reacted to the situation.
(1)	*Event participants viewed the events as a way to "speak up."*
(9)	Event participants have some of the lowest voting percentages in the entire country. They need to vote instead of "riot."

Table 6.2. (*cont.*)

Relevant assumptions	Argument
(9)	If every "rioter" voted, they "could turn around elections."
(9)	Lack of voting is the problem.
(9)	*It takes time to change the status quo through voting.*
(1)	Event participants were not thinking rationally; they were "just reacting."
(1)	You cannot excuse what people were doing just because they were not thinking rationally.
(1)	The events were fueled by "emotion and intellect" for only the first few hours.

End
(32:56)

Source: Analysis of verbatim transcript, MATES Group.

Table 6.3. *Average scores on looting, fires and arrests scales, by white-raced group.*

White-raced groups	Scale averages*		
	Loot1/loot2	Fires1/fires2	Arrest1/arrest2
MATES	9.5/9.5	9.5/9.5	2.3/2.5
DORM1	9.5/9.5	10.0/10.0	2.5/2.8
DORM2	7.8/7.8	8.0/7.8	4.8/6.5
DORM3	8.8/9.0	8.8/8.5	2.5/2.0
JILL	7.5/7.8	9.0/8.5	2.3/2.8

Note:
* Possible scale scores ranged from 1 to 10, with 1 indicating that informants felt the looting, fires or arrests were "right," and 10 indicating that informants felt each event-related activity was "wrong."
Source: Pre- and post-discussion surveys.

Table 6.4. *Key arguments emerging from* DORM1 *discussion, in order of emergence.*

Relevant assumptions	Argument
	Prompt 1
	It is obvious from the video that the causes of the events have not been resolved and probably won't be for decades.
	It is hard to explain something to your child that you cannot explain to yourself.
(4)	*It is not clear whether the events were caused by the Rodney King beating, "just outrage" or living in "raggedly conditions."*
(4)	*If we cannot understand exactly what caused the events we will have a hard time explaining them to our children.*
(1)	The use of violence is "totally wrong."
(1)	There are more "constructive" ways of showing your anger than burning property.
(7)	*Just because you see blacks and Latinos on television participating in the events does not mean that you should direct your hate toward these groups. All blacks and Latinos are not like those who participate in the events.*
	You have to teach your children morals at an early age, before they turn twelve years old.
(1)	Most people would say that the events were a "bad thing."
(4)	*It may be hard to explain the events to a child because many would say that the explanation depends on your perspective.*
	Prompt 2 (7:39)
(1)	Regardless of whether you are black, Latino or Asian it is "totally wrong" just to go out and "taunt" people.
(1)	You should not commit violence against others just because you don't agree with their opinions, or don't like their culture or race.
	Prompt 3 (9:15)
(1)	The events consisted of people taking out their aggressions in destructive ways.
(1)	You cannot "sugar coat" what happened by saying simply that event participants are bad and their victims are good. The real world is not so simple.

Table 6.4. (*cont.*)

Relevant assumptions	Argument
	Prompt 4 (10:17)
(12)	The people at FAME were protesting more "rationally" than those who were "venting their frustrations" in the streets.
	Prompt 5 (12:08)
(1)	The most important image in the video was state of "chaos" that was present.
(1)	*Talking might not be sufficient in some cases to "vent your outrage."*
(1)	Talking about the issues might not be sufficient, but burning down buildings is "wrong."
(1)	Taking out your frustrations by participating in the events is "unjustifiable."
(1)	Most event participants did not individually feel outrage. The events became a vent for all the anger that is in society and a "party" for participants.
(14)	*The media facilitated the events by covering them.*
(1)	There are better ways of protesting other than lighting fires.
(1)	It does not seem like event participants accomplished anything.
(12)	The events helped relieve some stress, but getting together and talking about solutions would be more constructive.
	Prompt 6 (16:15)
(14)	*Reporters and interviewees fell into the trap of "throwing out platitudes" rather than real answers.*
(14)	*Reporters oversimplified the events and possible solutions.*
(14)	Reporters oversimplified the events because it was hard to grasp what was happening at the time.
(14)	*Reporters statements were too "generalized" and "assuming."*
(14)	Reporters did not have time to formulate "eloquent statements" due to the nature of the events.

Table 6.4. (*cont.*)

Relevant assumptions	Argument
	Prompt 7 (18:55)
	It is hard to say what should or should not be done to address the events.
(1)	The events at Parker Center were like a "big, primal party."
(7)(6)	*The events were not simply caused by racial tensions because there were not just black and Latino participants.*
(7)	*There were whites and people from other races also participating at Parker Center.*
	Prompt 8 (21:03)
	Prompt 9 (22:25)
(1)	If you burn up your own neighborhood, you will destroy places to shop or find other services.
(1)	It is "wrong to burn things down."
(1)	It is "wrong" to destroy your own neighborhood.
(1)	*Event participants should have moved the events to Beverly Hills if they were outraged.*
	Prompt 10 (25:03)
(4)	We may never totally understand the events because it has been nearly a year and nothing has been resolved.
(1)(4)	Our perceptions of the events will change with time, as we view the events more "objectively."
	End (26:54)

Source: Analysis of verbatim transcript, DORM 1 Group.

Table 6.5. *Key arguments emerging from DORM2 discussion, in order of emergence.*

Relevant assumptions	Argument
	Prompt 1
(1)	It is "totally wrong" in all situations to steal.
(1)	Violence always results in rights violations.
(1)	The events were not a "war scene." We live in an orderly country.
(1)	It is self-evident that the events were "wrong."
(1)	Mobs "engulf" people.
(4)	Social circumstances prompted people to participate in the events.
(14)	*The media made "judgment calls" about the intentions and motivations of event participants.*
(6)	American racism and economic stratification led to the events.
(14)	*The media turned the events into a "freak show." They only showed fires and fighting.*
(14)(2)	*The media focused their coverage on people in South Central.*
(11)	The problems that led to the Watts riots were never addressed and eventually led to the events.
(14)	*The media "forgot" about causes and focused on actions.*
(1)	"Situations" cause people to participate in events like this, but the outcome may not benefit participants.
(1)	Mobs are never a "good thing."
(1)	In our type of society you can "big statements" without violence.
(1)	Event participants should have come together and formed some type of organization to address the problems underlying the events.
(1)	An organized protest would have led to an incredible amount of media coverage.
(1)	The "sick part of me" says that event participants should have moved the events to Beverly Hills.
(1)	Businesses will not want to return to South Central after the events.
(1)	Nothing has been gained from the events because they are going to bring the economy of the whole area "farther down."

Table 6.5. (*cont.*)

Relevant assumptions	Argument
(1)	Event participants should have attacked police stations instead of neighborhood businesses.
(1)	Mobs do not think before they act.

Prompt 2
(9:32)

(12)	The most important news in the video was the reactions to the rally at FAME.
(14)	*The media showed images of the events without providing context.*

Prompt 3
(10:44)

	The interviewee from Occidental College was a "joke" because she claimed to speak for a whole group – the black students on campus.
(8)	The ministers selected for interview by the media did not discuss the underlying causes of the events.
(4)	"Everybody" knew that the events would erupt if the verdict "came out the way it did."

Prompt 4
(13:28)

(14)	*The media showed images of fires over and over again.*
(6)	*Media coverage suggested that if you are white, "you don't belong down here" in South Central.*
(6)	*Everybody is human. You will not be shot for going into South Central just because you are white.*
(6)	*I will not get turned down in a South Central store because I am white.*
(6)	"They" do not get adequate service in stores "up here."
(14)	*Many people do not see the media's racism as problematic. This perspective leads to increased racism in society.*

Prompt 5
(16:15)

(1)	*The events were not "bad," but maybe other constructive tactics could have been tried by event participants.*

Table 6.5. (*cont.*)

Relevant assumptions	Argument
(14)	*The media's repeated showing of fires did not "tell us anything."*
(14)	*The media were just after ratings.*

Prompt 6
(18:40)

(14)	Reporters were doing their best to respond to the situation.
(14)	Biased coverage was not deliberate. The use of stereotypes and generalizations was subconscious. Reporters cannot help "the way they are."
(14)	Everybody has preconceptions about other people.
(14)	*The "bad part" about the media is that you expect newscasters to be more objective than the average person and they are not.*
(1)	Mob action is mob action, whether participants are poor and black or rich and white.
	You cannot put a "good" or "bad" label on people.
(1)	*The events were not "bad."*
(1)	The events were "bad."
(1)	The events were not "good."
(1)	If the events were not "good," then they were "bad."
(1)	*The situation is "never that clear," it is never an either/or situation.*
(1)	*The real situation is never similar to a "simple model."*
(1)	Death is inevitable, but the events did not have to happen.
(2)	If there had been more social programs in South Central, then the events may not have happened.
(1)	The events have not accomplished "anything."
(1)	Mobs are "intrinsically bad."
(1)	*The American Revolution was first defined as a mob activity.*
(1)	The American Revolution was not mob activity because participants had a plan.
(1)	*Event participants may have had a plan also.*
(1)	Police stations, judges and courts would have been attacked during the events if participants had had a plan.

Table 6.5. (*cont.*)

Relevant assumptions	Argument
(1)	*The buildings burned during the events may have been targeted as part of a plan.*
(1)	The events were "indiscriminate" – "everyone was hit."
(1)	*The fact that Korean businesses were "hit more than anyone else" suggests that event participants had a plan.*
(1)	*Koreans were "hit' because they do not keep their money in the community.*
(1)	*Event participants had a plan.*

End

(25:03)

Source: Analysis of verbatim transcript, DORM2 Group.

Table 6.6. *Key arguments emerging from DORM3 discussion, in order of emergence.*

Relevant assumptions	Argument
	Prompt 1
(1)	Violence is not "right;" it was "unnecessary" during the events.
	Everyone in America does not have the same rights that we do; some are poor and oppressed.
(6)	There are many different races in our culture. You must respect other people and their differences.
(1)	You cannot just destroy other people's businesses to show your dissatisfaction with the system.
(1)	It is "totally wrong" to beat up people just because they are a different color.
(1)	*We know some of the facts surrounding the events, but we do not truly know which activities were "wrong" and which were "right."*
(1)	Violence is "wrong."
	Both the police officers and the "rioters" were "wrong."

Table 6.6. (*cont.*)

Relevant assumptions	Argument
(1)	"The rioters in no way were right" for destroying their own communities.
(1)	Violence is never "the answer."
(1)	If event participants had opted to have a peaceful demonstration it would not have gained as much media coverage as the events did.
(1)	*The events were "destructive and sad," but they "made a point."*
(2)(1)	The events fostered "the stereotype" of people in South Central.
(2)(1)	The events represented a "poor trade-off" for participants between making a point and fostering negative stereotypes.
	The statements of the people at FAME suggest that a peaceful demonstration would have gained less media coverage than the events did.

Prompt 2

(6:32)

(4)	Buildings were burned during the events because people were upset about the King beating verdicts.
(4)	Justice "kind of fell apart" when the officers were found not guilty in the King beating case.
(4)	The verdicts were "wrong." Just seeing the tape was evidence enough.
	Some things are "still very wrong" in America.
(4)	*The events were not just caused by the King beating verdicts; they were the result of participants gaining more rights in society without corresponding improvements in their quality of life.*
(11)	The causes of the events are the same as those that led to the Watts riots. Conditions have not changed much since Watts. The King beating verdicts just reinforced this fact.
(14)	*"High key" media coverage of the King beating verdicts prompted blacks to "vent their anger."*
(14)	*Media coverage always leaves out "background information."*
(2)	The events were contained to a relatively small area of Los Angeles.

Table 6.6. (*cont.*)

Relevant assumptions	Argument
	The King beating video does not show the whole incident; it does not show King resisting arrest.
	We should look past what is legal and illegal to what is "right" and "wrong."

Prompt 3
(11:42)

(1)	The most important news in the video was that Los Angeles was in a "state of emergency."

Prompt 4
(12:48)

(1)	The events were not a war because participants were destroying themselves.
(1)	The most frightening image in the video was the one of Denny being pulled from his truck and beaten.
(1)	You would not expect to find the "total anarchy" you saw during the events in America, "the country of Democracy."

Prompt 5
(15:25)

Prompt 6
(18:42)

(14)	Because the video was live, it would be hard to manipulate the images in efforts to support a particular view of the events.
(14)	Seeing the events on television is much more "realistic" than hearing about them on the radio. Both options, however, are "nothing" compared to seeing the events in person.
(14)	*The media failed to stress that people should stay in doors and report any event activity to authorities.*
(14)	*The media failed to stress solutions to the events in their coverage.*
(14)	*The media seemed preoccupied with getting "exciting" footage.*
(14)	*Media coverage of the looting incited more looting.* People would have looted regardless of media coverage.

Table 6.6. (*cont.*)

Relevant assumptions	Argument

	Prompt 7 (21:26)
(14)	*Media coverage of the events led to an increase in the number of people participating in the looting.*
(4)	*People participated in the events primarily because they were upset at a system that was "just not paying off for them." The King beating verdict reinforced this feeling.*
	For every action there is going to be some reaction.
	Conditions were much worse in this society 100 years ago.
	There remains much work to be done in this society.
(14)	*Competition for viewers led the media to continually broadcast images of fires.*
	Prompt 8 (23:44)
(14)	Reporters did not seem "too affected" by the events.
(14)	*The media failed to stress restraint to viewers.*
(14)	*The media were preoccupied with ratings.*
(14)	*The media were "excited" about the events; they did not focus on the "personal" costs of the events.*
(14)	*The media have a responsibility to both report news and give advice.*
(14)	A reporter's job is simply to cover "what's going on." This is why reporters try not to get involved in the stories they cover.
(14)	*Detached coverage is appropriate if you are reporting to people outside the region who are not directly affected by the events. But if you are reporting to people in the immediate area of the events you have a "different responsibility."*
(14)	KTTV coverage was "good."
(14)	If a viewer were not in the area where the events are occurring, he or she would want to be "detached" from them like reporters.
	Prompt 9 (27:24)
(3)	Black officials were not "helping the situation."
	Looters were proud of what they were doing.

Table 6.6. (*cont.*)

Relevant assumptions	Argument
	Prompt 10 (29:19)
(1)	There are other ways of showing anger other than the activities at Parker Center.
	Prompt 11 (29:54)
	The statements of the minister and the woman from Occidental College were "just talk." Neither one did much to help the situation.
(3)	Community leaders took a stand *vis-à-vis* the events too late.
	If you do not talk about the events, you cannot improve the situation.
(14)	*The media did not offer reports about how the situation could be improved.*
	If you do not educate others about the events, then you cannot help improve the situation.
	End (31:41)

Source: Analysis of verbatim transcript, DORM3 Group.

Table 6.7. *Key arguments emerging from JILL discussion, in order of emergence.*

Relevant assumptions	Argument
	Prompt 1
(6)	The events were caused by racial tensions.
(7)	African Americans are not "bad" people. They had reasons for participating in the events.
(6)	The event were caused by race.
(7)	If a white child saw blacks beating up whites and starting fires on television he or she would be scared of blacks.
(7)	A child's perception of black people would depend on his or her interaction with them.
	Children are different today than they were a generation ago. They have more to "worry about" today.
(7)	Blacks felt that they must initiate the events.
	The events and the Rodney King incident were televised so much that it would be impossible to insulate children from them.
(7)(6)	*Even though blacks initiated the events, all blacks are not "evil." Likewise, all whites are not "evil" even though whites "sort of drove the whole racial tensions to where it is now."*
(6)	Your children will mimic your racial attitudes when they are growing up.
(6)	If a white child grows up in a neighborhood with only a few blacks, then he or she would not have formulated an opinion about blacks.
(6)	If a white child grows up in an area with Latino and black gangs he or she may think that all blacks and Latinos are "like this."
(1)	The events were "wrong."
(1)	There were two types of event participants, those who were protesting injustice and those who "cared more about stealing."
(1)	If participants had looted in a "rich area" they could have obtained better merchandise.
(1)	Event participants looted because they were poor.
(1)	Event participants should have moved the events to Simi Valley.

Table 6.7. (*cont.*)

Relevant assumptions	Argument
(1)	Simi Valley is too far away to be targeted.
(1)	The looting "wasn't right."
(1)	Arresting looters was "right" because they were committing crimes.
(1)	It is one thing to be angry and protest, but it is another thing to "just make an excuse just to go out and loot."
(1)	*Event participants have been expressing their opinions for years to no avail.*
(1)	Just because protesting had not been successful in the past does not mean that looting is justified now.
(1)	*Event participants tried legal means of protesting to no avail. Now they decided to try illegal means.*
(1)	It was "right" for them to loot as a means of protesting, but it is also "right" to arrest them because you cannot let crimes go unpunished.
(1)	*If you are being oppressed for years and no will listen, then you must act.*
(7)	If a white child watched news coverage of the events he might develop "bad feelings towards black people."
(4)	The King beating was a "unique" occurrence, not the type of incident that normally happens.
(6)	Race plays a major role in how people react to situations.
	Poor whites might perceive the events differently than more affluent whites.

Prompt 2
(23:39)

(12)	The most meaningful news in the video was that the blacks at FAME were saying that the situation could be addressed peacefully.
(7)	There was much disagreement within the black community regarding how the events should be handled.

Prompt 3
(25:20)

(1)	The most important news in the video concerned the "lawlessness" at the time.

Table 6.7. (*cont.*)

Relevant assumptions	Argument

	Prompt 4 (25:54)
(1)	The worst thing about the video was the images of people being beaten by event participants.
(14)	*When news reporters do not have their lines written for them, "stupid" analogies like the fighter pilot one usually result.*
(14)	*News reporters should just report the news and not their own vulnerability.*
	Prompt 5 (27:43)
	Statements of the people interviewed at FAME revealed the diversity of opinion within the black community regarding the events.
(1)(4)	The King beating verdict was "wrong," but there are better ways to protest.
(7)	The minister interviewed in the video is a good illustration of the fact that not all blacks are "out there on the street."
(6)	*The events were not simply caused by conflicts between blacks and whites.*
(13)	*The minister interviewed in the video was not "dealing in reality" because he rested his hopes for order on a "higher power."*
(3)	Black leaders should have been out among the people in the streets.
(3)	*Event participants would not have listened to black leaders.*
	Prompt 6 (29:59)
(14)	*KTTV reporters were "better than the anchor people" because they were not as "phoney" or "goofy."*
	End (30:52)

Source: Analysis of verbatim transcript, JILL Group.

Table 7.1. *Post-screening (pre-discussion) scale averages by group race.*

Race	Scale avg(stddv)		
(n)	Loot1	Fires1	Arrest1
Latino	8.3	8.7	3.7
(20)	(2.0)	(1.8)	(2.4)
Black	5.7	7.8	5.8
(25)	(2.2)	(2.4)	(2.5)
White	8.6	9.1	2.9
(20)	(1.4)	(1.1)	(1.7)

Source: Pre-discussion questionnaire.

Table 7.2. *Use of key pronouns in discussion of KTTV text, by group and race.*

	Uses per minute						
	We	Us	Our	They	Them	Their	Time
Latino-raced groups							
YOUTH	0.97	0.17	0.28	2.21	0.40	0.14	29:10
FAMILY	1.50	0.07	0.07	4.93	0.97	0.70	30:08
LATINA	2.07	0.48	0.24	5.41	0.21	0.41	29:30
MARIA (UCLA)	0.73	0.18	0.00	7.14	0.73	0.50	22:00
JULIO (UCLA)	1.67	0.05	0.38	2.33	0.67	0.33	21:20
Avg.		1.77			5.42		
Black-raced groups							
GANG	2.67	0.44	0.67	5.67	1.44	0.00	9:45
CHURCH	2.42	0.75	0.25	9.00	0.75	1.42	12:02
CORNER	1.26	0.22	0.17	15.67	1.87	0.00	23:27
KEISHA (UCLA)	1.50	0.31	0.15	5.15	0.85	0.54	26:34
NORTH (UCLA)	1.63	0.19	0.06	5.50	0.63	0.44	16:00
Avg.		2.54			9.79		

Table 7.2. (*cont.*)

	We	Us	Our	They	Them	Their	Time
				Uses per minute			
White-raced groups							
MATES (UCLA)	1.06	0.22	0.25	3.25	0.53	0.50	32:56
DORM1 (UCLA)	1.12	0.08	0.19	0.85	0.19	0.31	26:54
DORM2 (UCLA)	1.76	0.12	0.16	4.92	0.60	0.32	25:03
DORM3 (UCLA)	1.00	0.00	0.26	3.26	0.98	0.42	31:41
JILL (UCLA)	.67	0.10	0.23	2.53	0.80	0.57	30:52
Avg.		1.44			4.01		

Source: Computer search of verbatim transcripts.

Table 7.3. *"Solidarity" versus "distance" pronoun usage, by referent, group and race.*

Referents	YOUTH	FAMILY	LATINA	MARIA	JULIO	Total
			Number of solidarity pronouns ("we/us/our")			
			Latino-raced groups			
Blacks	0	0	0	0	0	0
Whites	0	0	0	0	0	0
Latinos	2	7	2	0	0	11
Americans	2	0	0	0	10	12
This group	2	12	14	13	19	60
Participants	0	0	0	0	0	0
People in SC	7	14	27	0	0	48

Table 7.3. (*cont.*)

	Number of solidarity pronouns ("we/us/our")					
	Black-raced groups					
Referents	GANG	CHURCH	CORNER	KEISHA	NORTH	Total
Blacks	13	33	15	33	7	101
Whites	0	0	0	0	0	0
Latinos	0	0	0	0	0	0
Americans	0	0	0	0	0	0
this group	3	0	2	4	14	23
participants	0	0	8	3	0	11
people in SC	0	0	2	1	0	3

	White-raced groups					
Referents	MATES	DORM1	DORM2	DORM3	JILL	Total
blacks	0	0	0	0	0	0
whites	0	0	0	0	0	0
Latinos	0	0	0	0	0	0
Americans	1	0	1	3	0	5
this group	20	17	6	2	10	55
participants	0	0	0	0	0	0
people in SC	0	0	0	0	0	0

	Number of distance pronouns ("they/them/their")					
	Latino-raced groups					
Referents	YOUTH	FAMILY	LATINA	MARIA	JULIO	Total
blacks	1	4	1	0	0	6
whites	0	0	0	0	0	3
Latinos	0	6	4	0	0	10
Asians	0	14	0	0	0	14
participants	24	35	26	107	12	204
media	15	38	84	18	8	163
police	15	2	1	5	0	23
authorities/ officials	6	2	4	23	2	37
system	0	0	0	0	0	0
people in SC	0	0	2	0	0	2

Table 7.3. (*cont.*)

	Number of distance pronouns ("they/them/their")					
	Black-raced groups					
Referents	GANG	CHURCH	CORNER	KEISHA	NORTH	Total
blacks	0	1	1	3	7	12
whites	1	20	0	9	5	35
Latinos	0	0	4	0	0	4
Asians	6	0	0	0	0	6
participants	21	12	76	4	20	133
media	7	46	51	37	32	173
police	1	8	15	0	6	30
authorities/ officials	0	0	2	9	0	11
system	0	4	5	3	0	12
people in SC	0	0	1	0	0	1

	White-raced groups					
Referents	MATES	DORM1	DORM2	DORM3	JILL	Total
blacks	1	0	4	7	21	33
whites	0	0	0	0	1	1
Latinos	0	0	0	0	0	0
Asians	0	0	1	0	0	1
participants	32	8	40	37	35	152
media	34	4	56	42	26	162
police	0	0	0	2	1	3
authorities/ officials	0	0	5	2	3	10
system	0	0	0	0	0	0
people in SC	0	0	1	0	0	1

Source: Computer analysis of verbatim transcript.

Table 7.4. *Results for regressions of support for event-related looting, fires and arrests on race and income (standard errors in parentheses, N=60).*

	Model 1 (loot1)	Model 2 (fires1)	Model 3 (arrests1)
Unstandardized coefficients			
Income	0.00 (0.00)	0.00 (0.00)	0.00 (0.00)
Black	−3.25** (0.79)	−1.63* (0.78)	3.43** (0.87)
Latino	−0.27 (0.87)	−0.20 (0.85)	1.65 (0.95)
Intercept	8.22	9.24	2.05
r-square	0.30	0.09	0.23
Adjusted r-square	0.26	0.04	0.18
Standard error of estimate	2.40	2.35	2.63
Standardized coefficients			
Income	0.03	−0.07	0.12
Black	−0.55**	−0.32*	0.56**
Latino	−0.04	−0.04	0.25

Notes:
* $p < 0.05$
** $p < 0.01$
Source: Pre- and post-discussion questionnaires.

Table 7.5. *Results for regressions of support for event-related looting, fires and arrests on race and gender (standard errors in parentheses, N=65).*

	Model 4 (loot1)	Model 5 (fires1)	Model 6 (arrests1)
Unstandardized coefficients			
Black	−3.13**	−1.26	2.94**
	(0.72)	(0.69)	(0.76)
Latino	−0.20	0.10	0.80
	(0.75)	(0.72)	(0.80)
Female	0.24	0.03	1.11
	(0.62)	(0.59)	(0.65)
Intercept			
r-square	0.27	0.07	0.26
Adjusted r-square	0.24	0.02	0.23
Standard error of estimate	2.40	2.31	2.55
Standardized coefficients			
Black	−0.54**	−0.26	0.48**
Latino	−0.03	0.02	0.12
Female	0.04	0.01	0.19

Notes:
* $p < 0.05$
** $p < 0.01$
Source: Pre- and post-discussion questionnaires.

Table 7.6. *Viewing activity, by group and race.*

	Viewing mode**	"Thugs"	"Drenched in blood"	News summary
		Viewing activity		
Latino-raced groups				
YOUTH	passive	—	—	gasp
FAMILY	animated	—	head shake	talk
LATINA	animated	talk	head shake	talk
MARIA (UCLA)	passive	—	—	talk
JULIO (UCLA)	animated	—	head shake	talk
Black-raced groups				
GANG	animated	talk/ laugh	—	laugh
CHURCH	animated	—	glances exchanged	talk
CORNER	animated	—	talk	talk
KEISHA (UCLA)	animated	talk	—	talk
NORTH* (UCLA)	animated	talk	?	talk
White-raced groups				
MATES (UCLA)	passive	—	—	talk
DORM1 (UCLA)	passive	—	—	—
DORM2 (UCLA)	passive	—	—	—
DORM3 (UCLA)	passive	—	—	—
JILL (UCLA)	passive	—	—	—

Notes:
 * Due to equipment malfunction, data for this group are based on screening notes.
 ** $p = 0.02$ (one-tailed); Fisher Exact Probability Test; whites versus non-whites.
Source: Analysis of screening videotapes.

Table 7.7. *Cases of attitude polarization, by group, race and scale.**

	Scale averages		
	Loot1/loot2	Fires1/fires2	Arrest1/arrest2
Latino-raced groups			
YOUTH	*9.3/10.0*	*10.0/10.0*	2.7/2.7
FAMILY	*9.8/10.0*	*10.0/10.0*	*1.0/1.0*
LATINA	8.8/8.8	8.5/8.0	6.3/5.5
MARIA	*7.3/7.8*	8.8/8.8	5.3/5.5
JULIO	*6.3/8.0*	*6.0/6.5*	3.0/4.1
Black-raced groups			
GANG	5.8/6.0	8.3/6.5	4.3/6.0
CHURCH	*8.8/9.4*	*8.6/9.1*	5.0/8.6
CORNER	4.0/5.2	9.0/9.7	5.7/6.0
KEISHA	4.6/5.0	5.2/6.0	7.4/8.6
NORTH	5.2/5.4	7.8/7.8	6.4/7.0
White-raced groups			
MATES	9.5/9.5	9.5/9.5	2.3/2.5
DORM1	9.5/9.5	*10.0/10.0*	2.5/2.8
DORM2	7.8/7.8	8.0/7.8	4.8/6.5
DORM3	*8.8/9.0*	8.8/8.5	*2.5/2.0*
JILL	*7.5/7.8*	9.0/8.5	2.3/2.8

Note:
* Italicized entries denote cases of polarization.
Source: Pre- and post-discussion questionnaires.

Table 7.8. *Cases of attitude convergence, by group, race and scale.* *

	Scale avg(stddy)		
	Loot1/loot2	Fires1/fires2	Arrest1/arrest2
Latino-raced groups			
YOUTH	*9.3/10.0*	*10.0/10.0*	2.7/2.7
FAMILY	*9.8/10.0*	*10.0/10.0*	*1.0/1.0*
LATINA (n = 4)	8.8/8.8	8.5/8.0	6.3/5.5 (3.8/1.7)**
MARIA	*7.3/7.8*	8.8/8.8	5.3/5.5
JULIO	*6.3/8.0*	6.0/6.5	3.0/4.1
Black-raced groups			
GANG	5.8/6.0	8.3/6.5	4.3/6.0
CHURCH	*8.8/9.4*	*8.6/9.1*	5.0/8.6
CORNER	4.0/5.2	*9.0/9.7*	5.7/6.0
KEISHA	4.6/5.0	5.2/6.0	*7.4/8.6*
NORTH (n = 5)	5.2/5.4 (3.2/2.3)**	7.8/7.8	*6.4/7.0*
White-raced groups			
MATES	9.5/9.5	9.5/9.5	2.3/2.5
DORM1	9.5/9.5	*10.0/10.0*	2.5/2.8
DORM2 (n = 4)	7.8/7.8	8.0/7.8	4.8/6.5 (3.3/2.1)**
DORM3	*8.8/9.0*	8.8/8.5	*2.5/2.0*
JILL	*7.5/7.8*	9.0/8.5	2.3/2.8

Note:
   * Italicized entries denote cases of polarization.
   ** Cases of attitude convergence.
Source: Pre- and post-discussion questionnaires.

Table 7.9. *Scale outcomes correctly predicted by polarization hypotheses, by race, group and scale.***

	Scale averages		
	Loot1/loot2	Fires1/fires2	Arrest1/arrest2
Latino-raced groups			
YOUTH	*9.3/10.0*	*10.0/10.0*	*2.7/2.7*
FAMILY	*9.8/10.0*	*10.0/10.0*	*1.0/1.0*
LATINA	*8.8/8.8*	8.5/8.0	6.3/5.5
MARIA	7.3/7.8	8.8/8.8	5.3/5.5
JULIO	6.3/8.0	6.0/6.5	*3.0/4.1*
Black-raced groups			
GANG	5.8/6.0	*8.3/6.5*	4.3/6.0
CHURCH	8.8/9.4	8.6/9.1	*5.0/8.6*
CORNER	4.0/5.2	9.0/9.7	*5.7/6.0*
KEISHA	4.6/5.0	*5.2/6.0*	7.4/8.6
NORTH	5.2/5.4	*7.8/7.8*	6.4/7.0
White-raced groups			
MATES	*9.5/9.5*	*9.5/9.5*	*2.3/2.5*
DORM1	*9.5/9.5*	*10.0/10.0*	*2.5/2.8*
DORM2	7.8/7.8	*8.0/7.8*	4.8/6.5
DORM3	*8.8/9.0*	*8.8/8.5*	*2.5/2.0*
JILL	7.5/7.8	*9.0/8.5*	*2.3/2.8*

Notes:
* Indicates cases where pre-discussion scores all fall on the same side of the scale.
** Italicized scale averages denote cases correctly predicted by polarization hypotheses.
Source: Pre- and post-discussion questionnaires.

Table 7.10. *Group racial composition, discussion dynamics and polarization/convergence outcomes, by race and group.*

	Racial make-up*	Discuss dynamic	Polarization/convergence (n = 3)
Latino-raced groups			
YOUTH	Lat (3)	unity	66.7%
FAMILY	Lat (5)	unity	100.0%
LATINA	Lat (4)	unity/ N vs B	33.3%
MARIA (UCLA)	Lat (3) wht (1)	M v N/JS	33.3%
JULIO (UCLA)	Lat (1) wht (3)	Lat v wht	66.7%
Black-raced groups			
GANG	blk (2) Lat (2)	blk v Lat	0.0%
CHURCH	blk (5)	unity	66.7%
CORNER	blk (6)	unity/ K vs D	33.3%
KEISHA (UCLA)	blk (5)	unity	33.3%
NORTH (UCLA)	blk (4) Mly (1)	unity	66.7%
White-raced groups			
MATES (UCLA)	wht (3) Tai (1)	J vs E/M	0.0%
DORM1 (UCLA)	Kor (2) Fil (1) wht (1)	unity	33.3%
DORM2 (UCLA)	wht (3) Lat (1) wht	Lat v wht	33.3%
DORM3 (UCLA)	wht (2) Chi (2)	unity	66.7%
JILL (UCLA)	wht (4)	M vs L/M	33.3%

Notes:

* wht = white; blk = black; Lat = Latino; Fil = Filipino; Tai = Taiwanese; Kor = Korean; Mly = Malaysian.

Source: Pre- and post-discussions questionnaires, analysis of verbatim transcripts and videotape.

Table 8.1. *Group SES, decoding mode and rate of opposition toward KTTV textual assumptions, by group and race.*

	SES	Discuss mode	Number of oppositional arguments/min
Latino-raced groups			
YOUTH	Low	referential	0.14 (4/29:10)
FAMILY	Low	referential	0.10 (3/30:08)
LATINA	Low	referential	1.02 (31/29:30)
MARIA (UCLA)	High	referential	0.73 (16/22:00)
JULIO (UCLA)	High	referential	1.03 (22/21:20)
Avg.			0.58 (76/132:08)
Black-raced groups			
GANG	Low	referential	1.44 (14/9:45)
CHURCH	High	metalinguistic	1.39 (17/12:02)
CORNER	Low	referential	0.68 (16/23:27)
KEISHA (UCLA)	High	referential/ metalinguistic	0.98 (26/26:34)
NORTH (UCLA)	High	referential	1.00 (16/16:00)
Avg.			1.01 (89/87:48)
White-raced groups			
MATES (UCLA)	High	referential/ metalinguistic	0.97 (32/32:56)
DORM 1 (UCLA)	High	referential	0.41 (11/26:54)
DORM 2 (UCLA)	High	referential/ metalinguistic	0.92 (23/25:03)
DORM 3 (UCLA)	High	referential	0.57 (18/31:41)
JILL (UCLA)	High	referential	0.32 (10/30:52)
Avg.			0.64 (94/147:03)

Source: Transcripts and post-discussion questionnaires.

Table 8.2. *Number of oppositional arguments, by group, race and assumption.*

Groups	Assumptions														TOT
	1	2	3	4	5	6	7	8	9	10	11	12	13	14	TOT
YOUTH						1				1				2	4
FAMILY								1						2	3
LATINA	4													27	31
MARIA	12													4	16
JULIO	14			1			1	1						5	22
Lat tot.	30			1		1	1	2		1				40	76
percent	40			1		1	1	3		1				53	100
GANG	4			6	1		1							2	14
CHURCH	1	1					1				2			12	17
CORNER	11		1	1										3	16
KEISHA	4			1	2		1	5						13	26
NORTH	9					1								6	16
Blk tot.	29	1	1	8	3	1	3	5			2			36	89
percent	33	1	1	9	3	1	3	6			2			40	99*
MATES	5			1		7	1		1					17	32
DORM1	2			3			2							4	11
DORM2	10					3								10	23
DORM3	2			2										14	18
JILL	3		1			1	1						1	3	10
Wht tot.	22		1	6		11	4		1				1	48	94
percent	23		1	6		12	4		1				1	51	99*
Gr. total	81	1	2	15	3	13	8	7	1	1	2		1	124	259
percent	31	0	1	6	1	5	3	3	0	0	1		0	48	99*

Note:
* Numbers do not add to 100 due to rounding error.
Source: Transcript of group discussions.

Table 8.3. *Usage of key terms, by group and race.*

	Latino-raced groups					
Terms	YOUTH	FAMILY	LATINA	MARIA	JULIO	Tot.
Riot(ing)(ers)	9	15	4	6	4	38
Uprising	0	0	0	0	0	0
Rebell(ion)(ing)	0	0	0	0	1	1
Rodney King	6	1	0	0	2	9
Verdict(s)	0	2	2	2	1	7
Thugs	0	0	13	0	0	13
Loot(er)(ing)	5	2	6	4	2	19

	Black-raced groups					
Terms	GANG	CHURCH	CORNER	KEISHA	NORTH	Tot.
Riot(ing)(ers)	10	4	9	2	3	28
Uprising	0	1	0	0	0	1
Rebell(ion)(ing)	0	0	0	5	0	5
Rodney King	9	6	6	1	1	23
Verdict(s)	0	0	0	5	6	11
Thugs	0	0	0	4	5	9
Loot(er)(ing)	6	3	10	3	3	25

	White-raced groups					
Terms	MATES	DORM1	DORM2	DORM3	JILL	Tot.
Riot(ing)(ers)	13	6	10	17	11	57
Uprising	0	0	0	0	0	0
Rebell(ion)(ing)	0	0	0	0	0	0
Rodney King	5	4	0	10	2	21
Verdict(s)	6	0	3	6	2	14
Loot(er)(ing)	12	1	0	7	17	37

Source: Computer analysis of verbatim transcripts.

Table 8.4. *Pre- and Post-discussion scale averages by group race.*

Race (n)	Scale avg.		
	loot	fires	arrest
Latino-raced (20)	8.3/8.9	8.7/8.7	3.7/3.8
Black-raced (25)	5.7/6.2	7.8/7.8	5.8/7.2
White-raced (20)	8.6/8.7	9.1/8.9	2.9/3.3

Source: Pre- and post-discussion questionnaires.

Notes

1 Introduction

1 Extracted from CNN coverage of President George Bush's address to the nation, Friday, May 1, 1992.

2 Horne (1995) presents a comprehensive analysis of the 1965 "riots" that erupted in the predominantly black Los Angeles neighborhood of Watts. Like the 1992 events, these events involved massive destruction: at least 34 people died, 1,000 or so were injured, and property damage from fire and "looting" was estimated at about $200 million. Moreover, these events were similarly connected to police brutality against blacks. But as Horne (1995) notes, there were also a number of other pressing issues – economic, cultural, and political – fueling the events. Indeed, there was much disagreement at the time over the nature of the events – although the label of "riots" seems to have become dominant over the years, some observers described the events as a "revolt," a "virtual civil insurrection," or "a veritable revolutionary movement" (pp. 36–37). In any case, the events marked a watershed in United States race relations, casting a heavy shadow on them ever since. For in-depth personal accounts of the 1965 events, see Bullock (1969).

3 Many observers attributed the outbreak of the events and the truce between the Crips and Bloods – two warring black gangs from South Central Los Angeles – to a climax in disenfranchisement among residents of the predominantly black and Latino community (see Hazen 1992). The combination of the Rodney King incident, worsening socio-economic conditions and two recent court decisions (as well as several earlier cases), many contended, nakedly exposed (in case some had forgotten or had not been convinced) the unjust nature of the system (see Johnson et al. 1992).

There had been a history of tensions between black residents and Korean business owners in South Central Los Angeles. In the same month that a camera videotaped Rodney King's beating by four white police officers, another camera captured the killing of Latasha Harlins, a 15-year-old black girl, by Soon Ja Du, a Korean liquor store merchant. Soon Ja Du had accused Harlins of attempting to steal a bottle of orange juice. After a brief struggle between the two, Harlins placed the bottle on the counter and turned to leave. Clearly visible on the store's security videotape, Soon Ja Du pulled out a handgun and shot Harlins in the back of the head.

Nine months later, a white superior court judge, Joyce Karlin, sentenced Soon Ja Du to five years probation and *no* jail time for the shooting. Meanwhile, in the Los Angeles suburb of Glendale – just five days after Soon Ja Du's sentencing – Brendan Sheen was sentenced to 30 days in jail for repeatedly kicking his dog. As the *Los Angeles Times* put it, "News accounts of Sheen's sentencing were not prominent, but in black communities the word filtered around" (Coffey 1992, p. 41). That is, many black observers wondered whether and to what degree the system valued black life.

4 The Simi Valley jury contained *no* black members. It was composed of ten whites, one Latino and one Asian American member (Berry 1994).

5 This proposition will be examined in detail in chapter 3, when I analyze one news operation's presentation of the events.

6 Here, I refer to "power" in the generic sense that Weber (1946) understood it: "the chance of a man or a number of men to realize their own will in a communal action even against the resistance of others who are participating in the action" (p. 180).

7 In the discussion below, what I identify as "Critical Media Studies" and the "Sociology of Race" should be understood as "ideal types" (Gerth and Mills 1958). I admittedly stereotype both traditions in order to draw attention to popular perceptions/criticisms of each tradition from within and from the position of the other. These perceptions/criticisms, I propose, help explain the unfortunate legacy described in the story.

8 Jhally and Lewis (1992) – an empirical study of race, class, audience reception and "The Cosby Show" – is a notable exception to this observation. But in 1992, the year this study was published, *Communications Abstracts* listed just ten journal articles on media *and* race out of a total of 1500 articles (less than 1 percent). Furthermore, only four of these articles even remotely resembled works in the Critical Media Studies tradition. And of these four articles, *none* was an empirical analysis of audience reception.

9 See McQuail (1987), Schroeder (1987), Carragee (1990) and Press (1992) for cogent accounts of Marxism's influence in the development of Critical Media Studies.

10 For detailed discussions and/or illustrations of orthodox Marxism's treatments of race, see Cox (1970), Tucker (1972), Banton (1977), Rex (1987) and Omi and Winant (1994).

11 From January 1974 to August 1993, for example, *Sociofile* listed just 189 journal articles on race *and* media out of a total of 9,668 articles mentioning "race," and 4,488 mentioning "media." Furthermore, only 20 of these articles were based on empirical studies (about one article per year). In short, the interplay of race and media has been marginalized as an object of study in mainstream sociology; few

studies have conceptualized media as an integral component of the process by which racial subjectivity is constructed and reproduced; fewer studies still have attempted to explore this interaction empirically.

12 Prager (1982) and Omi and Winant (1986, 1994) offer convincing accounts of the dynamic nature of racial meanings.

13 Inspired by the rhetoric of mass marketing and the pleasures of consumer culture, American social scientists in the 1940s began to question critical characterizations of mass media as all-powerful. After all, the implications of this view contradicted the age-old "American" ideal of democracy and fledgling notions of pluralism. What was needed, it seemed, was solid research (read *positivist* and *quantitative*) that could empirically test many of the assumptions concerning media effects that critical approaches had taken for granted over the years.

Lazarsfeld *et al.* (1965) obliged this need with their study of the media and voting behavior in the 1940 presidential campaign. Although conducted before the widespread introduction of television, the study's key finding – that mass communications are mediated by personal contacts in a "two-step flow" of communication – has been influential in American audience conceptualizations ever since (Gitlin 1978; Wright 1975). This pioneering study spawned the notably American "effects" tradition, producing a proliferation of empirical studies over the years concerned with quantifying specific media effects on specific audiences.

Accordingly, the "dominant paradigm" in American mass media research, Gitlin (1978) points out, assumes that the influence of mass media is paralleled by the influence of important others, that it is refracted through the personal environment of the ultimate consumer. Furthermore, because media messages are so refracted, the logic suggests, these messages at best merely help reinforce pre-existing beliefs and attitudes (e.g., Klapper 1960). In other words, the "classic" American research tradition depicted audience members as more powerful than media in the audience–media encounter. While this approach has spawned some noteworthy findings at the micro level concerning short-term media effects (i.e., effects that are meaningful to the researcher), it generally ignores long-term effects (Lowery and DeFleur 1983) and the meanings audience members attribute to their respective media experiences (Morley 1980). Furthermore, this tradition suffers from the lack of a theoretical framework that might link micro-level findings to macro-level issues such as "race" (Gitlin 1978; Morley 1980).

"Uses and gratifications" research (Rubin 1986) grew out of the dominant paradigm, a response to this tradition's lack of a "relevant theory of social and psychological needs" (Blumler and Katz 1974). This research, consonant with the dominant paradigm, conceptualizes audience members as active participants in the communication process, but assumes that no message can have an effect if audience members do not have a use for it. Accordingly, Blumler and Katz (1974) begin by focusing on the micro-level necessities addressed by mass media. That is, the central goal of these types of analyses is understanding how individual needs prompt media use and how these needs intervene between media messages and effects. Blumler and Katz (1974, p. 23) identify several such needs, including diversion, personal relations, personal identity and surveillance. But where do these needs come from? What are their social determinants? A behavioralist frame leaves these issues largely unexplored.

14 I also suspect that mainstream sociology may have marginalized media studies simply because it was perceived to be too difficult an enterprise. That is, by the canons of the positivist frame that continues to guide most mainstream work (Jankowski and Wester 1991), long term effects cannot be established due to the multitude of variables any given study could not control for (Schroeder 1987). Furthermore, analyses of meaning and interpretation immensely complicate efforts to achieve accepted levels of validity and reliability.

15 How we introduce sociology to undergraduates, it seems, reveals much about the fields that dominate the discipline. Of the nine prominent textbooks I reviewed recently for use in an introductory course, *all* had sections devoted to social institutions (e.g., "Marriage and family," "Education," "Religion," "Health and medicine," "The economic order," "The political order," "Science," and so on). But in *none* of the texts did these sections include chapters devoted solely to mass media. Only one of the texts (Kornblum 1994) considered mass media an important enough social institution to even warrant *mention* in a chapter title ("Education and Communications Media"). All of the texts, of course, included discussions of mass media, but these discussions were typically quite superficial and tended to be scattered amongst other material throughout the texts.

16 I take up the concept of "text" in more detail in chapter 2. For now, I will define "text" as simply a bounded set of written words, images, and/or audio composed by someone to be communicated to someone else.

17 Alarmed by the power of the great nation-state propaganda campaigns surrounding the First World War, theorists in the 1920s began to conceptualize society in the electronic-media age as a "mass" of atomized individuals (Gitlin 1978; Lowery and DeFleur 1983; McQuail 1987). The role that traditional norms and values played in social solidarity, it was believed, had begun to decline as increases in social differentiation and the division of labor led to an ever more bureaucratized and impersonal society. Weakened by anomie, the mass society was seen as fertile ground for media manipulation (Lowery and DeFleur 1983).

Accordingly, the theorists of the Frankfurt School believed that media messages – in "hypodermic" fashion – were injected directly into the minds of the masses for the purposes of persuasion (Adorno 1991a, 1991b; Gitlin 1978). Heavily influenced by their experiences in Hitler's Germany, these theorists viewed the audience, society at-large, as a powerless mass manipulated by the whims of the "power elite."

Subsequent conceptualizations of media and audience based on this model (e.g., Postman 1985; Parenti 1986; Herman and Chomsky 1988; Ewen and Ewen

1992) tend to be historically and textually based. While these studies are successful in linking media to broader socio-cultural processes, they generally fail to isolate the audience as an object of empirical analysis.

18 Some hard-line critical scholars question whether many of these projects are really just throwbacks to dominant paradigm views of the all-powerful audience (Gitlin 1990).

Fiske (1987a) is a critical scholar whose work is particularly suspect in this regard. His notion of "semiotic democracy" argues that television's accessibility to society at large – its commercial success – depends on its delegation of meanings and pleasures to its viewers. In other words, similar to uses and gratifications theorists (Blumler and Katz 1974), Fiske seems to argue that viewers are able to freely choose between the potential meanings emerging from television programs in order to meet their most salient needs and desires. If viewers were not able to do this, Fiske's logic continues, they would have little use for a large number of televised programs – i.e., this material would be inaccessible – and the television medium could not be as profitable as it obviously is. But while Fiske is undoubtedly correct that viewers are able to actively produce meanings from the media programs they consume, it is unlikely that this activity takes place in an environment of perfect freedom. As many scholars have pointed out, the range of meanings that may be potentially produced from a program is constrained by the domain of privileged meanings embedded in it (Hall 1973; Morley 1974, 1980, 1992). Morley (1993) offers a concise discussion of the "pitfalls" of "active audience theory."

19 Incorporating many of the insights of "mainstream" Critical Media Studies, and adopting empirical research techniques often associated with the dominant paradigm, British cultural studies in the late 1960s and early 1970s re-conceptualized the relation between media and audience. The Birmingham School's brand of cultural studies (e.g., Hall 1973; Morley 1974; 1980) accepted the critical notion that media messages ultimately served the interests of societal hegemony, but rejected the idea that these messages were injected directly into the minds of the masses. Echoing a key tenet of the dominant paradigm, these theorists treated audience members as active participants in the communication process. Media messages, according to this approach, were polysemic *texts*, tapestries of encoded meanings from which audience members make "dominant," "negotiated," or "oppositional" decodings in accordance with the exigencies of their personal environments (Hall 1973; Morley 1974; 1980). In short, the outcome of the media experience was conceptualized as a never-ending struggle between viewers and texts.

Against this theoretical backdrop, Morley (1980) presents an "audience ethnography (cf. Morley 1974)" that sought to link differential decodings of a popular British public affairs program to differences in socio-economic status among viewers. Thus he screened an episode of *Nationwide* for twenty-nine different groups – including black college students, factory line workers, and business executives – that he later questioned in focus group interviews. He had assumed that there would be more uniformity in decoding the *Nationwide* text within groups than across them. Morley's findings largely supported this assumption, although he discovered that key sociological categories such as race, class or gender – in and of themselves – were not the best predictors of group decoding strategies. What was more important, he surmised, was the "influence of the discourses and institutions in which [audience members] are situated" (p. 137). Left unanalyzed by Morley was just *how* these situational conditions contribute to differential decoding behaviors. That is, Morley failed to explore how social interaction gives meaning to these conditions and subsequent decodings.

20 By "positivism," I mean objectivist notions of social reality that model research methods after those found in the natural sciences. Jankowski and Wester (1991) provide a succinct overview of the evolution of dominant methods in the social sciences, from 1890 to the present.

21 Omi and Winant (1994) insightfully categorize major sociological works on race into three major paradigms: ethnicity, class and nation. By examining influential works in the literature, the scholars demonstrate that the ethnicity paradigm has been dominant throughout most of this century. Only during the 1960s, on the heels of turbulent social movements, the analysis reveals, did the class and nation paradigms seriously challenge the hegemonic power of the ethnicity paradigm. Many recent works illustrate the continuing influence of the ethnicity paradigm on social scientific conceptualizations of race (e.g., see Lieberson 1980; Espiritu 1992).

22 The affinity between these understandings and how most sociological studies conceptualize race (i.e., in static terms) seems to be no mere coincidence. Many observers have accused social scientists of shying away from questions that cannot be readily quantified (i.e., Schroeder 1987) or of confusing "whatever is being studied with the set of methods suggested for its study" (Mills 1959, p. 51).

23 Several media scholars have described what appears to be signs of a convergence between social scientific and critical approaches to the field (Jensen 1991; Jankowski and Wester 1991; Livingstone 1993). But by all accounts, this convergence is far from being realized to the degree that it might.

24 I specify "British" Cultural Studies for the following reason: Cultural Studies as commonly practiced today in the United States tends to either privilege textual analysis at the expense of empirical analysis (Hall 1992) or downplay issues of political economy in the name of affirming audience resistance (Budd *et al.* 1990).

25 A debate continues to rage in the Critical Media Studies literature concerning "pseudo" versus "real" resistance. This debate will be explored in chapter 2, as the theoretical framework for analysis is developed.

26 Informants racially identified themselves.

2 Media, race and resistance

1 In their prologue, for example, Ewen and Ewen (1992) describe a rather illuminating series of hypothetical encounters that demonstrate how various media

reference one another, how their boundaries ultimately blend together to shape actors' perceptions of social reality.

2 See Newcomb (1984), Fiske (1987), Mellencamp (1990) and Morley (1992) for lucid arguments concerning the elusive boundaries of texts.

3 These questions, of course, entail coming to terms with the power of media to impose a particular view of reality on audiences versus the tendency/ability of audience members to resist, to embrace alternative understandings.

4 By "ideology," I simply mean background assumptions, commonsense definitions, and taken-for-granted justifications that *generally* serve to support and reproduce a given status quo. This definition is not meant to imply, as Althusser (1971) suggests, that ideology's positioning of historical subjects is all-encompassing or inescapable.

5 By "medium," I mean "any social or technological procedure or device that is used for the selection, transmission, and reception of information" (Altheide and Snow 1979, p. 11). *Mass* media, it follows, are those "directed toward audiences that are relatively large and heterogeneous and whose members are anonymous so far as the communicator is concerned" (Wright 1975, p. 78). Television, of course, is the prime example today.

McQuail (1987) identifies six generic functions of mass media in society (pp. 52–53): mass media literally extend our vision ("window"); they help us make sense of otherwise ambiguous events ("interpreter"); they relay information and opinions ("platform"); they select out certain pieces of information for attention, while ignoring others ("filter"); they reflect back to society an image of itself ("mirror"); and they cloak truths in the service of propaganda or escapism ("screen or barrier").

6 This conceptualization of culture, of course, presupposes a *conflict* (as opposed to *order*) view of society (cf. Horton 1982). That is, while culture is rightly understood as the patterning/order that informs and flows from meaningful action (cf. Alexander 1990), the underlying meanings are continually contested, making order at any given point in time precarious, unstable (cf. Gramsci 1971).

7 A brief review of television's introduction into US life illustrates how the medium has taken the nation by storm. In 1939, television made its grand entrance onto the historical scene as RCA demonstrated the new technology at the World's Fair in New York. Television technology, however, was closely related to another technology – radar – which was being developed by GE for the military. For a brief period between 1941 and 1942, television made a limited commercial appearance, only to eventually suffer the same fate as its elder sibling, radio (Barnouw 1982). That is, in 1942 the manufacturing of television sets was halted as America delved deeper into World War II.

At the war's end in 1945, manufacture of television sets began again in earnest. A new network player, the American Broadcasting Companies (ABC) had quietly entered the fray in 1943, at the height of the war years. Television sets again went on sale in 1946, and by 1947, NBC and CBS had found commercial sponsors for their network newscasts (Barnouw 1982). In short, commercial television – the mass medium as we know it – was well under way.

By 1951, movie theater attendance began to drop for the first time in US television cities, leading to a epidemic of theater closings (Barnouw 1982; Sklar 1975). By 1953, the national networks were finally beginning to take shape; by 1956 and 1957 a boom in licensed stations left nearly 85 percent of the homes in the nation with television. By 1963, a Roper survey found for the first time that the majority of US residents got their news from television, not newspapers (Barnouw 1982). Today, practically every home in the US has a television set, and these sets are turned on for an average of over seven hours per day (Kellner 1990).

8 Lipsitz (1990) identifies an important way in which media and lived experiences have become intertwined:

> The very same media that trivialize and distort culture, that turn art into commodities, and that obscure the origins and intentions of artists also provide meaningful connection to our own pasts and to the pasts of others ... Time, history, and memory become qualitatively different concepts in a world where electronic mass communication is possible. Instead of relating to the past through a shared sense of place or ancestry, consumers of electronic mass media can experience a common heritage with people they have never seen; they can acquire memories of a past to which they have no geographic or biological connection. This capacity of electronic mass communication to transcend time and space creates instability by disconnecting people from past traditions, but it also liberates people by making the past less determinate of experiences in the present.
> (p. 5)

9 Cultural considerations aside, the flow of television programming first and foremost serves commercial interests. That is, television seeks to win the attention of large numbers of viewers so that this attention might be sold to advertisers (Gitlin 1985). The various channels thus compete for viewers, necessitating "rational" measures of program popularity, of advertising potential (see Meehan 1990, for a revealing critique of the television ratings industry).

10 I purposefully use Althusser's (1971) concept of "hail" in conjunction with the term "receive" to characterize the text-audience encounter as I see it. That is, a text hails or greets viewers in order to interpellate them in ways consistent with the text's preferred meanings. But real viewers are active participants in the process, and the act of receiving the text may or may not result in the interpellation(s) intended by the text's producer.

11 Moreover, as Morley (1992) argues, contradictory/inconsistent subject positions or interpellations also exist. Just because a viewer inhabits the subject position most fully inscribed in a given text does not mean that they necessarily subscribe to the ideologies embedded in the text. The text in question may be received by the viewer from within the preferred subject position, yet contradicted by the viewer's relation to other texts and discourses.

12 Recent contributions to the media literature have advocated a "reworking" of the decoding model that first takes into account "the question of viewers' positive or negative response to the text as a particular cultural form – do they enjoy it, feel bored by it, recognize it as at all relevant to their concerns?" Thus many studies now explore "genres" (form) rather than "meaning-systems" (content). Accordingly, the analytical focus might be on which "sectors or milieux of a society favour or resist 'penetration' by a range of different particular ideological forms (Morley 1992, pp. 126–30)." The cultural competencies different sectors have available to them thus become objects of analysis. This insight is incorporated into my analysis below (see chapters 4 through 8).

13 In other words, these perspectives apply theories of society, culture, and mind to "portray what the [audience] member's actions will have come to by using the stable structures – i.e. what they *came* to – as a point of theoretical departure from which to portray the necessary character of the pathways whereby the end result is assembled" (Garfinkel 1967, p. 68).

14 While Newcomb (1984) is quite convincing in its elaboration of the dialogic nature of television, I believe it overstates the degree to which hegemony theory contains resistance, the degree to which it "gestures toward the complexities of textual and social processes, but expands at will to explain complexity in conventional terms of dominance" (p. 37). This depiction of hegemony theory suggests that the theory ultimately equates resistance with pseudo-resistance. In fact, I submit, hegemony theory accomplishes just the opposite. I discuss this issue in more detail below, when I contrast the work of Althusser (1971) and Gramsci (1971) on the question of resistance.

15 An important component of subjectivity, of course, is *racial consciousness* – "a set of political beliefs and action orientations" arising out of "the awareness of having ideas, feelings and interests similar to others who share the same [raced] characteristics" (Gurin *et al.* 1980, p. 30).

16 For example, scholars such as Cox (1970), Bonacich (1972), Wilson (1978), Rex (1987), and Hechter (1986) understand "race" primarily in economic terms, as the outcome of competition between groups in society. But a major problem with this group of theories is that in their rush to explain the totality of social relations in terms of economics, they essentially fail to adequately account for the autonomous influence of non-economic forces. The result, more often than not, consists of rather deterministic models of "empty places" (Hartmann 1981, p. 10) that fail to explain *why* certain individuals, rather than other individuals, occupy the positions they do in society. Accordingly, social actors are portrayed as "judgmental dopes" (Garfinkel 1967, p. 68) whose actions are determined in "behavioralist" (Prager 1982, p. 106) fashion by economic forces. Situational meaning and understanding – critical components of agency – are left untheorized or conveniently dismissed as "false consciousness."

Psychological and cultural approaches to "race" often attempt to address the problem of meaning ignored by economic approaches, but this group of studies often fail to *clearly* link their models to material conditions. Key examples of this school include Park (1950), Frazier (1957), Gordon (1964), Gergen (1968), and Myrdal (1982).

17 For example, Spivak (1987), Hall (1988), hooks (1990), and Goldberg (1990) all focus on breaking the chains of "race" and center anti-essentialism as a strategy.

18 According to Farr and Moscovici (1984), a representation is a "given definition, common to all members of the community to which we belong" (p. 5). As such, representations "conventionalise the objects, persons and events we encounter" (p. 7), imposing themselves upon us "with an irresistible force" (p. 9). Although these definitions or paradigms are "taken for granted" (p. 4), they often turn out to be illusory. Representations are created by individuals and groups "in the course of communication and co-operation" (p. 13), in order to make sense of empirical circumstances. But once created, "they lead a life of their own, circulate, merge, attract and repel each other, and give birth to new representations, while old ones die out" (p. 13).

19 In order to underscore the importance of this point, I will in the remaining pages use the term "race-as-representation" to refer to "race," and append the term "raced" to common racial labels (e.g., "Latino-raced," "black-raced" and "white-raced"). In short, I employ this rather cumbersome language in order to highlight the *continual* formation of race-as-representation in the US, and to remind the reader that individual identity is in large measure constituted and reconstituted by reference to race-as-representation. (As Hall (1988) and others have pointed out, class, gender, and sexuality are other important frames of reference for identity.)

20 Allen (1994) notes that an implicit agreement was struck between white elites and white workers guaranteeing that, no matter how bad circumstances became, the latter would not fall below the level of non-white workers. For elites, this agreement meant increased economic stability and labor force control; for white workers, it amounted to psychic compensation for economic oppression.

21 Over the years, as "blacks" have struggled for self-determination and an autonomous identity, group-embraced racial labels (e.g., "Negro," "black," "African-American") have been coined, abandoned and embraced anew.

22 Harris (1987) adds that European notions of African inferiority arose soon after contact between the continents. This belief, as Hacker (1992) notes, continues to influence US race relations today: "What other Americans know and remember is that blacks alone were brought as chattels to be bought and sold like livestock" (p. 14).

23 Native Americans have always belonged to what anthropologists might describe as a "race" (Hacker 1992). But the "racialization" of this group seems to have switched into a higher gear in recent years. That is, during the 1960s, "there was a return to traditional religious and spiritual concerns. Cultural nationalism helped to link distinct groups who were racialized as one monolithic entity" (Omi and Winant 1986, p. 105). The result? "Between 1970 and 1990, the

number of persons claiming tribal antecedents rose from 827,268 to 1,516,540, which works out to more than three times the growth rate for the nation as a whole" (Hacker 1992, p. 5).

24 In this sense, Heritage (1984, p. 115–117) points out, norms possess a "double constitution" property. That is, actors have the choice of either (1) sustaining the "life-as-usual" stance identified by the norm or (2) breaching this stance. The latter option requires accounting work as breaches of the norm are generally regarded by actors as reflections of "significant real dispositions, opinions, characters, commitments and beliefs." When actors wish to avoid the latter consequence, they "will engage in the 'perceivedly normal'/normatively provided for conduct." Note that internalization of the norm is not required to facilitate adherence to the norm.

25 Admittedly, this distinction may a bit of an overstatement on my part, a stereotyping of different formulations within the symbolic interactionism school. That is, an important forerunner of this perspective, W. I. Thomas, seems to appreciate the link between micro-level agency and macro-level structures: "There is always a rivalry between the spontaneous definitions of the situation made by the member of an organized society and the definitions which his society has provided him" (Thomas 1972, p. 332). Nonetheless, in an influential statement on the symbolic interactionism position, Blumer (1969) seems to downplay the significance of such structures, focusing, instead, on the interpretations flowing from interaction: "Human group life is a vast process of such defining to others what to do and of interpreting their definitions; through this process people come to fit their activities to one another and to form their own individual conduct. Both such joint activity and individual conduct are formed *in* and *through* this ongoing process; they are not mere expressions or products of what people bring to their interaction or of conditions that are antecedent to their interaction" (p. 10 original emphasis).

26 A critique that applies to both Prager (1982) and Omi and Winant (1986, 1994), it seems, is that the theory of representations (cf. Farr and Moscovici 1984) leads to tautological exercises when used to frame empirical analysis (Potter and Litton 1985). For example, these positions generally posit that the meanings of social phenomena can only be interpreted on the basis of representations; yet, in empirical studies, the *existence* of representations must be derived from an analysis of the social phenomena they supposedly explicate. Nonetheless, as Kuhn (1962) points out, "circularity is characteristic of scientific theories" (p. 90). That is, we cannot "prove" what we think we know without relying upon paradigms specifying the relation between cause and effect. And these paradigms, of course, are themselves the "unproven" explanations for our conclusions. In short, when weighed against the insights of the theory, this critique seems to be less than fatal.

27 This point has also be made in a number of theoretical works over the years. For example, Blumer (1969) argues that the media encounter is shaped by a process of "collective definition" (p. 188). More recently, Lindlof (1988) argues that

audience decoding is a socially coordinated practice influenced by viewer membership in "interpretive communities" (p. 81).

28 Collier *et al.* (1991) review the history of the social psychological tradition in the US, highlighting the general failure of small group research, in particular, to take into account the "historical, ideological, and economic context" of study participants (p. 193). See appendix A for a discussion of how this study attempts to manage these limitations.

29 Myers and Lamm (1975) point out that this theory explains why groups that are already quite extreme on a particular issue often do not show as much attitude polarization as less extreme groups.

30 For example, in his discussion of racist discourse, Goldberg (1990) distinguishes between representations and the explanations and expectations that undergird them. Goldberg says:

> The discourse of racism does not consist simply in descriptive representations of others. It includes a set of hypothetical premises about human kinds (e.g., the 'great chain of being,' classificatory hierarchies, etc.), and about the differences between them (both mental and physical). It involves a class of ethical choices (e.g., domination and subjugation, entitlement and restriction, disrespect and abuse). And it incorporates a set of institutional regulations, directions, and pedagogic models (e.g., apartheid, separate development, education institutions, choice of educational and bureaucratic language). Norms or prescriptions for behavior are contextually circumscribed by specific hypotheses, ethical choices, regulations, and models.   (p. 300)

31 See Fiske (1987) for a cogent discussion of horizontal and vertical intertextuality. The first involves common axes such as genre and character, while the second refers to specific references in one or more texts to another.

32 For example, see Gray (1995) for a lucid discussion of the stakes behind media representations of blacks and the American dream.

33 For example, as an "African-American" male, I have personally experienced real changes in society that emerged on the heels of the Civil Rights and Black Power movements; I cannot simply label these movements pseudo-resistance because they were not successful in producing a radical victory over bourgeois economics, politics and ideology. I can, however, understand these movements as progressive intrusions, as important victories in an on-going struggle against the multi-faceted forces of oppression in society.

34 From time to time, of course, news texts support views that certain elites find objectionable. Indeed, the news media are routinely attacked from the Right as well as Left for their coverage (Parenti 1986). But these Right-wing attacks tend to obfuscate the observation that news depictions generally support status quo versions of reality. In the end, the *content* of viewer opposition toward news texts, and how that content reflects on hegemonic discourses, should always be considered prior to declaring such opposition "resistance."

35 Some viewers may oppose news reports on the basis of poor execution – that is, "unprofessional" news gathering and reporting techniques, writing, and so on. At the same time, these viewers might generally respect the legitimacy of journalism as a profession and institution. "Opposition" in this case would *not* constitute "resistance."

36 Bagdikian (1992) lucidly establishes the links between capitalism, media industry concentration and the myth of objective news coverage.

37 Given the hypermediation of the events, the present study might be seen as a *strong* test of the polarization hypothesis.

3 The KTTV text

1 The political implications of this analysis – the power of media texts to justify, reinforce, and impose status quo versions of reality on audience members (i.e., the ideological power of media texts) – are explored in chapter 8.

2 Promoting the concepts of "semiotic democracy" and "producerly text," Fiske (1987, p. 95) ultimately treats the television text as a creation of audiences. That is, "reading and talking about television are part of the process of making a *text* out of it and are determinants of what *text* is actually made" (p. 15, emphasis added.) In other words, like sound is to the proverbial tree falling in the forest, so are texts to audiences: they do not exist *as-socially-meaningful-text* until they are processed by audiences.

Criticisms of this position abound (for example, see Morley 1992). In fact, Fiske himself seems to respond to these criticisms by refining his conceptualization of "text" in more recent works. For example, Fiske (1994a) distinguishes between the "industrial text" (the one produced and distributed for profit by the cultural industries) and the "popular text" (the one produced by audiences as they engage the industrial text). This conceptualization gives the pre-audience text definite boundaries, and justifies its study as an object in its own right.

3 KTTV-TV, Channel 11, owned and operated by Fox Broadcasting Co., was the only local television station in Los Angeles to cover the Rodney King beating trial in its entirety. For this reason, I limited my search for textual data to KTTV's coverage. The specific extract used in the study originally aired between about 9:43 pm and 10:00 pm on the first night of the events (April 29). This 17-minute text was selected from the day's more than fourteen hours of coverage for its rich footage, interviews, and reporter comments. KTTV averaged a modest viewership rating of 4.8 and 9.0 share for the period spanning its initial report of the verdicts and 10 pm.

4 This trucker, Reginald Denny, became an important symbol of racial tension in the aftermath of the events. As study interviews were being conducted, the Los Angeles news media vigorously covered developments in the criminal cases against the black-raced youth who allegedly attacked Denny.

5 The social implications of these expectations and explanations are considered in chapter 8.

6 In order for researchers to benefit from this exploration, to understand what a sign "means" from the perspective of the text, they would still have to "know" something of the social context in which the sign arises. For this reason, of course, I necessarily walk a narrow line between performing an "objective" reading of the KTTV text and one based on my own ideological predispositions as an audience member.

7 Jensen (1991) objects to the "Saussurean dualism of signifier and signified" (p. 40). Instead, he argues, Pierce's tripartite model of sign, object and interpretant (i.e., the sign in a person's head used to interpret other signs) is more "social" in that it explicitly recognizes meaning as a continuous process shaped by actors' consciousness. In my mind, the *probabilistic* signifier- signified model offered by Eco (1979) gets us to the same place. That is, this model offers no guarantee that specific signifiers will be linked by actors to specific signifieds. In fact, in this model, different semantic fields act much like Pierce's interpretants – they make different readings of signifiers (i.e., Pierce's signs) possible. But while the notion of interpretant points to individuals, the notion of semantic fields seems to point to something beyond the individual. In this sense, Eco's (1979) model actually appears to be more "social" than the one championed by Jensen (1991).

8 I present assumptions in the forms I do because these are the forms I feel are most directly implied by actual textual arguments. In theory, of course, other analysts might derive an infinite number of differently worded assumptions from these same arguments. But because each of these alternatively worded forms would ultimately work to support the *same* originating argument, I expect the choice of assumption wording to have little bearing on my ultimate findings – as long as these alternative forms are linked to the same arguments that I have identified. Finally, in order to minimize researcher bias, I established my assumption forms prior to reviewing informant arguments.

9 Numbers in parentheses refer to the location of the extracted quote in the KTTV transcript (see appendix C).

10 The stylebook adds that "in some stories that involve a conflict, it is equally important to specify that an issue cuts across racial lines" (p. 167).

11 Telephone interview with Jose Rios, December 16, 1993.

12 One of the KTTV reporters, Christine Devine, noted in an interview with the researcher that she is partly of African descent. Her "racial" appearance, however, was somewhat ambiguous for many study informants.

13 This is a dominant signifier-signified relationship in the text, despite Reverend Washington's observation – which was *not* acknowledged by the interviewers – that other raced groups were participating in the events.

4 Latino-raced informants and the KTTV text

1 For example, see Espiritu (1992) for a discussion of the politics surrounding census racial classification. See also, table 12, *The American Almanac: Statistical Abstract of the United States, 1994–1995,* US Bureau of the Census.

2 Officially recognized "races" are limited to the following: White, Black or Negro, Asian or Pacific Islander, Indian (American), Eskimo, Aleut, Other race (Espiritu 1992).

3 All names were changed to protect informant identities.

4 Group members responded that the event-related looting and fires were "wrong," and that event-related arrests were "right."

5 Early in the discussion, however, one of the informants, Felix, briefly challenged this emerging consensus about causes: "I think that the way we're telling it, it's not about Rodney King or race . . . It's about people trying to come up with money, with things, freeloading. Because that's what it's really all about."

6 Group members responded that the event-related fires and looting were "wrong," and that event-related arrests were "right."

7 Denotes an episode of loud, simultaneous talking among group members.

8 *Malcolm X*, by black-raced director Spike Lee, was released in the fall of 1992.

9 Informants blamed this low level of education in the area on the "messed up" school system in Los Angeles.

10 Denotes an episode of laughter.

11 A fifth group member was excluded from this analysis because he was not present for the group discussion that followed the screening.

12 I classified this group as "Latino" because Julio, who identified himself as Latino, was the center of the network.

13 One group member, Tom, suggested that KTTV's choice of Reverend Washington as an authority on the events was misguided because religious leaders are rarely well-informed regarding socio-political issues.

5 Black-raced informants and the KTTV text

1 For example, see table 12, *The American Almanac: Statistical Abstract of the United States, 1994–1995*, US Bureau of the Census.

2 I classified this group as "black-raced" because half of its members were black-raced, the center was administrated primarily by black-raced workers, and the woman who organized the group was black-raced. The significance of racial heterogeneity for this group is discussed below and in chapter 7.

3 Prior to the screening and discussion, James and Deshon repeatedly asked how long the interview would take, warning that they had other plans to attend to soon. At the conclusion of the interview, both informants disappeared from the center, despite the researcher's offer to provide them with a ride home. The Latino-raced informants, in contrast, remained at the center long after the interview and accepted a ride home from the researcher.

4 See Hecht *et al.* (1993) for an insightful discussion of the role that "cool" – "not letting the other know what you are thinking or feeling" (p. 132) – plays in "black" culture and communication. Majors and Billson (1992) suggests that black-raced males, in particular, use "being cool" as an ego boost for themselves, as an innovative strategy for surviving in a racist society.

5 Harlins is the 15-year-old black-raced girl who was shot and killed by a Korean-raced liquor merchant in South Central Los Angeles (see chapter 1).
6 Tim was probably predisposed to discussing the text in a metalinguistic mode because of his role as a youth minister at First AME, the church's activist stance in the community, and the criticism's leveled at the church's rally by interviewees in the text.
7 In the post-discussion questionnaire, however, Tim blamed the events on sensationalized news coverage. Another informant, Daryl, blamed the events on greed: "The rebellion started mostly because of people's greed [i.e., looting]. They used the King verdicts as an excuse for personal gain." Both informants' comments in the discussion, however, are more consistent with those of the other informants regarding the role of racism.
8 Indeed, one of the informants took issue with the text's and the questionnaires' characterization of the events as "riots." He crossed out each reference to "riots" in the questionnaires and replaced it with "rebellion."
9 This intersection was identified by the media as the flashpoint of the events (see discussion of the KTTV text in chapter 3).
10 Although there was no explicit discussion of systemic causes, one informant briefly pointed out that "the people was just tired of everything."
11 This group had very little discussion of event-related fires. The one direct reference to the fires concerned media coverage of them. In contrast, a large portion of its discussion was focused on event-related looting.
12 But, as I noted earlier, other black-raced informants seemed to understand the events as a "rebellion" (see chapter 8 for a more detailed discussion of terminology). Moreover, despite using the term "riot" during discussion, an informant in the CHURCH group crossed out the word "riots" everywhere it appeared on the questionnaires and replaced it with "rebellion." This behavior did not occur in any of the other-raced groups.
13 *Roots,* of course, is the 1977, eight-night mini-series about a black-raced family's experiences during slavery in the US. Garnering one of the largest television audiences in US history, the program, according to Bogle (1989, p. 338) "may have altered the popular imagination" about race relations in the nation. *Jungle Fever* is a controversial 1991 film by black-raced director Spike Lee that explores problems associated with interracial dating and relationships.
14 Due to equipment problems, I was unable to videotape this group's screening of the text. My discussion of screening highlights for the group is thus based on notes I took at the time.
15 One prominent example of informant opposition to the text as-construction is when informants criticized the anchor's labeling of people in the intersections as "thugs."
16 Kelley (1994) convincingly documents the prominence of Ice Cube and other rappers in black youth culture.
17 The CHURCH group was the lone black-raced exception to this rule.

6 White-raced informants and the KTTV text

1 Denny is the white-raced trucker attacked by black-raced youths in the Florence and Normandie intersection.

2 Informants felt that event-related looting and fires were "wrong," and that the arrests were "right."

3 Linda was a UCLA student who lived on the informants' dormitory floor during the events. Many students became upset with her for participating in looting.

4 Later in the discussion, Marcia described the events as little more than an annoyance, one that caused the cancellation of Mardi Gras, a popular UCLA carnival.

5 Tom failed to report his age on the questionnaire, but he appeared to be similar in age to the other group members.

6 I classified this group as "white" because it contained at least one white-raced member and did not contain any black-raced or Latino-raced members. The consequences of group racial heterogeneity for the analysis are discussed in chapter 7.

7 Perhaps this latter finding is explained by the observation that pre-interview ties in this group were quite weak compared to other study groups. This group was organized by an Asian-raced student who was hired to identify groups of students who all knew each other well. This group only marginally met the criterion. That is, the bond that all members shared in common was that they lived on the same dormitory floor and participated together in floor activities. But the lone white-raced informant, Bill, noted that he did not know any of the other informants "well." He noted that he frequently talked with John, had spoken with Brad "once or twice," and did not know Tom "at all." All other informants categorized one another as floormates.

8 One informant failed to respond to the religiosity item on the questionnaire.

9 This observation does not appear to be a function of infrequent interaction. Like the previous group (DORM 1), this group was organized by an Asian-raced student who was hired to identify groups of students who all know each other well. Also like the previous group, the primary bond that members of this group shared in common was that they lived on the same dormitory floor and participated together in floor activities. But this group seemed to have much stronger pre-interview ties than the previous group. Most of the members reported having frequent contact with one another, especially with Gloria, the resident assistant.

10 Gloria challenged this view of the events by arguing that the American Revolution was "first defined as a mob" that lacked a clear plan.

11 See Postscript for a discussion of Latino immigration to Los Angeles and Proposition 187.

12 I classified this group as "white-raced" because it was composed of two white-raced members and did not contain any black-raced or Latino-raced members.

The consequences of group racial heterogeneity for the analysis are discussed in chapter 7.

13 Like the two previous groups (DORM1 and DORM2), this group was organized by an Asian-raced student who was hired to identify groups of students who all know each other well. Likewise, the primary bond that all members shared was that they lived on the same dormitory floor and participated together in floor activities. But one of the informants, Margo, reported that she did not know other group members "that well." The other informants described one another with varying degrees of familiarity. In short, compared to other groups in the study, the pre-interview ties of this group seemed rather weak.

14 *Little Man Tate* was directed by Jody Foster and released in 1991.

7 Raced ways of seeing

1 About 10 percent of the "black" and "white" respondents, and about 7 percent of the "Asian" and "Hispanic" respondents viewed the events as composed of *both* "protest" and "looting/crime."

2 To formally establish this connection, of course, the zero-order correlation between the two items would have to be computed.

3 Three of the five white-raced groups (MATES, DORM1 and DORM3) contained one or more Asian-raced members. These informants held views very similar to their white counterparts regarding the events.

4 Only the most salient referents were included in the table – that is, those that clearly pertained to racial categories, participation in the events, or solidarity with or distance from the "system." A sizable number of pronouns/referents were classified as "ambiguous" and dropped from the analysis.

5 It was not clear from these discussions whether or not Latino-raced informants actually understood "people who live in South Central Los Angeles" as being synonymous with "Latinos." Furthermore, one of the Latino-raced groups (FAMILY) talked about Salvadorans as if they were distant others (3 uses), suggesting that the raced identity I have labeled "Latino" might be more fully understood and embraced by informants as "Mexican."

6 One of the Latino-raced groups (JULIO) also talked about heterosexuals as if they were distant others (4 uses). This finding is consistent with my earlier observation in chapter 4 that sexual orientation might be one of the more salient bonds between members of the group.

7 I used multiple regression with dummy variables rather than ANOVA to test the significance of experimental groupings because the two procedures provide equivalent results (Hays 1988), and I find the interpretation of regression coefficients to be more useful for this particular analysis. Formally, I violate the independence assumption of the General Linear Model by treating members of the study groups as independently drawn cases (Hays 1988). Thus, I treat the following results as, at best, a conservative test of "race," SES and gender effects

on the dependent variables. In short, I consider these results only in conjunction with other evidence.

8 The median family income for the zip code in which each informant's parents currently lived served as a proxy for family income (see appendix A).

9 For each model, the dependent variable was an attitudinal scale ranging from 1 to 10, with 1 indicating that informants viewed the event-related activity as "right" and 10 indicating that they felt it was "wrong" (see appendix A).

10 See previous note.

11 This conclusion, of course, holds only for the specific event-related activities explored in the study – looting, fires and arrests. Moreover, these activities were only analyzed along the "right"/"wrong" continuum. Alternative considerations of these and other activities may very well register significant differences along gender or class lines.

12 This expectation, of course, presupposes that the assumptions embedded in the KTTV text are congruent with popular discourses concerning the events, and that black-raced informants would anticipate this congruency on the part of news media.

13 Just as I observed the black-raced and Latino-raced groups to be more animated than the white-raced groups during the screening of the KTTV text, I also found them to be more animated than white-raced groups during the subsequent discussions. That is, the rates of laughing episodes and simultaneous talking episodes among black-raced and Latino-raced groups were considerably greater than among white-raced groups. These rates on average were nearly equal for black-raced and Latino-raced groups – about one episode of laughter per minute and a little more than 1.6 episodes of simultaneous talking per minute. Among white-raced groups, in contrast, the rate of laughter episodes was only about 0.64 per minute, while the rate of simultaneous talking episodes was only about 0.38 per minute.

14 Non-white-raced groups were significantly more likely than white-raced groups to be animated during the screening (i.e., visibly react at two or more of the key points in the text), $p = 0.02$ (one-tailed); Fisher's Exact Probability Test.

15 $p > 0.56$ (one-tailed); Fisher's Exact Probability Test. Sample of black-raced and Latino- raced groups divided into high (above \$25,000) and low (below \$25,000) family income groups.

16 Across all study groups, however, there appeared to be no significant relationship between reception mode and opposition rate, $p > 0.09$ (one-tailed); Fisher's Exact Probability Test. Sample divided into high versus low opposition groups (see chapter 8) and animated versus passive viewing groups.

17 See Condit (1994) for a compelling argument in favor of considering "polyvalence" as an important dimension of audience decoding (p. 430).

18 Quote extracted from Ellen's statements in the MATES group.

19 Morley (1992) discusses differences in viewing styles between men and women, but to my knowledge, little has been written on differences in viewing styles by "race." In any event, in this case, I suspect that the observed racial differences

in viewing styles are more a function of textual content than generic differences in how members of different raced groups view television.

20 These hypotheses include (see chapter 2 and appendix A):

1. Decoding polarization will only occur in groups where the pre-treatment decodings among viewers fall on the same side of a 10-point scale (i.e., either between 1.0 and 5.0 *or* between 6.0 and 10.0).
2. Group averages for a decoding scale that are relatively low before discussion (i.e., between 5.0 and 3.0 on a 10-point scale) will *decrease* in magnitude after discussion.
3. Group averages for a decoding scale that are relatively high before discussion (i.e., between 6.0 and 8.0 on a 10-point scale) will *increase* in magnitude after discussion.
4. Extreme pre-discussion decodings (i.e., average group scores above 8.0 *or* below 3.0) will result in little if any polarization after discussion.

21 I treat the former class of variables (group origin and racial make-up) as initial ("time zero") group characteristics; I treat the latter class of variables (discussion dynamics and polarization outcomes) as outcome variables influenced by these initial group characteristics, results of the group negotiation and norming process.

22 $p > 0.48$ (one-tailed); Fisher's Exact Probability Test. The sample was divided into groups originating in South Central Los Angeles and those originating at UCLA. "High polarization" groups had scores greater than or equal to 66.7% (polarization on two or more of the three scales), while "low polarization" groups had scores less than 66.7% (polarization on only one or none of the three scales).

23 $p > 0.39$ (one-tailed); Fisher's Exact Probability Test. The sample was divided into groups composed of individuals all identifying as members of the same raced groups and those where at least two of the members identified differently. "High polarization" groups had scores greater than or equal to 66.7% (polarization on two or more of the three scales), while "low polarization" groups had scores less than 66.7% (polarization on only one or none of the three scales).

24 The NORTH group is the exception among the racially heterogeneous groups exhibiting high rates of polarization. That is, this group – like the other black-raced groups – *did* center race in its discussion. The one non-black-raced informant in the group, Dara, often played Devil's advocate during the group's negotiation of the events and text. Perhaps the intensity of the ties that group members shared – most had been friends since high school – was enough to overcome this dissension.

25 $p = 0.03$ (one-tailed); Fishers Exact Probability Test. Sample divided into groups whose discussions were marked by unity and those marked by repeated disagreement between two or more members. "High polarization" groups had scores greater than or equal to 66.7% (polarization on two or more of the three

scales), while "low polarization" groups had scores less than 66.7% (polarization on only one or none of the three scales).

26 According to Oboler (1992), "Latino-Americans are growing up in the border-lands of at least two cultures and are affected by and aware of the discrimination and prejudice against them as *Latinos*" (p. 20, original emphasis). For this reason, I chose to use the label "Latino" to refer to informants who were of Mexican or other Spanish-surnamed descent. I must acknowledge, however, that some of the informants I labeled "Latino" did not understand themselves in this way (see chapter 4). Informants in the FAMILY group, for example, saw themselves as "Mexican" and were openly hostile toward Salvadorans – another group usually subsumed under the "Latino" label. In short, heterogeneity within the Latino-raced population may make it difficult for researchers to know a priori the boundaries of the relevant ingroup for informants.

27 Highlighting this point, perhaps, one black-raced informant (Tim from the CHURCH group) refused to identify himself as "African-American." Instead, he wrote in his preferred raced identity as "black" (see chapter 5).

28 Indeed, Asante (1976) argues that black-raced viewers used television coverage of the "black movement" in the 1960s as an instrument for receiving the latest information on the struggle and for rallying the black-raced masses.

8 Meaning-making and resistance

1 Consistent with the general lack of metalinguistic decoding across the groups, only one group (JULIO) specifically referred to "Fox" or "KTTV" by name. In other words, the text was generally not treated by informants as a text constructed by *someone*. Instead, it was discussed as a somewhat generic depiction of the events.

2 The cutting point of 0.81 is midway between the overall sample mean and median values for oppositional-arguments-per- minute. Tables 4.2, 4.4–4.7, 5.2, 5.4–5.7, 6.2, and 6.4–6.7 (appendix E) present a complete listing of these arguments.

3 Although these mean values suggest that black-raced groups offered considerably more oppositional arguments per minute than either Latino-raced or white-raced ones, the relationship is not significant at the 0.05 level ($p > .16$ [one-tailed], Fisher's Exact Probability Test). Sample dichotimized into black-raced versus non-black-raced groups and high versus low-opposition groups.

4 $p = 0.05$ (one-tailed); Fisher's Exact Probability Test. Sample divided into those using referential and metalinguistic (at least partially) decoding modes. "High opposition" groups had a rate of at least .81 oppositional arguments per minute, while "low opposition" groups had a rate lower than .81.

5 $p > 0.33$ (one-tailed); Fisher's Exact Probability Test. Sample divided into blacks and non-blacks. "Metalinguistic" groups made at least partially metalinguistic decodings prior to specific prompting, while "referential" groups slipped into a metalinguistic mode only after specific prompting, if at all.

6 p = 0.15 (one-tailed); Fisher's Exact Probability Test. Sample divided into low SES (family income below $25,000) and high SES (family income above $25,000) groups. "Metalinguistic" groups made at least a partially metalinguistic decoding of the text, while "referential" groups failed to make metalinguistic decodings prior to specific prompting, if at all.

7 The Latino-raced members in the group, however, challenged the assumption.

8 "Riot" was nonetheless the favored term in the CHURCH discussion, while "rebellion" was favored in the KEISHA discussion.

9 See Fiske (1994b) for a compelling discussion of the role the term "looting" plays in the discourses of criminality and of property rights. I briefly review the former role below.

10 Individuals were categorized by racial group membership.

11 Scales ranged from 1 to 10, with 1 indicating "right" and 10 indicating "wrong."

12 For examples, see appendix C, transcript of the KTTV text, statements 4, 5, 8, 13, 20.

13 Interview with Jose Rios, March 25, 1993.

14 Interview with Christine Devine, April 14, 1993.

15 Nonetheless, most local television stations later touted their "riot" coverage in promotional advertisements designed to attract future news audiences.

16 Number in parentheses refers to location of the quote in the KTTV transcript (appendix C).

17 In a comparative study of media discourse, van Dijk (1993) notes that "ethnic" events are typically "topicalized" by media, divorced from the larger social context. These events, he argues, "are covered in such a way that negative action of Them, e.g., violence, is topicalized; and possible social explanations of ethnic conflict that reflect negatively on Us, such as discrimination or causes of poverty, are de-topicalized in news reports" (p. 249). In the end, van Dijk (1992) argues, "If discrimination or prejudice still exist, it is treated as an incident, as a deviation, as something that should be attributed to, and punished at the individual level. In other words, institutional or systemic racism is denied" (p. 95).

18 As is often the case in breaking stories of this magnitude, when the events began to slow down, KTTV's interpretive and analytical coverage began to increase.

19 President George Bush, *Los Angeles Times*, May 1, 1992, p. A10.

20 California Governor Pete Wilson, *Los Angeles Times*, May 1, 1992, p. A1.

21 Los Angeles Mayor Tom Bradley, *Los Angeles Times*, May 2, 1992, p. A1.

22 The Kerner Commission was organized by President Johnson to review the causes of a series of urban riots that erupted in the summer of 1967 (National Advisory Commission on Civil Disorders, 1968). The Commission recommended that the media: "Improve coordination with police in reporting riot news through advance planning, and cooperate with the police in the designation of police information officers, establishment of information centers, and development of mutually acceptable guidelines for riot reporting and the conduct of media personnel" (p. 21).

23 See Johnson *et al.* (1992) for a comprehensive discussion of this "multi-ethnic rebellion" (p. 2)

24 See Harrington (1984) for a compelling analysis of how the tactic of "blaming the victim" lies at the core of conservative political projects.

25 The motivations and understandings of event participants and sympathizers may also be gleaned from a reading of event-related graffiti and signs posted on black businesses. I observed countless such notices as I explored event-touched areas on April 30. Some examples: "Crips and Bloods Together Forever;" "LA Revolucion"; "Blacks and Mexicans United"; "Black- Owned, I'm Pissed Too"; "Fuck Tha Police." See Hazen (1992) and Coffey (1992) for photos.

26 Horne (1995) cites a survey released soon after the 1965 events which suggested that most black-raced respondents living in the area embraced counter-hegemonic understandings of the events – despite the destruction of community resources, despite the eminent flight of "white" businesses from the area. Sixty-two percent of these respondents saw the events as "Negro Protest," 56 percent thought the events had "a purpose," 38 percent described them "in revolutionary rhetoric," and 56 percent thought the events were "intended to be a blunt message delivered to the 'power structure'" (p. 335). Indeed, before a "white backlash" in California placed Ronald Reagan in the governor's mansion, several event-generated "concessions" were granted to black-raced residents of the area. For example, a major medical center was constructed in the area (Martin Luther King/Drew), a campus of the California State University system originally slated for affluent Palos Verdes was built in nearby Dominguez Hills, and black-raced women and men were being hired by the mainstream press in unprecedented numbers. And granting the problems associated with the black-raced nationalist movements gaining strength on the heels of the 1965 events (Horne 1995), many of these movements nonetheless provided counter-hegemonic voices and galvanized black-raced opposition to a growing "white backlash."

27 See Horton (1982) for a cogent discussion of *conflict* versus *order* perspectives on social relations.

28 For example, a survey conducted soon after the events by the Los Angeles County Human Relations Commission suggests that residents on its mailing list considered KTTV's coverage of the events to be among the most accurate and fair local coverage.

29 For example, see *The American Heritage Diction of the English Language, Third Edition*, New York: Houghton Mifflin Company, 1992.

30 When I mentioned to several pre-test informants that I was conducting research on "the rebellion," they clearly did not know what events I was referring to. But as I described the events, each of the informants quickly realized what I was talking about: "Oh, you mean the riots." Indeed, several of these same informants expressed rather counter-hegemonic understandings of the events, despite their use of the "hegemonic" term.

31 See Omi and Winant (1994) for a compelling analysis of the links between "colorblind" platforms and neo-conservative politics.

32 As one informant in the CHURCH group put it: "It's [the King beating incident] the law, it's the whole system." And the police who attacked King, another group member added, "just hide behind their badge."

Postscript

1 *Los Angeles Times*, August 27, 1992, p. F1.
2 Extracted from CNN coverage of President George Bush's address to the nation, Friday, May 1, 1992.
3 At least one commentator predicted that the events would lead to voters "retiring Bush in favor of Clinton" (West 1993). Indeed, despite the campaigns' overt focus on jobs and the economy, anecdotal evidence seems to support the notion that the Los Angeles events played a major role in the outcome. Black voters from South Los Angeles, for example, spoke candidly of the events and how they understood their votes for Clinton as a repudiation of Bush and his administration's neglect of urban areas (*Los Angles Times*, November 4, 1992, p. A16).
4 See table 448, *The American Almanac: Statistical Abstract of the United States, 1994–1995*, US Bureau of the Census.
5 Roughly 80 percent of black-raced voters in California cast their ballots for Clinton, compared to 12 percent for Bush; among Latino-raced voters, 51 percent cast their ballots for Clinton and 27 percent for Bush. Among white-raced voters, 43 percent cast their ballots for Clinton and 33 percent for Bush. Finally, Clinton's smallest margin of victory in California – 5 points – was amongst Asians: 45 percent cast their ballots for Clinton and 40 percent cast their ballots for Bush (*Los Angeles Times*, November 5, 1992, p. A1).
6 *Los Angeles Times*, November 4, 1992, p. A1.
7 See Johnson *et al.* (1992), table 3. Of the 9,456 persons arrested between April 30 and May 4, 1992 by the LAPD and Sheriff's Department, 3,492 were Latino-raced. By way of comparison, 2,832 black-raced persons were arrested in the same period.
8 *Los Angeles Times,* May 6, 1992, p. F1.
9 California Ballot Pamphlet, November 8, 1994.
10 See tables 8 and 10, *The American Almanac: Statistical Abstract of the United States, 1994–1995*, US Bureau of the Census.
11 The racial/ethnic breakdown for Los Angeles' population in 1990 was as follows: "Hispanics," 39.9 percent; "blacks," 14.0 percent; "American Indian, Eskimo and Aleut," .5 percent; "Asian, Pacific Islander," 9.8 percent; "whites" and others, 35.5 percent. Source: table 46, *The American Almanac: Statistical Abstract of the United States, 1994–1995*, US Bureau of the Census.
12 See *The Tarnished Golden Door*, Civil Rights Issues in Immigration, US Commission on Civil Rights, September 1980, Washington, D.C.
13 Exit polling, as the *Los Angeles Times* (November 10, 1994, p. A1) put it, suggests that "it was white California that spoke" in the Proposition 187 victory. Latino-raced voters rejected the legislation 77 percent to 23 percent,

while roughly half of black-raced and Asian-raced voters opposed the legislation.

14 *Los Angeles Times*, November 9, 1994, p. A26.
15 Los Angeles Times, November 21, 1995, p. A1.

Appendix A

1 All Westside college students attended the University of California, Los Angeles (UCLA). These informants were males and females aged 18–24.
2 Five of the groups (three white-raced, one Latino-raced and one black-raced) were actually organized by non-group members. Each of these groups nonetheless met the minimum study requirement for inclusion: group members all knew one another, frequently watched television together *or* discussed important issues with one another.
3 These data come from the second of two questionnaires that were administered to informants (see appendix D).
4 The consequences of group racial heterogeneity for the analysis are discussed in chapters 4 through 6 (when audience ethnographies are presented for the groups), and in chapter 7 (when "raced ways of seeing" are more systematically explored). For now, groups are classified a priori by the raced identification of the first-stage informant or group organizer.
5 This study defines "audience ethnography" in the tradition of Morley (1974, 1980, 1992) and other studies that have attempted to explore how audiences find meaning in media texts. While audience ethnographers rarely immerse themselves in their informants' culture to the degree that more traditional ethnographers do, they too are "interested in understanding and describing a social and cultural scene from the emic, or insider's, perspective" (Fetterman 1989, p. 12).
6 Interviews were conducted between December 1992 and March 1993.
7 Due to the imposed parent scenario, I assumed that the tendency for informants to offer politically correct responses would be balanced by a heightened sense of *personal* responsibility. The question of interest thus becomes the following: How did informants use race-as-representation to meet this responsibility, to make sense of what they saw? My analysis of the videotapes suggests that informants indeed took the prompt seriously and avoided offering contrived responses for the sake of political correctness.
8 The following additional prompts were issued when discussion stalled:

1) What do you feel is the most important news reported in the video?
2) What was good about the video?
3) What was bad about the video?
4) How do you feel about the people who were interviewed in the video?
5) How do you feel about the news reporters in the video?

9 The researcher, a black-raced male, conducted the interviews of the black-raced groups, while a Latina-raced women trained by the researcher conducted the

interviews of the Latino-raced groups. Interviews of the white-raced groups were conducted by three different individuals trained by the researcher: MATES was interviewed by a white-raced student at UCLA; DORM1, DORM2, and DORM3 were interviewed by an Asian-raced student at UCLA; JILL was interviewed by a white-raced graduate student at UCLA.

10 As Fiske (1989b) notes: "Oral culture is a product of its immediate social formation, so the way that television is talked about provides us with two sorts of clues – clues about how television is being assimilated into the social formation and how that social formation is read back into the text, and clues about which meanings offered by the text are being mobilized in this process" (p. 66).

11 The researcher coded approximately 865 group arguments prior to analyzing group patterns. Another coder, trained by the researcher, independently agreed with the researcher's codings in 85 percent of the cases.

12 I assume in the analysis that the median family income for the zip codes in which informants' parents lived is a more valid measure of SES than responses based on informant knowledge/recall. Furthermore, I assume that using a median value for the zip code is preferable to actual family income for this analysis because it may provide us with a picture of the broader socio-economic environment in which informants were embedded – the ways of life to which informants were exposed as they were growing up around their neighbors.

13 Separate models were tested for gender and SES effects due to the small size of the sample relative to the number of predictor variables.

14 That is, in these intervening months, informants undoubtedly had many opportunities to discuss the events within their networks.

15 The cutting points used for dichotomizing the variables are described in chapters 7 and 8.

References

Adorno, Theodor 1991a, "The Schema of Mass Culture," in J. M. Bernstein (ed.), *The Culture Industry: Selected Essays on Mass Culture*, London: Routledge.

1991b,"How to Look at Television," in J. M. Bernstein (ed.), *The Culture Industry: Selected Essays on Mass Culture*, London: Routledge.

Alexander, Jeffrey C. 1981, "The Mass Media in Systemic, Historical and Comparative Perspective," in Elihu Katz and Thomas Szesko (eds.), *Mass Media and Social Change*, Beverly Hills: Sage.

1990, "Analytic Debates: Understanding the Relative Autonomy of Culture," in J. C. Alexander and S. Seidman (eds.), *Culture and Society: Contemporary Debates*, Cambridge: Cambridge University Press.

Allen, Theodore W 1994., *The Invention of the White Race, Volume One: Racial Oppression and Social Control*, London: Verso.

Altheide, David L. and Robert P. Snow 1979, *Media Logic*, Beverly Hills: Sage.

Althusser, Louis 1971, *Lenin and Philosophy and Other Essays*, New York: Monthly Review Press.

1990, *Philosophy and the Spontaneous Philosophy of the Scientists and Other Essays*, London: Verso.

Ang, Ien 1989, "Wanted: Audiences. On the Politics of Empirical Audience Studies," in E. Seiter, H. Borchers, G. Kreutzner, and E. Warth (eds.), *Remote Control: Television, Audiences, and Cultural Power*, London: Routledge.

Asante, Molefi Kete 1976, "Television and Black Consciousness," *Journal of Communication* Autumn, 137–141.

Bagdikian, Ben H. 1992, *The Media Monopoly*, Boston: Beacon Press.

Baldwin, James 1961, *Nobody Knows My Name*, New York: Laurel.

Banton, Michael 1977, *The Idea of Race,* London: Tavistock.

Barnouw, Erik 1982, *Tube of Plenty: The Evolution of American Television,* Oxford: Oxford University Press.

Baudrillard, Jean 1988, "The Masses: The Implosion of the Social in the Media," in M. Poster (ed.), *Selected Writings by Jean Baudrillard,* Palo Alto: Stanford University Press.

Berger, Arthur Asa 1990, *Agitpop: Political Culture and Communication Theory,* New Brunswick NJ: Transaction Publishers.

Berger, John 1973, *Ways of Seeing: Based on the Television Series with John Berger,* New York: Viking Press.

Berry, Mary Frances 1994, *Black Resistance, White Law: A History of Constitutional Racism in America,* New York: Penguin.

Bienenstock, Elisa Jayne, Phillip Bonacich and Melvin Oliver 1990, "The Effect of Network Density and Homogeneity on Attitude Polarization," *Social Networks* 12,153–172.

Blea, Irene I. 1988, *Toward a Chicano Social Science,* New York: Praeger.

Blumer, Herbert 1969, *Symbolic Interactionism: Perspective and Method,* Berkeley: University of California Press.

Blumler, Jay and Elihu Katz 1974, *The Uses of Mass Communication,* Beverly Hills: Sage.

Bobo, Lawrence, James H. Johnson, Melvin L. Oliver, James Sidanius and Camille Zubrinsky 1992, "Public Opinion Before and After a Spring of Discontent: A Preliminary Report on the 1992 Los Angeles County Social Survey," in *UCLA Center for the Study of Urban Poverty Occasional Working Paper Series,* Los Angeles: UCLA Institute for Social Science Research.

Bogle, Donald 1988, *Blacks in American Films and Television: An Illustrated Encyclopedia,* New York: Fireside.

Bonacich, Edna 1972, "A Theory of Ethnic Antagonism: The Split Labor Market," *American Sociological Review* 37, 547–559.

Bradburn, Norman M. 1983, "Response Effects," in P. Rossi, J. Wright, and A. Anderson (eds.), *Handbook of Survey Research,* San Diego: Academic Press.

Brunsdon, Charlotte and David Morley 1978, *Everyday Television: "Nationwide.",* London: British Film Institute.

Budd, Mike, Robert M. Entman and Clay Steinman 1990, "The Affirmative Character of U.S. Cultural Studies," *Critical Studies in Mass Communication* 7, 169–184.

Bullock, Paul 1969, *Watts: The Aftermath. An Inside View of the Ghetto by the People of Watts,* New York: Grove Press.

Carragee, Kevin M. 1990, "Interpretive Media Study and Interpretive Social Science," *Critical Studies in Mass Communication* 7, 81–96.

Coffey, Shelby III (ed.) 1992, *Understanding the Riots: Los Angeles Before and After the Rodney King Case,* Los Angeles: Los Angeles Times.

Collier, Gary, Henry L. Minton and Graham Reynolds 1991, *Currents of Thought in American Social Psychology,* New York: Oxford University Press.

Condit, Celeste Michelle 1994, "The Rhetorical Limits of Polysemy," in H. Newcomb (ed.), *Television: The Critical View,* New York: Oxford University Press.

Cox, Oliver C. 1970, *Caste, Class and Race,* New York: Modern Reader Paperbacks.

Cramer, M. Richard and Howard Schuman 1975, "We and They: Pronouns as Measures of Political Identification and Estrangement," *Social Science Research* 4, 231–240.

Dahlgren, Peter 1988, "What's the Meaning of This? Viewers' Plural Sense-Making of TV News," *Media, Culture and Society* 10, 285–301.

Dates, Jannette L. and William Barlow 1990, *Split Image: African-Americans in the Mass Media,* Washington, DC: Howard University Press.

Davis, Mike 1990, *City of Quartz: Excavating the Future in Los Angeles,* New York: Vintage Books.

1992, "Burning All Illusions in LA," in D. Hazen (ed.), *Inside the LA Riots,* Institute for Alternative Journalism.

Dentler, Robert A. 1992, "The Los Angeles Riots of Spring 1992: Events, Causes, and Future Policy," *Sociological Practice Review* 3:4, 229–244.

DuBois, William E. B. 1965, *The Souls of Black Folks,* in *Three Negro Classics,* New York: Avon.

Durkheim, Emile 1965, *The Elementary Forms of the Religious Life,* New York: Free Press.

Durkheim, Emile and Marcel Mauss 1903, *Primitive Classification,* Chicago: University of Chicago Press.

Eco, Umberto 1979, *A Theory of Semiotics,* Bloomington: Indiana University Press.

Emery, Edwin and Michael Emery 1978, *The Press and America: An Interpretative History of the Mass Media,* Englewood Cliffs: Prentice-Hall.

Epstein, Edward Jay 1973, *News From Nowhere: Television and the News,* New York: Vintage Books.

Erickson, Bonnie H. 1988, "The Relational Basis of Attitudes," in Barry

Wellman and S. D. Berkowitz (eds.), *Social Structures: Network Approach,* Cambridge: Cambridge University Press.

Espiritu, Yen 1992, *Asian American Panethnicity: Bridging Institutions and Identities,* Philadelphia: Temple University Press.

Estrich, Susan 1989, "The Hidden Politics of Race," *The Washington Post Magazine,* April 23, 20–25.

Ewen, Stuart and Elizabeth Ewen 1992, *Channels of Desire: Mass Images and the Shaping of American Consciousness,* Minneapolis: University of Minnesota Press.

Fanon, Frantz 1967, *Black Skin, White Masks,* New York: Grove Press.

Farley, Reynolds and Walter R. Allen 1989, *The Color Line and the Quality of Life in America,* New York: Oxford University Press.

Farr, Robert M. and Serge Moscovici 1984, *Social Representations,* Cambridge: Cambridge University Press.

Feagin, Joe R. and Hernan Vera 1995, *White Racism,* New York: Routledge.

Featherstone, Mike 1991, *Consumer Culture and Postmodernism,* London: Sage.

Festinger, Leon, Stanley Schachter and Kurt Back 1965, "The Operation of Group Standards," in H Proshansky and B. Seidenberg (eds.), *Basic Studies in Social Psychology,* New York: Holt, Rinehart and Winston.

Fetterman, David M. 1989, *Ethnography: Step by Step,* Newbury Park: Sage.

Fine, Gary Alan and Sherryl Kleinman 1983, "Network and Meaning: An Interactionist Approach to Structure," *Symbolic Interaction* 6:1, 97–110.

Fishman, Mark 1980, *Manufacturing the News,* Austin: University of Texas Press.

Fiske, John 1987a, *Television Culture,* London: Routledge.

1987b, "British Cultural Studies," in R. Allen (ed.), *Channels of Discourse: Television and Contemporary Criticism,* Chapel Hill NC: University of North Carolina Press.

1989a, *Understanding Popular Culture,* Boston: Unwin Hyman.

1989b, "Moments of Television: Neither the Text Nor the Audience," in E. Seiter, H. Borchers, G. Kreutzner and E. Warth (eds.), *Remote Control: Television, Audiences, and Cultural Power,* London: Routledge.

1994a, "Ethnosemiotics: Some Personal and Theoretical Reflections," in H. Newcomb (ed.), *Television: The Critical View,* New York: Oxford University Press.

1994b, *Media Matters: Everyday Culture and Political Change,* Minneapolis: University of Minnesota Press.

Foster, Hal 1985, *Recodings: Art, Spectacle, Cultural Politics,* Port Townsend, Washington: Bay Press.

Franklin, John Hope 1965, "The Two Worlds of Race: A Historical View," in T. Parsons and K. Clark (eds.), *The Negro American,* Boston: Beacon Press.

Frazier, E. Franklin 1957, *The Negro in the United States,* New York: Macmillan.

Gabriel, Teshome H. 1988, "Thoughts on Nomadic Aesthetics and the Black Independent Cinema: Traces of a Journey," in *Blackframes: Critical Perspectives on Black Independent Cinema,* Cambridge MA: The MIT Press.

1993, "Ruin and The Other: Towards a Language Of Memory," in H. Naficy and T. Gabriel (eds.), *Otherness and Media: The Ethnography of the Imagined and the Imaged,* New York: Harwood Academic Publishers.

Gans, Herbert 1979, *Deciding What's News,* New York: Pantheon.

Garfinkel, Harold 1967, *Studies in Ethnomethodology,* Cambridge: Polity Press.

Geertz, Clifford 1973, *The Interpretation of Cultures,* New York: Basic Books.

1983, *Local Knowledge: Further Essays in Interpretive Anthropology,* New York: Basic Books.

General Social Survey (GSS) 1990, *General Social Surveys, 1972–1990: Cumulative Codebook,* Principal Investigator, James A. Davis; Director and Co-Principal Investigator, Tom W. Smith, Chicago: National Opinion Research Center.

Gergen, Kenneth J. 1968, "The Significance of Skin Color in Human Relations," in J. H. Franklin (ed.), *Color and Race,* Boston: Beacon Press.

Gerth, H. H. and C. Wright Mills 1958, *From Max Weber: Essays in Sociology,* New York: Oxford University Press.

Gitlin, Todd 1978, "Media Sociology: The Dominant Paradigm," *Theory and Society* 6:2, 205–253.

1980, *The Whole World is Watching,* Berkeley: University of California Press.

1985, *Inside Prime Time,* New York: Pantheon.

1990, "Who Communicates What to Whom, in What Voice and Why, About the Study of Mass Communication?" *Critical Studies in Mass Communication* 7, 185–96.

Goldberg, David Theo 1990, "The Social Formation of Racist Discourse," in D. Goldberg (ed.), *Anatomy of Racism,* Minneapolis: University of Minnesota Press.

Goldstein, Norm 1994, *The Associated Press Stylebook and Libel Manual*, Reading, MA: Addison-Wesley.

Goodwin, Andrew 1992, "Truth, Justice and Videotape," in D. Hazen (ed.), *Inside the L.A. Riots: What Really Happened – and Why It Will Happen Again*, Institute for Alternative Journalism.

Gordon, Milton 1964, *Assimilation in American Life*, New York: Oxford University Press.

Gramsci, Antonio 1971, "The Intellectuals," in Q. Hoare and G. Nowell Smith (eds.), *Selections From the Prison Note-books of Antonio Gramsci*, New York: International Publishers.

Gray, Herman 1993, "The Endless Slide of Difference: Critical Television Studies, Television and the Question of Race," *Critical Studies in Mass Communication* 10, 190–197.

1994, "Television, Black Americans, and the American Dream," in H. Newcomb (ed.), *Television: The Critical View*, New York: Oxford University Press.

1995, *Watching Race: Television and the Struggle for "Blackness,"* Minneapolis: University of Minnesota Press.

Grossberg, Lawrence 1993, "Can Cultural Studies Find True Happiness in Communication?" *Journal of Communication* 43:4, 89–97.

Gurin, Patricia, Arthur H. Miller and Gerald Gurin 1980, "Stratum Identification and Consciousness," *Social Psychological Quarterly* 43:1, 30–47.

Gwaltney, John Langston 1980, *Drylongso: A Self-Portrait of Black America*, New York: Random House.

Hacker, Andrew 1992, *Two Nations: Black and White, Separate, Hostile, and Unequal*, New York: Ballantine Books.

Hall, Stuart 1973, "Encoding and Decoding in the Television Discourse," Birmingham: Centre for Contemporary Cultural Studies.

1986, "Gramsci's Relevance for the Study of Race and Ethnicity," *Journal of Communication Inquiry* 10:2, 5–27.

1988, "New Ethnicities," in K. Mercer (ed.), *Black Film, British Cinema*, London: Institute of Contemporary Arts.

1989, "Cultural Identity and Cinematic Representation," *Framework* 36, 68–81.

1992a, "Cultural Studies and its Theoretical Legacies," in L. Grossberg, C. Nelson and P. Treichler (eds.), *Cultural Studies*, London: Routledge.

1992b, "Race, Culture, and Communications: Looking Backward and Forward at Cultural Studies," *Rethinking Marxism* 5:1, 10–18.

Hallin, Daniel C. 1984, "The Media, the War in Vietnam, and Political Support: A Critique of the Thesis of an Oppositional Media," *Journal of Politics* 46:1, 2–24.

Hare, Nathan 1973, "The Challenge of a Black Scholar," in J. A. Ladner (ed.), *The Death of White Sociology*, New York: Random House.

Harrington, Michael 1984, *The New American Poverty*, New York: Penguin.

Harris, Joseph E. 1987, *Africans and Their History*, New York: Penguin.

Hartmann, Heidi 1981, "The Unhappy Marriage of Marxism and Feminism," in L. Sargent (ed.), *Women and Revolution*, Boston: South End Press.

Hays, William L. 1988, *Statistics*, New York: Holt, Rinehart and Winston.

Hazen, Don (ed.) 1992, *Inside the L.A. Riots: What Really Happened – and Why It Will Happen Again*, Institute for Alternative Journalism.

Heath, Stephen 1990, "Representing Television," in Patricia Mellencamp (ed.), *Logics of Television: Essays in Cultural Criticism*, London: BFI Publishing.

Hecht, Michael L., Mary Jane Collier and Sidney A. Ribeau 1993, *African American Communication: Ethnic Identity and Cultural Interpretation*, Newbury Park: Sage.

Hechter, Michael 1986, "Rational Choice Theory and the Study of Race and Ethnic Relation," in J. Rex and D. Mason (eds.), *Theories of Race and Ethnic Relations*, Cambridge: Cambridge University Press.

Heritage, John 1984, *Garfinkel and Ethnomethodology*, Cambridge: Polity Press.

Herman, Edward S. and Noam Chomsky 1988, *Manufacturing Consent: The Political Economy of the Mass Media*, New York: Pantheon Books.

hooks, bell 1990, *Yearning: Race, Gender and Cultural Politics*, Boston: South End Press.

Horne, Gerald 1995, *Fire This Time: The Watts Uprising and the 1960s*, Charlottesville: University of Virginia Press.

Horton, John 1982, "Order and Conflict Theories of Social Problems as Competing Ideologies," in N. Yetman and C. Steele (eds.), *Majority and Minority*, Boston: Allyn and Bacon.

Inglis, Fred 1990, *Media Theory: An Introduction*, Oxford: Basil Blackwell.

Iyengar, Shanto and Donald R. Kinder 1987, *News that Matters*, Chicago: University of Chicago Press.

Jankowski, Nicholas W. and Fred Wester 1991, "The Qualitative Tradition in Social Science Inquiry: Contributions to Mass Communication Research," in K. B. Jenson and N. W. Jankowski (eds.), *A Handbook of Qualitative Methodologies for Mass Communication Research*, London: Routledge.

Jaynes, Gerald David and Robin M. Williams, Jr. 1989, *A Common Destiny:*

Blacks and American Society, Washington DC: National Academy Press.

Jensen, Klaus Bruhn 1991, "Humanistic Scholarship as Qualitative Science: Contributions to Mass Communications Research," in K. B. Jensen and N. W. Jankowski (eds.), *A Handbook of Qualitative Methodologies for Mass Communication Research,* London: Routledge.

Jhally, Sut and Justin Lewis 1992, *Enlightened Racism: The Cosby Show, Audiences and the Myth of the American Dream,* Boulder, CO: Westview Press.

Johnson, James H., Cloyzelle K. Jones, Walter C. Farrell, Jr. and Melvin L. Oliver 1992, "The Los Angeles Rebellion, 1992: A Preliminary Assessment from Ground Zero," in *UCLA Center for the Study of Urban Poverty Occasional Working Paper Series,* Los Angeles: UCLA Institute for Social Science Research.

Katz, Elihu and Paul F. Lazarsfeld 1955, *Personal Influence: The Part Played by People in the Flow of Mass Communications,* New York: Free Press.

Kellner, Douglas 1990, *Television and the Crisis of Democracy,* Boulder, CO: Westview Press.

Kelly, Robin D. G. 1994, *Race Rebels: Culture, Politics and the Black Working Class,* New York: The Free Press.

Klapper, Joseph 1960, *The Effects of Mass Communication,* New York: The Free Press.

Knoke, David and James H. Kuklinski 1982, *Network Analysis,* London: Sage.

Kornblum, William 1994, *Sociology: In a Changing World,* New York: Harcourt Brace.

Kuhn, Thomas S. 1962, *The Structure of Scientific Revolution,* Chicago: University of Chicago Press.

Lazarsfeld, Paul, Bernard Berelson and Hazel Gaudet 1965, *The People's Choice,* New York: Columbia University Press.

Lieberson, Stanley 1980, *A Piece of the Pie: Blacks and White Immigrants Since 1880,* Berkeley: University of California Press.

Liebes, Tamar and Elihu Katz 1988, "Dallas and Genesis: Primordiality and Seriality in Popular Culture," in James W. Carey (ed.), *Media, Myths, and Narratives: Television and the Press,* Beverly Hills: Sage.

1993, *The Export of Meaning: Cross-Cultural Readings of Dallas,* Cambridge: Polity Press.

Lindlof, Thomas R. 1988, "Media Audiences as Interpretive Communities," *Communication Yearbook* 11, 81–107.

Lippman, Walter 1922, *Public Opinion,* New York: Harcourt, Brace and Company.

Lipsitz, George 1990, *Time Passages,* Minneapolis: University of Minnesota Press.

Livingstone, Sonia M. 1993, "The Rise and Fall of Audience Research: An Old Story With a New Ending," *Journal of Communication* 43:4, 5–12.

Lowery, Shearon and Melvin L. DeFleur 1983, *Milestones in Mass Communication Research,* New York: Longman.

McManus, John 1990, "How Local Television Learns What is News," *Journalism Quarterly* 67:4, 672–683.

McQuail, Denis 1987, *Mass Communications Theory: An Introduction,* London: Sage.

Madhubuti, Haki R. (ed.) 1993, *Why L.A. Happened: Implications of the '92 Los Angeles Rebellion,* Chicago: Third World Press.

Majors, Richard and Janet Mancini Billson 1992, *Cool Pose: The Dilemmas of Black Manhood in America,* New York: Touchstone.

Marin, Gerardo and Barbara VanOss Marin 1991, *Research with Hispanic Populations,* Newbury Park: Sage.

Martinez, Elizabeth 1990, "There's More to Racism Than Black and White," *Z Magazine,* November, 48–52.

Marx, Karl 1972, "The German Ideology," in R. Tucker (ed.), *The Marx and Engels Reader,* New York: W. W. Norton.

Meehan, Eileen R. 1990, "Why We Don't Count: The Commodity Audience," in P. Mellencamp (ed.), *Logics of Television: Essays in Cultural Criticism,* London: BFI.

Mellencamp, Patricia (ed.) 1990, *Logics of Television: Essays in Cultural Criticism,* London: BFI.

1990, "TV Time and Catastrophe, or Beyond the Pleasure Principle of Television," in P. Mellencamp (ed.), *Logics of Television: Essays in Cultural Criticism,* London: BFI.

Mencher, Melvin 1981, *News Reporting and Writing,* Dubuque, Iowa: W. C. Brown and Co.

Mills, C. Wright 1959, *The Sociological Imagination,* London: Oxford University Press.

Morley, David 1974, "Reconceptualizing the Media Audience: Towards an Ethnography of Audiences," Birmingham: Centre for Contemporary Cultural Studies.

1980, *The 'Nationwide' Audience,* London: BFI.

1992, *Television, Audiences and Cultural Studies,* London: Routledge.

1993, "Active Audience Theory: Pendulums and Pitfalls," *Journal of Communication* 43:4, 13–19.

Moscovici, Serge and Marisa Zavalloni 1969, "The Group as a Polarizer of Attitudes," *Personality and Social Psychology* 12:2, 125–135.

Myers, David G. and Helmut Lamm 1975, "The Polarizing Effect of Group Discussion," *American Scientist* May-June, 297–303.

Myrdal, Gunnar 1982, "An American Dilemma," in N. Yetman and C. Steele (eds.), *Majority and Minority*, Boston: Allyn and Bacon.

National Advisory Commission on Civil Disorders 1968, *Report of the National Advisory Commission on Civil Disorders*, New York: Bantam Books.

Newcomb, Horace M. 1984, "On the Dialogic Aspects of Mass Communication," *Critical Studies in Mass Communication* 1, 34–50.

Noel, Peter 1992, "When the Word is Given," in D. Hazen (ed.), *Inside the L.A. Riots*, Institute for Alternative Journalism.

Oboler, Suzanne 1992, "The Politics of Labeling: Latino/a Cultural Identities of Self and Others," *Latin American Perspectives* 75:19, 18–36.

Omi, Michael and Howard Winant 1986, *Racial Formation in the United States From the 1960s to the 1980s*, New York: Routledge and Kegan Paul.

1993, "The Los Angeles 'Race Riot' and Contemporary U.S. Politics," in R. Gooding-Williams (ed.), *Reading Rodney King, Reading Urban Uprising*, New York: Routledge.

1994, *Racial Formation in the United States From the 1960s to the 1990s*, New York: Routledge.

Parenti, Michael 1986, *Inventing Reality: The Politics of the Mass Media*, New York: St. Martin's Press.

Park, Robert 1950, *Race and Culture*, Glencoe, IL: The Free Press.

Postman, Neil 1985, *Amusing Ourselves to Death: Public Discourse in the Age of Show Business*, New York: Penguin.

Potter, Jonathan and Ian Litton 1985, "Some Problems Underlying the Theory of Social Representations," *British Journal of Social Psychology* 24, 81–90.

Prager, Jeffrey 1982, "American Racial Ideology as Collective Representation," *Ethnic and Racial Studies* 5, 99–119.

Press, Andrea 1990, "The Active Viewer and the Problem of Interpretation: Reconciling Traditional and Critical Research," *Communication Yearbook* 15, 91–106.

1991, *Women Watching Television: Gender, Class, and Generation in the American Television Experience*, Philadelphia: University of Pennsylvania Press.

Radway, Janice 1984, *Reading the Romance: Women, Patriarchy, and Popular Literature,* Chapel Hill: University of North Carolina Press.

Rex, John 1987, *Race Relations in Sociological Theory,* London: Routledge and Kegan Paul.

Robinson, Cedric J. 1993, "Race, Capitalism, and the Antidemocracy," in R. Gooding-Williams (ed.), *Reading Rodney King, Reading Urban Uprising,* New York: Routledge.

Rottenberg, Annette T. 1985., *Elements of Argument: A Text and Reader,* New York: St. Martin's Press.

Rubin, Alan M. 1986, "Uses, Gratifications, and Media Effects Research," in J. Bryant and D. Zillman (eds.), *Perspectives on Media Effects,* Hillsdale NJ: Lawrence Erlbaum Associates.

Schroeder, Kim Christian 1987, "Convergence of Antagonistic Traditions? The Case of Audience Research," *European Journal of Communication* 2, 7–31.

Schudson, Michael 1978, *Discovering the News: A Social History of American Newspapers,* New York: Basic Books.

1982, "The Politics of the Narrative Form: The Emergence of News Conventions in Print and Television," *Daedelus* 3:4, 97–111.

Skerry, Peter 1993, *Mexican Americans: The Ambivalent Minority,* New York: Free Press.

Sklar, Robert 1975, *Movie-Made America: A Cultural History of American Movies,* New York: Random House.

Spivak, Gayatri Chakravorty 1987, *In Other Worlds: Essays in Cultural Politics,* New York: Methuen.

Strinati, Dominic 1995, *An Introduction to Theories of Popular Culture,* London: Routledge.

Tice, Carol 1992, "Helicopter Journalism," in D. Hazen (ed.), *Inside the L.A. Riots: What Really Happened – and Why It Will Happen Again,* New York: Institute for Alternative Journalism.

Toulmin, Stephen Edelston 1958, *The Uses of Argument,* Cambridge: Cambridge University Press.

Tuchman, Gaye 1978, *Making News: A Study in the Construction of Reality,* New York: The Free Press.

Turner, Patricia A. 1993, *I Heard It Through the Grapevine: Rumor in African-American Culture,* Berkeley: University of California Press.

van Dijk, Teun A. 1992, "Discourse and the Denial of Racism," *Discourse and Society* 3:1, 87–118.

1993, *Elite Discourse and Racism,* Newbury Park: Sage.

Waters, Mary C. 1990, *Ethnic Options: Choosing Identities in America,* Berkeley: University of California Press.

Weber, Max 1958a, "Class, Status, Party," in H. H. Gerth and C. Mills (eds.), *From Max Weber: Essays in Sociology,* New York: Oxford University Press.

1958b "Science as Vocation," in H. H. Gerth and C. Mills (eds.), *From Max Weber: Essays in Sociology,* New York: Oxford University Press.

Wellman, Barry and S. D. Berkowitz 1988, *Social Structures: A Network Approach,* Cambridge: Cambridge University Press.

West, Stan 1993, "How the L.A. Uprising Will Affect the '92 Election," in H. Madhubuti (ed.), *Why L.A. Happened: Implications of the '92 Los Angeles Rebellion,* Chicago: Third World Press.

White, Mimi 1987, "Ideological Analysis and Television," in R. Allen (ed.), *Channels of Discourse: Television and Contemporary Criticism,* Chapel Hill: University of North Carolina Press.

Williams, Raymond 1975, *Television: Technology and Cultural Form,* New York: Schocken.

Willis, Paul 1977, *Learning to Labor: How Working Class Kids Get Working Class Jobs,* New York: Columbia University Press.

Wilson, William Julius 1978, *The Declining Significance of Race,* Chicago: University of Chicago Press.

Winant, Howard 1994, *Racial Conditions: Politics, Theory, Comparisons,* Minneapolis: University of Minnesota Press.

Wright, Charles 1975, *Mass Communication,* New York: Random House.

Index